AF594731

The Challenge to Human Rights in Colombia

MY EXPERIENCE

CECILIA L. ZARATE-LAUN

EDITED BY JACK LAUN AND DAVID KAST

LITTLE CREEK PRESS

MINERAL POINT, WISCONSIN

Little Creek Press
5341 Sunny Ridge Road
Mineral Point, WI 53565

ORDERING INFORMATION
Quantity sales. Special discounts are available on quantity purchases by corporations, associations, and others. For details, contact info@littlecreekpress.com

Orders by US trade bookstores and wholesalers.
Please contact Little Creek Press or Ingram for details.

Printed in the United States of America

Cataloging-in-Publication Data
Names: Cecilia Zarate-Laun, author
Title: The Challenge to Human Rights in Colombia: My Experience
Description: Mineral Point, WI Little Creek Press, 2025
Identifiers: LCCN: 2025900142 | ISBN: 978-1-955656-91-7
Classification: BIOGRAPHY & AUTOBIOGRAPHY / Cultural & Regional
BIOGRAPHY & AUTOBIOGRAPHY / Memoirs
BIOGRAPHY & AUTOBIOGRAPHY / Social Activists

Book design by Little Creek Press

This book is dedicated to Fr. Javier Giraldo of the Jesuit think-tank CINEP in Bogota, Colombia, and Prof. Noam Chomsky, linguist emeritus from MIT and progressive social critic, both of whose support, encouragement and deep friendship uplifted Cecilia to the strength of her own voice.

Foreword

Jack Laun

This book is a compendium of articles and case studies written by Cecilia Lucia Zarate-Laun over the space of 40 years, from 1977 through 2017, during the last 30 of which she was Program Director for the Colombia Support Network (CSN). She and I were co-founders of CSN together with Joseph Swaja, a member of the Madison, Wisconsin, City Council. Joseph left Madison and CSN activity shortly after our initial meeting at the Ivy Inn's restaurant in Madison, which has long since disappeared. I met Cecilia while she was studying for her Master's Degree in Nutritional Science at the University of Wisconsin.

Cecilia trained as a nutritionist at the Universidad Nacional de Colombia in Bogotá and, upon graduation in 1966 as a member of the university's first promotion of nutritionists, was hired as a professor in the university's nutrition department. After teaching for a few years combined with work as a nutritionist in the Misericordia Children's Hospital in Bogotá, Cecilia received a scholarship to study nutrition at the University of Wisconsin-Madison, and in 1975 obtained a Master's Degree in Nutritional Science from the University of Wisconsin-Stevens Point.

Cecilia returned to Colombia upon receiving her degree and again taught nutrition, this time at the Jorge Tadeo Lozano University. In 1976, she and I were married in the town of Girón, near Bucaramanga in Cecilia's home department (province) of Santander. Shortly thereafter she was appointed the nutritionist for the Colombian Government's National Nutrition Plan, within the National Planning Department. In 1977, Cecilia and I returned to Wisconsin, my home state. Our home was a lake home on Elkhart Lake, where we spent the next 27 years. Cecilia worked in Madison during the week where, in 1978, she and I and some friends started a food business, Coquitos Corporation. The company made four principal varieties of empanadas, which were sold fresh from a food cart at the Memorial Library Mall of the University of Wisconsin and frozen at supermarkets in the Madison and Milwaukee areas.

At the same time, Cecilia began to act on her concern about the threats to rural communities and human rights leaders in Colombia, where civil conflict between guerrilla organizations and the Colombian government had been underway since 1964. In fact, interparty violence between followers of the Liberal Party and those of the Conservative Party had begun in 1946, when Conservative Mariano Ospina Pérez won the Presidential election by receiving more votes than either of the two candidates running on the Liberal Party ticket, Jorge Eliécer Gaitán and Gabriel Turbay. Ospina had received fewer votes than the two Liberal Party candidates together. When Turbay died in France in 1947, Gaitán became the Jefe Único, or sole leader, of the Liberal Party and, with substantial popular support, was the overwhelming favorite to win the 1950 presidential election. He was assassinated on April 9, 1948, as he came out of his law office in downtown Bogotá, by a lone gunman, Juan Roa Sierra, who may have been hired to kill Gaitán. However, proof of this has not been made public.

At the time of Gaitán's murder, an important meeting of the Pan American Union was being held in Bogotá. At that meeting the creation of the Organization of American States (OAS) was decided upon, with U.S. Secretary of State George Catlett Marshall in attendance. The immediate reaction to the assassination of Gaitán was rioting in Bogotá, called the *Bogotazo*, which destroyed a large part of the city. What followed was an increase in violence in rural areas as Conservative Party-linked gangs attacked Liberals, who then responded with violence.

This is relevant to this book because Cecilia's father and mother were followers of the Liberal Party, and when Cecilia was three years old, in 1949, a torch-bearing gang acting for the Conservatives burned her family's farmhouse down, causing her family to flee. Her father later abandoned the family, and Cecilia, her mother and four sisters spent years living from year to year in different small communities where her mother taught school. A part of Cecilia's passion for human rights came from herself being a victim of the violence in the countryside. Cecilia described what happened as follows in a 2016 note:

"I also want to share something very painful to me which I experienced as a child. My parents had two homes, one in a town called Capitanejo and another on a farm called El Totumito. When violence came to our home area in 1949, which was near the beginning of the current war, armed men set the farm's house on fire. At that time my mother had just given birth to my sister Martha, and was resting with her after she was born at that house. She, along with some helpers, baby Martha, my two other sisters and I had to spend the night hiding in a cave watching the bandits setting fire to everything, including the tobacco that was grown on the farm. They were looking to kill my parents and us children. My parents' crime? They were helping peasants to learn how to read and write and were activists for human issues. We also had to flee from the house in the town of Capitanejo, leaving everything behind and never returning. There was lots of suffering after that, but thanks to the kindness of my aunt Rebeca, we were able to survive in the city of Bucaramanga.

"The fact that we were basically refugees developed in me from early childhood a sense of duty toward Colombia and the incredible suffering of its people. The Colombian government and elites are the first who should apologize for their main responsibility for what has happened during all these painful years, due to their selfishness and greed without compassion. All the injustices and cruelty motivated the creation of guerrilla movements. As time passed by, the war became more and more cruel. I am talking about three groups responsible for the violence: the Army, the paramilitaries and the guerrillas."

Most of the articles that follow come from the years in which Cecilia worked as Program Director for Colombia Support Network in Madison. But the initial impetus for her writings and for a number of talks she gave on the situation in Colombia came from her work with the Women's International League for Peace and Freedom (WILPF). She joined the Madison Chapter of WILPF and was thereafter named to the U.S. National Board of WILPF. She was also chosen to be a member of the Quakers' Latin American Committee. The first essay in this collection of writings by Cecilia came about through an invitation she received to speak to a meeting organized by a WILPF chapter in Watsonville, California. The talk was given in both English and Spanish before an enthusiastic audience that gave her a standing ovation when she finished her presentation. The English text of her talk follows.

PART A

PART B

PART C

PART D

PART E

PART F

PART A

Cecilia's View of Society and Critique of Colombia's Situation and its Institutions. In this first part of the book we have collected together articles that present Cecilia's views on what Colombia should be and of the history of the country and important issues facing it, as well as a description of one of the most important institutions protecting the rights of Colombians, the Defensoría del Pueblo.

SEPTEMBER 26, 1991

Participatory Democracy:
A Latin American Dilemma

Talk Presented at the Opening Meeting of the Pájaro Valley Chapter of The Women's International League for Peace and Freedom
Watsonville, California

In light of the collapse of the governments of Eastern Europe, a lot of ink has been spilled trying to demonstrate euphorically the "defeat" of socialism and the "triumph" of capitalism. Capitalism has been described in almost poetic terms as the maximum expression of the economic as well as political evolution of humanity.

Once the euphoria has passed and we stop to think a little about the reality of the situation, questions occur to us, such as: Was Eastern Europe really socialist? Is the capitalist system the answer for reaching happiness in this life? Are capitalism and democracy synonymous? These questions become sharper and sharper in view of the daily newspapers we receive and read. Can it be that we have reached happiness as a human race and we do not realize it? Is it that the Utopia has arrived and we do not appreciate it?

Doubts arise with greatest intensity when we read the news about the so-called Third World and particularly about Latin America. The majority of Latin American democracies arose at the beginning of the Nineteenth Century as the inevitable product of the collapse of the Old Order as a result of the French Revolution. The ideas of Rousseau and the Encyclopedists permeated the thick walls of the Spanish Empire, and in spite of the Inquisition, crossed the seas, the jungles and the rivers to arrive at the sleepy capitals of the vice-royalties where fervent minds and hearts absorbed them as the law and began, with ideas as their banner, the Wars of Independence.

The ideas of Rousseau about participatory democracy are as vital and fresh today as they were three centuries ago. According to Rousseau, democracy is not decreed but rather built. It is a result of a permanent struggle in society where an educating process ought to exist that constantly prepares the citizen to construct a participatory and egalitarian society. In that society there ought to be vigilance over its representatives for the purpose of assuring the common good. In emphasizing values such as solidarity, civic spirit, altruism, respect for diversity and freedom of expression, participatory democracy would be the expression of a balanced, just and egalitarian society. Up to this point, these ideas could be expressed also in socialist theories, signifying that in essence, socialism and capitalism could have the same democratic ideals.

Divergencies begin when the economic manifestations of the two types of societies are analyzed. Obviously, one does not live by altruism, and every human being has to fulfill his or her basic needs for food, clothing, housing, health and education. The problem really lies in whether there is or is not a balance between the economic system and the political system. The two must complement each other in order for participatory democracy to be real. In this respect one may ask: Is capitalism the ideal economic system for the flourishing of participatory democracy?

A participatory democracy by definition ought to be inclusive and not exclusive in order that the mechanisms of decision-making not become inflexible. But in the capitalist system economic privileges and capital are concentrated in the hands of a few people. This guarantees an exclusive political control, and as a result brings with it a shortage of participatory democracy, leading to the result that leaders respond to the minorities who put them in power and not to the democratic majority. Rights of powerful minorities go against the welfare of the poor majority. Because the poor people do not have investments to protect, they are unprotected politically and economically, and their interests do not coincide with those necessary to have a "stable climate" which would favor economic expansion and investments. In addition, as time passes, the global economy becomes more and more interrelated, and as a result, modern technology has inevitably converted the entire world into a small town where the primary objective is to protect the interests of multinational corporations. Besides this, the conglomerates of the communications media control information and do not respond to their listeners, readers or public in general. They limit the information reported, but it is necessary to have this information unrestricted in a participatory democracy.

The Latin American democracies serve as a perfect example to demonstrate the incongruency of a democracy with a capitalist system such as we now know it. This example illustrates at the regional level what happens at the global level in North-South relations.

Due to telluric convulsions, this small planet of ours has the raw materials that humanity needs spread out over diverse parts of the globe. The majority of these are located in the Third World. The problem is that the countries of the global North assume that they are the owners of the natural resources of the Third World, and they value those resources at a relatively low price. After the Napoleonic Wars, Latin America began to depend almost exclusively upon England for its imports. Once the wars of independence had ended, the situation was accentuated due to the complete English domination of their competitors on the European continent. When England declined, this exclusive monopolistic dominion passed into the hands of the United States, which throughout the last century has exercised hegemonic control over the Western Hemisphere.

The United States says it has a commitment to democracy and liberty, which is a myth. But it continually speaks of this myth. A vital component of the foreign policy of the United States with respect to Latin America is intervention in defense of privileges for the purpose of maintaining a stable climate for its economic expansion and the benefit of its investments. Participatory democracy? No. Democracy American-style, in which the hopeless situation of the poor majority has long been aggravated and where, according to Monseigneur Arturo Rivera y Damas, the Archbishop of San Salvador, "the market economy makes the poor poorer." The problem with the model of democracy American-style lies in that this system "helps" the poor without threatening the basic structure of power, leaving the free market to "trickle down" benefits without making reforms in social welfare or agrarian reform.

The problem of agrarian reform, for example, is vital in a continent such as Latin America where the distribution of land was carried out before independence in the form of concessions given by the sovereigns of Spain to the Conquistadors. In this form the future was prepared for a caste of privileged persons who are never going to consent to a redistribution of lands out of their own goodwill.

Thus, American-style democracy is contradictory because in having as an objective stability and security of economic investments only, it is denying the same stability and security to the majority of the people when it refuses to eliminate the roots of their poverty. How can there be peace when the great majority of the people of the continent are denied basic necessities of economic justice, food and work? Unless we are speaking of the peace of the cemeteries after the physical elimination of any person who dares to ask questions!

The American-style democracy which the United States imposes upon Latin America, using coercive methods when it is not using direct military intervention, has four elements. Upon seeing these in practice, we find they contradict the definition of participatory democracy. These elements are economic, political, ideological and religious.

In the economic sphere, privatization is emphasized, and as a result, the role of government is reduced. The belief is that the very invisible hand of the market functions automatically to balance inequalities. Programs of social welfare are diminished, especially in the areas of health, education and the environment, affecting the two-thirds of the population that lives in conditions of poverty. Unemployment and malnutrition rise, with terrible consequences for the most vulnerable sectors of the population such as women, children and the elderly. Children especially are victims of a silent genocide that does not appear on the front pages of the newspapers.

The environment shares the destiny of the poor people because erosion, deforestation and the poisoning of the environment with pesticides increased during the decade of the 1980s due, in great part, to the models of development imposed upon the region. Thus, the lack of food, clothing, education and health created discontent and, as a result, labor tensions. This is not a secure climate for capitalist investments. The tensions lead to protests, which generate a severe repression and a culture of resistance. These are not exactly what Rousseau had in mind when he spoke of participatory democracy.

In addition to increasing the poverty of the masses, the capitalist economic policies in Latin America do not give priority to industrialization. This creates a crisis for the small and medium industries of the Latin American countries, generating more unemployment and poverty. Priority is placed upon assisting foreign companies to which preferential treatment is given by means of exemption from payment of taxes, subsidies, elimination of regulations which require care of the environment and, in general, creating "a climate of business" which maximizes profits, as for example by using cheap labor in free trade zones.

The international financial institutions, such as the International Monetary Fund, the World Bank and the Inter-American Development Bank, impose economic policies that generate inflation, low wages and unemployment. They also bring pressure to bear upon the governments of the region, resulting in their total dependency, which creates more poverty and oppression, with consequent restrictions on the political system. With the economic situation described above, the use of force remains as the only solution for repressing revolts.

At the political level, the unholy alliance between the United States government and the Latin American elites not only emphasizes the apparatus of national security, the Army and the Police, but goes to almost theatrical extremes to demonstrate the legitimacy of the particular Latin American government. American-style democracy signifies only elections every so often. It is not important that these elections, with desperate people as voters, are carried out in fraudulent form by the purchase and sale of votes in return for money, food, a scholarship or a zinc roof. Photographs which show the long lines of voters are circulated around the world by the "free press" purporting to show democracy at work. But what these photographs do not show is that the results of these elections, which are praised as the triumph of democracy, are really a tribute to the effectiveness of terror.

The façade is democratic. The reality is the sadistic terror imposed by Latin American armies. These armies are armed, trained, advised and financed by the United States, which defines itself as a model democracy within the ideological frame of reference of national security. The armies of Latin America are really invading armies within each country. Their so-called defense activities are carried out not against an external enemy but rather against an internal "enemy" through the physical extermination of peasants, labor leaders, social workers, journalists, priests, nuns, political activists, artists, writers and intellectuals... in effect any person who dares to think. These persons are tortured in a savage way and what is even worse, often *disappeared* without a trace. They follow the foggy road. They are the mark of American-style democracy in Latin America. Whatever Eastern European activists such as Lech Walesa, Vaclav Havel and Alexander Dubcek may say, if they had been living in El Salvador, Colombia,

Guatemala or Peru, they would have been *disappeared* a long time ago, taken away by men dressed as civilians and armed to the teeth.

When in Latin America an attempt has been made to experiment with participatory democracies, as in the cases of Chile or Nicaragua, the United States, with excessive cruelty and inhumanity, has vented its fury against the country of the moment until it has destroyed the experiment. At times this has led to pathetic situations, as in the case of Nicaragua, where the United States considered itself threatened by a very small, sparsely populated country.

The ideological control of the population should not be left to pass unperceived. It is exercised through the communications media, which, in the hands of the local power structure allied with foreign investors, have an absolute cultural domination over the population. They impose a different culture, oriented towards consumption and violence, upon the Latin American societies.

Freedom of expression is one of the most important manifestations of a participatory democracy. Large daily newspapers and radio and television networks in Latin America are in the hands of families or of persons who defend the *status quo* above the interests of the majority. Besides being profitable businesses that depend upon profits from advertising, the mass media act as informal ministries of culture and information, deforming the popular ideology in accord with their economic and political interests. The press of Eastern Europe, so much criticized for being censored, pales in comparison to the Latin American mass media in its self-censorship. Besides this, the influence of the biased international news agencies is to filter the truth and not report events affecting the daily life of the majority. When some newspaper or radio station has the courage to publish the truth, death squads come to carry out their mission of destruction, demolishing buildings and assassinating journalists. There are many who have been the heroes of liberty of expression who have sacrificed themselves on the altar of American-style democracy.

The other important component to consider is that of religion. From a military point of view, the Third World is without defense against the North. Although it appears romantic, the confrontation in the present modern world has passed to the spiritual level. Individualism, consumerism, competition and destruction of the sense of community, which are characteristics of capitalism, can only be balanced by strength, hope and the sense of human dignity and community that come from the teachings of religion.

Since the beginning of the Conquest, the destiny of Latin America has been tied to the influence of the Roman Catholic Church. The cross and the sword were its symbols. The Church traditionally has been one of the most conservative forces of the continent, allied absolutely with the centers of power, the oligarchic classes and the owners of the great landed properties. The traditional teaching throughout centuries was that of telling the poor people that they should have patience with the will of God on this earth, because in the next life they would receive their compensation.

The fresh winds of renovation that came with the Second Vatican Council, the examples of the worker priests in Europe and the situation of the masses in Latin America gave rise to profound analyses of religious activists who saw the necessity of altering the role of the Church and of bringing it closer to the suffering of the poor people. Beginning with the Latin American Bishops' Conference (CELAM), which took place in Medellín in 1968, the Church declared "a preferential option for the poor," altering in that way the equation of centuries of alliance among the Church, the military and the wealthy people.

Medellín marked the beginning of the *Theology of Liberation*. For the first time in the history of the Church, total liberation of the human being was talked about as were changes in the political, economic and social structures. There was a profound renovation because the mission of the Church began to be seen as evangelical, announcing the freedom of God to humanize and liberate human beings. The new Church would not be arrogant and authoritarian but rather at the service of the poor. Communities called Ecclesiastical Base Communities (EBC) began to be framed. These are small groups of Christians who meet to read the Gospel, converse, meditate and discover the roots of their sufferings. They begin to see the message of salvation as a liberation which ought to begin now, in this world, and to connect it with the oppression and exploitation of their daily lives.

After meditation comes practice. Many labor unions, community organizations and neighborhood groups that organize schools, health centers, and food production, all at the service of the poor, never would have been founded without the support of the Church.

Little by little, this religious activism was being converted into a political revolution, which the assassinated Salvadoran Jesuit Xavier Gorostiaga called "the logic of the masses" versus "the logic of capitalism." Rousseau would have called it participatory democracy. However, this logic produced an ideological, theological and political offensive against the EBC on the part of the ecclesiastical hierarchy.

Another unforeseen consequence of this activism is that the continent is being invaded by religious movements and electronic churches originating in the United States, which tend to emphasize individual religious experiences, a private spirituality and American-style democracy. The press, the military and the politicians constantly call the activity of the Ecclesiastical Base Communities "communist." There are thousands of activists of the EBC who have "disappeared" throughout the length and breadth of the continent.

Sadly, the Vatican, and particularly John Paul II, who enthusiastically support the political activities of the Catholic Church in Eastern Europe and especially in Poland, do not seem to understand that the communism of Eastern Europe was not so very different from the authoritarian capitalism of Latin America, and they condemn and reproach the religious leaders of the Theology of Liberation.

CONCLUSIONS

A participatory democracy cannot exist if there is not a political and economic balance in society. When the lack of economic balance generates poverty for the majority of the population, this signifies that participatory democracy is impossible because the economic power controls the political power and as a result, the majority is not represented in the decision-making process.

The model of American democracy is not a model of participatory democracy because it is based economically on an authoritarian and privileged capitalism that does not tolerate popular participation. It is a demagogic democracy which in the name of democracy looses wars against countries that are looking for their self-determination, and in doing that, those countries cannot remain as democracies for very long without beginning to repress their own people.

Latin America in particular ought to look to its own roots to give life again to participatory democracy. The pre-Columbian indigenous peoples represented the greatness and dignity of the common man. A sense of community, dignity, mutual respect and solidarity were characteristics of some of these societies which, although primitive, empirically showed some of the most important aspects of participatory democracy.

1995

Historical Roots of the Conflicts in Latin America

Dedicated to Edith Ballantyne,
General Secretary of Women's International League
for Peace and Freedom (WILPF) for her dedication to
the cause of peace and justice in Latin America

In this essay, I intend to demonstrate that the present state of affairs in Latin America originates in the history of the continent itself and that the present conflicts go back to the roots of the continent and should not be surprising to us. I also propose to compare the history of the two Americas, the Anglo-Saxon one and the Latin one, to show that from the very beginning they were destined to become the one more racist, and the other more classist. Finally, I would like to suggest ways for WILPF to plan a strategy in Latin America based upon the principles that move this venerable organization: peace, justice and freedom for all.

In the beginning, Asiatic people emigrated for unknown reasons from Asia to the American continent, crossing the Bering Strait. They arrived at Alaska and then went on to Canada and the United States. But without technology and with the miserable winters of the temperate zone, they kept going down to the tropics, where the warm climate, the luxurious plant growth and the absence of seasons facilitated their daily life of fishing and hunting until something marvelous happened: The discovery of corn made them settle down to live from agriculture and to develop new ways of life.

Before I describe the different groups, I would like to say that the American continent should be approached from a different point of view than the one used in studying, for example, the development of Western Europe. In America there are almost no ancient records to guide us; there was no contact with other civilizations outside the hemisphere and no exchange with other nations. The living exchange that happened on the shores of the Mediterranean that set up contact between Phoenicians, Greeks, Romans, etc., never happened in the Americas.

Archeology is the science which rediscovers the great cultures of the continent's past. The folk arts and crafts, the ruins, fragments of pottery, basketry, shrines and sanctuaries reveal majestic cultural products that show the psychology and growth of these peoples. Beyond these, they had a desire to mystify and create tradition, then convert it into legend, legend into religion, religion into art. No man ever lived closer to earth than in the ancient cultures of the Americas. In them man accepted life as he found it and his unity with nature was almost complete. As John A. Crow says: "A wonderful plastic sense was innate in all of this people, and all of this people had a hand in creating and enjoying their art." (Crow, pg. 5) It was part of their daily life; for them use could not be separated from beauty. This total integration is what was then and is now their greatest strength. Art was a pure expression of feeling of the folk. There were not individual artists in every field, but in all fields art itself was what was great.

With this in mind, we will take an imaginary trip to the ancient cultures. First there were the Mayans, called the Greeks of the New World. They were the architects, mathematicians and astronomers that produced a calendar so exact that it was more accurate than and superior to any calendar used during the Christian era. They had a refined system of sculptured hieroglyphics to express themselves. Unfortunately, many manuscripts were destroyed by the Spaniards as evil documents of idolatrous people. The books of Chilam Balam and Popol Vuh tell of their legendary and mythical history. They built magnificent pyramid-temples decorated with stone and wood carvings, perhaps among the finest in the ancient world, where sculptures, brilliant frescoes together with jade and featherwork, textiles and pottery are the admiration of mankind. For the Mayans, religion and art were blended with a refinement not achieved by any other group in the Americas. Today, they still live on among their descendants, the Indians and mestizos of Central America.

The Incas were the children of the Sun. They were the largest and most closely integrated native population. They had a superlative system of agriculture, fine arts and crafts, and a social organization unequaled in the Americas. There was no poverty, no hunger, no unemployment and no crime in their land. Life was a cooperative enterprise and everything was common; they had no sense of private property and the Inca had absolute power, being God and Pope at the same time. For this reason, the Conquest was a brutal shock for them. They lived in a land of deep gorges and gigantic mountains with a barren and difficult soil, but in the land of the Incas, everything was inferior except man. The Incas were magnificent engineers who built terraces, roads and bridges. They were astronomers and surgeons who practiced trepanning skulls. They were also fine weavers. Their direct descendants live in the highlands of Peru and Bolivia.

The Aztecs were warriors outstanding in the arts, crafts and mosaics. In 1325, they founded the City of Tenochtitlan, today's Mexico City. They were violent oppressors, dominated by a bloody religion that demanded human sacrifices which contributed to their defeat because their neighboring Indians allied themselves with the Spaniards to defeat the hated Aztecs.

The Chibchas of Colombia were a pacific and developed group, outstanding in gold work. It is said today by some foreign governments that Latin America needs constant foreign aid to develop, but as we have seen here, the continent has the capacity to grow by itself without the World Bank or USAID (United States Agency for International Development).

The other side of our roots comes from the Iberian Peninsula. There are years in the history of countries that are of crucial importance, and certainly 1492 was one in the history of Spain. First, that year the Spaniards defeated the Moors after a crusade of eight centuries beginning in 711. Also in 1492, they expelled non-converted Jews after eight centuries of coexistence. In addition, in that year they also discovered America, published the first grammar of a romance language and had a Spaniard as Pope.

The Portuguese were great navigators who pushed the Moors out first, and because they were a stopping place for the Crusaders, Portugal became the crossroads of Europe and a slave trading center. So, when people from these two nations, Spain and Portugal, came to America, they gave of themselves completely; they practiced racial fusion, were intolerant of minority thinking, were extraordinary warriors, navigators and explorers, but were the worst statesmen and economists mankind has seen.

The Conquest period was a brutal and bloody enterprise dominated by two obsessions: gold and souls. The human elements that made it so were soldiers and priests, thus combining fortune seekers with spiritual crusaders who established two characteristic institutions that reflected their ideas: the *encomienda* and the Mission.

I will proceed now to compare the Spanish and Portuguese way of conquest with the English colonization of North America. While the English colonies of North America were settled by families, man and wife, the Spanish and Portuguese never brought women with them. Women came only at a later period. While the Pilgrims came as religious minorities seeking political and religious freedom for their families, the Spanish and Portuguese came as zealous crusaders seeking converts, gold and slaves. The English came as settlers to till the soil and endure hard labor. The relative absence of an Indian population in the land settled by the English meant absence of labor, since one million primitive nomads spread over the United States and Canada cannot be compared with the 40 to 50 million organized, economically productive Indians in Latin America with strong central governments. There the Indian was and still is the dominant element. The alternative, for Spain and Portugal, was to incorporate the natives into society, and crusading priests started from the beginning a work of assimilation which could be considered the most powerful force shaping Latin-American character. To diminish the power of the Catholic Church outside the realm of religion is the grossest of errors.

The imperial conquest by Spain and Portugal was carried out on the Roman model. They imposed their language, religion and culture over millions of colonial subjects of different race and level of development. In contrast, the English never treated the Indians as an integral part of the same state or society. The English colonies were small, growing colonies, where there was no gold or silver, and they were left to develop and grow by themselves with no heavy taxation. Spain and Portugal borrowed funds in Europe which they sought to repay in gold and silver from their colonies. They established strict commercial monopolies, heavy taxes and a political blend of church and state. Exploitation, oppression, scarcity and improvidence started with the arrival of Spaniards and Portuguese in the New World.

The contact of both worlds brought a demographic hecatomb. According to Santayana, in Latin America the Catholic Church "was a very human institution in regard to the foibles and emotions of the animal man." (Crow, pg. 213) To sin was human and an understandable human weakness, but to disbelieve was a crime. In Anglo-Saxon North America, the Puritans turned this statement the other way around: They were obsessed with sex. They had illicit relations with women of different races, but they were clandestine, and if children were born, they refused to recognize them. "The Puritan was intolerant in what he thought was an expression of his weakness." (Crow, pg. 151) Consequently, Puritan settlers were strong in muscle, bone and fiber but lacking in egalitarian spiritual direction. The result was a racist society.

In Latin America, Spain and Portugal, located in the Mediterranean, were used to centuries of mixing. They were intolerant toward other religions and toward political and economic changes in the structure of society, and they could not coexist with different believers. The consequence was an authoritarian society. As this analysis shows, both the North American and South American societies were intolerant, but on different issues.

With relation to land and labor, the orders of the Spanish Crown and the Portuguese Crown were to be friendly, to convert the Indians to the Catholic Church, to collect tribute, pay for their work, to not enslave them but to consider them subjects of the Crown. But the kings were far away, and many abuses were reported in the colonies. The Crown then decided to resuscitate the feudal concept of *encomienda* or trusteeship by which the *encomenderos* had to set up schools for their wards, or *encomendados*, teach them Spanish, Catholic religion, and the "art of civilization."

In practice, Spaniards came to realize that the greatest of all spoils of the New World was Indian labor and they used the Indians to work the mines, in agriculture and as domestic servants. Since the Indians had no concept of wages, private property, money or accumulation, it was easy for the Spaniards to describe the Indian labor as "allowing the natives certain tasks." Their society became two separate groups, one that had property, economic and social privileges and did not have to work versus the other group with no property, no privileges and that was consigned to hard work. These are the ancestors of the peons of the modern hacienda. Thus the colonial society was a feudal society formed of layers of castes regulated in such a way that the lower castes would have little opportunity for economic growth, social progress or democratic ideas. At the top were the natives of the Iberian Peninsula, then came the Creoles, then the mestizos, then the indigenous peoples and finally Negro slaves. This was, in fact, the expression of an economic caste system, not racial, but deeply embedded in the unwillingness of the Spanish and Portuguese to take part in manual labor. Long accustomed to being the conqueror-soldiers, they left to others the ignoble task of working with their hands. [Editor's note: "Creoles," as used above, refers to Spaniards born in the Americas.]

Labor was seen as degrading. Spain's King Carlos III, the enlightened Bourbon King, even issued a decree which stated that a man can engage in mechanical or agricultural labor without losing social caste. Yet this feeling of work as degrading is still so strong in Latin America today that upper-class people will not so much as carry a piece of paper in public. By holding this belief and acting on it, idleness became a virtue and economic exploitation a necessity.

Since the Crown was the owner of all the land, it was distributed as grants before independence, in contrast with North America where land was distributed after independence.

As a consequence of all of the above factors, the forms of assimilation took an odd shape in Latin America. In a way, the Spaniards inverted values. As an example, Christian values were inverted or falsified and became a means of subjugation. One could be a Christian, and be a man but be a slave, and at the same time, Indian values, such as collective solidarity, were eliminated. In this way, glorification of the soldier brings incipient militarism, and propagation of faith brings political and social intolerance. The rules of the game were, and still are, exaltation of personal rule, disrespect for impersonal law, disdain for manual labor and a psychology of exploitation. All these characteristics have deep roots in the Iberian past and are difficult to overcome easily.

Of course, when one considers the reality of the historic moment when this occurred, one thinks that never before were such chaotic circumstances presented to an imperial power on such a big scale. Everything was an obstacle: conquest, distance, race, geography, religion, government and economics. John A. Crow puts it this way: "Never before had the problems of race confronted a nation on such a scale and never before or since have they been moved toward a solution with less racial bitterness." (Crow, pg. 256)

The Catholic Church with its clergy brought teachers, architects, engineers, writers, scientists, moral censors and viceroys, since separation of Church and State was unthinkable. There was only one Church; you had to believe in it or you were a heretic. If you were a dissenter, you were sent directly to the dungeons of the Inquisition. The Catholic Church undertook defending the Indians, who were declared human beings from the very beginning. Segregated churches for different colors of skin were not permitted since the church taught that in God's eyes we are all equal. Although later the Church became wealthier and upper-class minded, from time to time it came back to its defense of the Indians.

In Latin America, the place of the pioneers was taken from those born on the Iberian Peninsula, along with their government, culture and religion, while the territory to be assimilated was the mass of Indians and Blacks. The Church established schools for Indians and mestizos to teach them to read and write and to teach religion. In the English colonies education was popular, but the problem of educating the people could not be compared with that in the Spanish and Portuguese colonies because there was a world of difference between educating a few thousand English-speaking children to read and write in their own language and the problem in Latin America to attempt to convert, instruct and assimilate millions of primitive Indians into the mainstream of an entirely different and foreign cultural system.

Spain had four viceroyalties: New Spain (modern-day Mexico and much of Central America and North America), New Granada (modern-day Venezuela, Colombia, Ecuador), Peru (modern-day Peru and parts of Ecuador, Colombia, Chile) and La Plata (modern-day Argentina, Chile, Bolivia, Paraguay, Uruguay). The first university was founded in 1538 in Santo Domingo, 98 years before Harvard's founding. In 1553, San Marcos was founded in Lima and soon there were a total of 23 universities in Latin America. They were modeled after medieval universities in Spain, and the curriculum was heavily oriented towards the Humanities. There was a life of extravagant luxury in the colonies, and art was very important, as it is today. When these two peoples, the Spanish and Portuguese colonizers on one hand and the indigenous peoples on the other, got together, they combined two very artistic groups. The illiterate Pueblo of the Iberian Peninsula, which has absorbed so many currents into its soul and body, had become in its own right a great creative artist. As John A. Crow writes in *The Epic of Latin America*, pgs. 297ff, "the deep undercurrent of folk art was as varied and wealthy as any in the world, since nothing in history seems able to blot out the creative and artistic feeling which springs constantly and forever from the genius of a great people." On the same pages he mentions that the German philosopher Hegel expressed many of the same views. These feelings came intact to the New World, where they met another folk culture of almost equal value, and the two began to blend into one, into mestizo art, which is Latin America's breath of life.

Although there were abortive rebellions against the Spanish Empire, such as Túpac Amaru's in Peru or that of the Comuneros in Colombia, because of the systematic exploitation and enforced vassalage of the lower classes, these were not successful. Rousseau, Montesquieu and Voltaire inspired liberalism in North and South America, and the North American Revolution was an example. The struggle for Spanish-America's independence was definitely a revolt of the classes, not of the masses. It was a cruel, bloody and implacable affair where only a few minds, among them the keen and brilliant mind of Simón Bolívar, understood the real meaning of the words "freedom" and "democracy."

An interesting difference between the North American Revolution and the struggle for independence in Spanish America was the role of women. In spite of Machismo, women were directly active in the fight against the Spanish Crown and several were shot by the Spaniards. In the United States, on the other hand, women's roles were more traditional. Women engaged in activities supporting the struggle, such as making clothes for the soldiers, but did not actually fight against the British troops.

Another important difference between the revolutionary leaders in Spanish America and those in the United States was that the former liberated their slaves as a symbol in the struggle for independence, whereas most of the latter did not.

Today in the Republican period, the countries of Latin America have small elites who are direct descendants of the *encomenderos*, and the masses have little education, no equality before the law and no free choice in voting. Today, there is a little more consciousness of rights and education, but the Latin-American countries need a process of restructuring of values, and that is not simple or easy. Latin America needs to awaken its consciousness to seek its soul and to elevate its people to the greatness of their own inheritance.

In conclusion, the following fundamental differences between Latin America and the United States must be taken into account in explaining what is happening in Latin America and the often faulty perception of that reality in the United States:

1. The Spanish colonization had to deal with huge indigenous populations, unlike the English colonization. The result was the development of a class-based society in Latin America, while a race-based society was developed in the United States.
2. British colonization typically was one where the colonist did not mix with

the indigenous people, whereas Spanish colonizers typically did intermix with indigenous people.

3. The Spanish colonies, unlike the English, were known to be very rich in minerals. As a result, the Spanish tried vigorously to prevent contact of their colonies with other people. This phenomenon did not occur to the same degree in the British colonies.
4. The Spanish colonizers avoided manual labor as being demeaning, whereas the English settlers embodied a work ethic. The result is that in Latin America there is a reluctance of the rich to mix with the poor, so that the very concept of decision-making by a majority vote has traditionally been unacceptable to most Latin American leaders.
5. From the earliest days of the Spanish American colonization, Church and State were present in a symbiotic, interdependent relationship. It was impossible to imagine the State without political support of the Church hierarchy in most cases. In the United States, on the other hand, the Churches have traditionally been divorced from political control of the State.

The Women's International League for Peace and Freedom (WILPF) in Latin America should be committed to using peaceful means for:

1. An educational campaign to inform the people of their civil rights;
2. Instruction of the people in what democracy means and how it works;
3. Committing itself to the fight for human rights;
4. Collaborating with liberation theologians to increase the consciousness of the poor and oppressed people in Latin America;
5. Emphasizing women's and children's rights to become more vocal in the defense of women's rights and the knowledge of their oppression, and to participate actively in civil life;
6. Vocalizing opposition to foreign intervention in military training and for reorientation of government expenditures from the military to health and education programs;
7. Committing itself to fostering a dialogue between the social classes and promoting greater understanding among social classes;
8. Promoting the development of solidarity among the different peoples of Latin America.

BIBLIOGRAPHY

Berryman, Phillip. *The Religious Roots of Rebellion*, Orbis Books, Maryknoll, New York, 1984.

Crosby Jr., Alfred W. *The Columbian Exchange*, Greenwood Press, Westport, Connecticut, 1975, 1980.

Crow, John A. *The Epic of Latin America*, University of California Press, 4th Edition, 1992.

Hobsbawn, E.J. *The Age of Revolution*, New American Library, New York, 1962.

Mariátegui, José Carlos. *Siete Ensayos de Interpretación de la Realidad Peruana*, Casa de las Américas, La Habana, Cuba, 1973.

Pereyra, Carlos. *Historia de la America Española*, Editorial "Saturnino Colleja," S.A., 1920.

Von Hagen, Victor. *Los Aztecas: Hombre y Tribu*, Editorial Diana, México, 1964.

Von Hagen, Victor. *World of the Maya*, New American Library, New York, NY, 1960.

Zárate-Laun, Cecilia. "The Jesuits and Their Influence on Education in Latin America," paper for a course in History of Medicine in Latin America, unpublished manuscript, 1984.

1998

Human Rights, Ecology, and Globalization from the War Front

The region of the Colombian Pacific Coast is a region of great ecological importance for humanity which, at this moment, confronts an ecological and cultural disaster. This paper, inspired by the first draft of the Women's International League for Peace and Freedom (WILPF) paper on globalization, seeks to demonstrate at a micro level the devastating consequences which the process of globalization implies for the countries of the periphery, in this case Colombia.

CHARACTERISTICS OF THE COLOMBIAN PACIFIC COAST

The Colombian Pacific Coast contains four departments, or provinces, but it is in general known by the generic name of Chocó, and it forms by itself a geographic and demographic entity. The Chocó is located between the frontiers of Colombia with Panamá to the north and Ecuador to the south. To the east it borders the western mountain range of the Andes, including the mountains of the Baudó and the Darién, the watershed of the Atrato and San Juan Rivers as well as the region of the upper Sinú and San Jorge Rivers. The coastal region of the Pacific Ocean is 1,300 kilometers long and its total surface area is 7,100 square kilometers, which represents 6.2 percent of the total territory of Colombia. Approximately 900,000 persons live in this region, 40 percent of them in five urban centers and a little more than half of the population in small communities dispersed along the rivers and the sea coast. Ninety percent are Afro-Colombians, five percent are mestizos, and the remaining five percent are indigenous of the Emberá, Tule, Waunana, Katió and Cuna nations.

It is the region of the highest rainfall in the country (between 5,000 and 12,000 millimeters per year), varying by sub-region, and has close to three-quarters of its territory covered by tropical forests. The greater part of the territory lies in the Department of Chocó (which gives its name to the region and is the farthest north of the four departments comprising it), the Department of Antioquia[1] and the coast of the Departments of Nariño, Cauca and Valle del Cauca. The region of the Chocó is of global importance for its biodiversity, containing 7,000 to 8,000 species of plants and at least 600 species of birds, almost equal to that of the United States and Canada combined. A large number of the species are endemic, that is to say, they are only found in the Chocó, making the Colombian Pacific one of the regions with the highest concentrations of endemic species in the world, consequently making it one of the richest reserves of biodiversity on the planet. Forty-seven percent of the reptile population is endemic, and in just the region of Anchicaya, 525 species of butterflies have been reported. Cut off from the rest of Colombia by the Andes Mountain Range and by the impenetrability of its territory, this isolation has been a double-edged sword because although it has helped to protect its biodiversity, it remains one of the poorest and most unhealthy places in Colombia. Eighty percent of the territory is covered by tropical forests, swamps and rivers.

HISTORY OF THE CHOCÓ

For the last 500 years, the Chocó has suffered all kinds of invasions and sackings, conforming to a permanent history of conquest, colonization and resistance on the part of the indigenous population. The Chocó has been used as a dispensary from which natural resources have been taken, always trying to integrate it into the international mercantilist system. Spanish, English, French, Scots, North Americans, Syrians, Lebanese and Colombian nationals have always tried to exploit this region.

---

1. Editor's Note: Cecilia often combined the Department of Antioquia with the four Chocó region departments because of the connected conditions and political/economic problems they shared.

The Spanish invaded the Chocó beginning in the Sixteenth Century. Santa María la Antigua in the Darién was founded in 1510 by Vasco Núñez de Balboa, being the first Spanish city founded as a city and bishopric in mainland South America. From near this city, from the mountains of the Darién, Balboa glimpsed and later "discovered" the Pacific Ocean. Fourteen years later the settlement was destroyed by Cuna Indians as a reaction to the policies of extermination and pacification of the Spanish. The Sixteenth Century was a century of continuous struggle for the control of territory between the European invaders and indigenous ethnic groups. In the Seventeenth Century, the Spanish realized the immense mineral potential of the Chocó, since the hot and humid forests of the Chocó, with its rivers Atrato and San Juan, their tributaries and other rivers down the length of the Pacific, have been the traditional sources of gold in Latin America.

Near the end of the colonial period a second metal was discovered, invariably united to gold: platinum. Before the exploitation of gold in the Chocó, platinum was an element totally unknown to humanity. The first samples of the metal were sent to Spain in 1740, and in 1751 it was recognized as a new element. The Spanish Crown, sensing a new source of income, established the first monopoly for production of platinum in the world. The Chocó remained the only source of platinum on the planet until 1820, when deposits of the mineral were discovered in Russia.

In 1536, Pascual de Andagoya, one of the lieutenants of Pizarro, founded the port of Buenaventura, which is still the principal Colombian port on the Pacific Ocean, close to the recently founded city of Santiago de Cali. Soon the Chocó had its indigenous population parceled out in *encomiendas*, private property of the Spanish miners. An *encomienda* comprised groups of indigenous entrusted to a Spanish merchant whose obligation to treat them well and teach them the Catholic religion was repaid by tribute and service, in gold and products and labor.

While the Chocó was consolidated for mineral production, the valleys of Cauca and Popayán were used for the development of large haciendas producing sugar cane and cacao. The Indians began to rebel against the forced labor of the mines and the haciendas. In 1640 there was a revolt which forced the temporary abandonment of some mines.

The indigenous manpower was reduced due to the disastrous mortality caused by their mistreatment and by epidemics of viruela (smallpox), sarampion (measles) and typhoid fever. In 1590, according to colonial chroniclers, the population diminished to one-tenth its size prior to the Conquest. Thus in the middle of the Sixteenth Century, black slaves from the coasts of Guinea, the Congo, Western Sudan and Angola were introduced, becoming the fundamental tool in the enterprise of extracting natural resources.

With the African slaves, colonial mining exploitation was established through the so-called *Reales de Minas*, which were large tracts of land granted by the Crown to the conquistadores (the Spanish conquerors). The decimated indigenous peoples made pacts to provide food to the mining enclaves in return for respecting their territories.

The slaves also rebelled, fleeing the mines and forming free settlements called Palenques in the interior of the mountains from which they continually attacked the mine production and sought the liberation of other slaves. In this form, those ex-slaves called Cimarrones succeeded in impairing the economic interests of the European colonizers. The Nineteenth Century produced political independence from Spain, promoted by the *criollos* (descendants of Spaniards born in America) to gain power and control over national territory. Thus the Viceroyalty of Nueva Grenada passed from being a colony to being the Republic of Colombia. However, this did not change the Pacific region because it only produced a simple change of hands. The structures of domination and the extractive economy continued. Slavery was abolished on January 10, 1852.

At the end of the Nineteenth Century, new extractive processes began when concessions were granted to English and North American companies to extract minerals, fine woods, tagua (vegetable ivory), rubber and other resources. In the Twentieth Century, mechanized mineral mining was rapidly consolidated, carried out by mining companies such as International Mining Company and South American Gold and Platinum Company, which had subsidiaries in all the Pacific and Lower Cauca.

The Afro-Colombian and indigenous communities have shared the territory of the Chocó since the colonial period when it became a refuge for escaped slaves. The black population lives in urban centers and rural areas all along the banks of the rivers, surviving through agriculture, fishing and artisanal mining. All of what is produced, plus gold, are sent to relatives in the town who sell the products, take care of their young relatives who go to study in the town and so forth. It is a symbiotic relationship. They transport by rivers, which act as highways where hand-made canoes transport bananas and even school children.

The indigenous communities are less visible. The majority are rural and live in small settlements in clearings in the forest or along small rivers. They hunt, fish and grow different crops or gather plants from the jungle. Historically, the two communities have coexisted more than integrating with one another. Only recently has there been a more organized collaboration.

THE CHOCÓ AND THE PROCESSES OF GLOBALIZATION

Since the Eighteenth Century, the extractive system of the Pacific plus the slave trade established a commercial dynamic linking Europe, Latin America and Africa. This produced the basis for an accumulation of capital which generated profits and made possible the technological advances which later gave origin to the first forms of capitalist production. In other words, the gold and silver of Latin America allowed the bases for development of capital.

From the establishment of Santa María la Antigua by Balboa, policies of extermination, pacification and integration into the international mercantilist system were initiated in the Chocó. Today, 500 years later, this process has not ended and the spontaneous colonization via missions, tourism and the programs of the Colombian government, under the banner of "development of the Chocó," are a threat to the Afro-Colombian and indigenous communities that are the collective owners of the Chocó and have cared for their forests for 500 years for the whole of humanity

PLAN PACíFICO

The Pacific Coast is the object of an ambitious plan of "development" known as Plan Pacífico. The object is very simple: Exploit the vast natural resources of the Chocó for development programs and to pay the external debt. The Plan's objective is to open and economically modernize the Pacific. It indicates there is need to open the productive system to world markets in order to stimulate the private sector and reduce the intervention of the state, to create a climate of greater liberty for business.

Plan Pacífico includes the following:

1. **The construction of highways.**

   More than 11 highways are planned or are under construction, the majority of them conceived for just two purposes: either to permit more access to the sea from the Andean region through cutting of forests or to improve communications from North to South. The most notable case is the finishing of the Pan-American Highway, for which the remaining 108 kilometers needed will be completed—the famous Tapón del Darién (Darién Gap). This highway represents the greatest dream of the promoters of neo-liberalism and free trade because it will unify the Americas from Alaska to Chile. The Darién Gap is one of the most fragile and important ecological reserves in the world, as its swamps and forests host a great variety of still unclassified plants and animals that provide very important evidence for the study of biological links between North America and South America via the land bridge of the Darién. The highway would directly affect the lives of the Emberá and the Tule indigenous communities as well as accelerate the deforestation of the region.

All of these highways would guarantee to big capital the continuous flow of raw materials and merchandise to the Pacific and all along the length of the Americas.

2. **Oil pipelines.**

   Pipelines are planned for both oil and gas. The multi-pipeline (poliducto) from the Bay of Málaga, which is almost finished, will bring the oil of the Eastern Andes and the Amazon region to western Colombia. When it was publicly announced, a very strong protest from the Afro-Colombian community was provoked because it would cause irreparable damage to local ecosystems and would hurt the natural base of their economies.

3. **Hydroelectric projects.**

   At least six hydroelectric projects are proposed, with a number of small reservoirs. These projects will have disastrous consequences for the environment and society. One of the plans is to divert the waters of the polluted Cauca River, which carries all the industrial waste of the city of Cali, to the pristine waters of the Calima River, which is very rich in wildlife.

4. **Ports.**

   Plans have been developed to expand the port of Buenaventura and create a Naval Base in the Bay of Málaga for the clear purpose of protecting present and future projects from civil protests or from the guerrillas.

5. **Inter-oceanic canal.**

   The most spectacular of the projects is the construction of an inter-oceanic canal which would cross Colombia from the extreme north of the Pacific region to connect the Atlantic and Pacific Oceans. A railroad complex is also proposed for the transportation of cargo, and parallel or overlapping highways, pipelines and multi-pipelines, which would connect two super ports, one in the Gulf of Urabá on the Caribbean Sea and the other in Cupica Bay on the Pacific Ocean. In this way access would be guaranteed to the two seas in one project which would be more efficient than the Panama Canal and which would fulfill the functions of a dry canal. The ecological implications I do not need to emphasize more and the project signifies extinction of the Emberás, Katíos and Tules plus the disappearance of the banks of the rivers where the Afro-Colombian population lives.

6. **Commercial exploitation of natural resources.**
   Wood: The Pacific produces more than 58 percent of the wood for domestic use and foreign markets. Especially sought after are the cativo species (Prioria copaifera) and abarco (Cariniana pyriformis). These are sold domestically and exported to Venezuela, the United States and England.
7. **Mining.**
   About 28 percent of the inhabitants of the Chocó live from mining. Furthermore, gold has been exploited using artisanal methods that do not damage the environment. Recently mechanical excavators have begun to be used. These constitute a serious threat because they excavate large quantities of soil, causing erosion and contamination of water, ruining the traditional miners.

Even though Plan Pacífico has been given an ecological component, and "sustainable development" and "conservation of natural resources" are spoken of, the reality is that the region is suitable for, or fits, the opening of markets recommended by the International Monetary Fund (IMF) and international banks.

HOW PLAN PACÍFICO IS TO BE IMPLEMENTED

In what follows I cite a paragraph from a report by La Comisión Interclesial de Justicia y Paz (The Inter-Church Commission of Justice and Peace) describing the holocaust suffered by the people of the Chocó.

Since February of 1997, the civilian population of the Chocó has been intimidated, kidnapped and threatened by groups who identify themselves as paramilitaries or "self- defense forces" and who force the people to leave their lands and abandon their livestock and their crops. They tell the people clearly that they have to leave "because of the canal."[2] Some die en route through the jungle, especially children. As a method of intimidation, some persons taken at random are executed in front of the community to force them to leave.

In its testimony before the Commission on Human Rights of the United Nations in Geneva during its 53rd Session, Pax Christi international cited the case of the small community of Bijao where the youth Marino López was decapitated and dismembered to force the terrified population to leave. Simultaneously, the areas were bombarded by the Armed Forces of Colombia, also forcing the people out. Like a modern Balboa, General Rito Alejo del Río, Commander of the Seventeenth Brigade of the Colombian Army, declared that he could not guarantee the return of the thousands of refugees—especially women and children—who up until today live in refugee camps. The abandoned hamlets are occupied by the Army and the paramilitaries. The cruel methods create a concentration of land in the hands of owners unknown up to this moment.

Now comes one of the most insidious consequences of globalization: the change that obligatorily follows at the individual level. People are forced, willingly or unwillingly, to participate in the market economy. The new refugees who before were self-sufficient have to leave to sell themselves as a work force or as prostitutes to survive and transform into consumers. The new residents of the villages are people who do not have the emotional and sacred ties to the land that the previous residents had, and as a result do not take care of nor protect it from the planned projects. On the contrary, they are part of the projects. Thus a "mutation" is created in the people, who begin to believe that if they do not participate in the market economy—that is, if they do not have money or a Visa or American Express card—they are not human beings. Little by little, humanity is transformed into a collection of passive consumers alienated by television, sports as business, the necessity of buying useless electric appliances for the home (electrodomesticos) and playing computer games. The children of the Chocó grew up listening to the so beautiful stories and legends of their ancestors. But now they will be molded to buy the toys of Walt Disney. In other words, globalization and neoliberalism signify the death of the human spirit and the triumph of the material. Politically this is reflected in passive multitudes who do not question anything and who have the mentality of slaves.

2. Editor's note: That is, "because of the Atrato Canal, to be built where you now live." As of 2024, the canal has still not been built.

THE WAR FRONT

What is happening in the Chocó is also happening in the length and breadth of Colombia. The refugees of the Chocó have become part of the one and one-half million refugees and displaced people throughout the country.

The violence in Colombia is not the result of a struggle to survive with scarce resources. The abundant resources of the country are distributed in a form totally unequal, with some sectors in absolute misery, while the land is concentrated in vast properties. The options for those in poverty are the guerrillas or the traffic in drugs. The crisis of Colombia is fundamentally a political crisis where the guerrillas, the paramilitaries and the Colombian Army are confronting one another under a framework of very weak democratic institutions.

In Colombia, to defend life—through activities of human rights, labor unions, campesino (farmer, peasant) organizations or ecological organizations—routinely signifies seeking death. He who criticizes the economic policies or the political structures is equated with being "subversive" and becomes the focus of a national network of assassins who, since 1988, have assassinated or executed or disappeared 33,300 persons, with an average of 10 per day, according to the Comisión Colombiana de Juristas (Colombian Commission of Jurists).

If one compares the 9,000 political murders in Argentina during the eight years of the military dictatorship there or the 3,000 political murders during the 17 years of Pinochet in Chile, the average of 3,000 political murders per year since 1988 presents a pathetic picture of the "Colombian democracy." Imagine if it had been a military dictatorship!

In 1997 alone there were 185 massacres, according to the Comite Permanente para la Defensa de los Derechos Humanos (Permanent Committee for the Defense of Human Rights). Summarizing, the war in Colombia is against the poor.

Since 1989, Colombia has been the number one country in Latin America in receipt of military help from the United States in spite of the fact that the Colombian Army has never hidden the fact that its fundamental objective is to fight the guerrillas and the "subversives." Instead of supporting human rights, the government of the United States provides military aid to the Colombian Army, which is guilty of horrible human rights violations by means of paramilitaries directly linked to the military, such as Carlos Castaño, who sent his paramilitaries to the Chocó. The campesinos expelled from their lands go to the Amazon region to cut down the tropical forest and to plant coca to survive. The drug traffic is the direct result of the desperation of poverty. To treat this problem militarily is not the solution. To look at Colombia only from the perspective of drugs is to blind ourselves to the social, political and military dynamics of the country. Doing so produces confusion around the theme of the realities and causes of the drug problem in Colombia and the United States.

Ironically, the globalization of the world economy is not developed to serve the necessities or demands of the majority but rather to serve the caprices or *conspicuous consumption* of a minority. Thus, if the majority does not have money to buy products defined as necessities by the geniuses of the market, these persons do not exist. In other words, merchandise is only produced to obtain profits and not to produce goods and services for humanity, which was the origin of the bartering or exchange system. As the refugees from the Chocó cannot buy at GAP or from Nike, they don't exist.

Economic power with globalization becomes stronger than political power–or said in a better way, the economic power of the minorities is converted into political power serving their minority interests. Thus democracy in its essence is being lost because decisions are centralized in the salons of the corporations, and the much-criticized "central planning" of the socialist system ironically becomes a reality for the "western democracies," because over time it becomes increasingly difficult for a state to impose corrections on the global market to correct deficiencies. The Colombian state receives many external pressures to open up the Chocó for the world economy and the "free market" of the Americas.

Another aspect of this theme is that as the multinationals compete with one another, work becomes not a right but almost a favor, and to have work in conditions inferior to those in other countries is seen as a privilege. From this perspective, the refugees of the Chocó must obligatorily work for whatever the corporations wish to pay them.

The Chocó now will no longer relate stories as an oral tradition but as a commodity to obtain money. The subsistence economy has ended, and one needs money to buy Coca-Cola.

And so, little by little, the last objective of globalization is reached, which is to transform all of us into individual consumers for whom fraternity is unknown, solidarity is unknown, and compassion for one another is unknown.

PART B

Cecilia's analysis of the conflict in Colombia, its causes, and her evaluation of developments affecting it.

1996

Clarifying the Obscurities in Colombia's Human Rights Crisis[1]

"Therefore, we are living the greatest of injustices: that which occurs when the criminal, without fear, brags about his criminal acts..."

— Jaime Córdoba Triviño (Defensor del Pueblo)
Ombudsman for the Colombian Government, Speech, September 7, 1995

Sipping a cup of dark Colombian coffee, I sat down on a cold Wisconsin night to read the Lawyers' Committee for Human Rights evaluation of the most recently published United States State Department Report on different countries' human rights situation.[1)]

The United States State Department hails Colombia as one of Latin America's oldest and most durable democracies. A few specks here and there, true, but as a whole, one of the most stable and solid democracies in the hemisphere.

Perhaps it is the oldest, since the battle of Boyacá on August 7, 1819, won by Simón Bolívar's Army, was the first defeat of the proud Spanish Royal Army and the beginning of the end for the Spanish Empire in the Americas. The most stable? Perhaps, thanks to the same Army. The most solid? It depends on your

1. Editor's note: Superscript numbers such as [1)] or [2)] refer to Bibliography entries. Superscript entries such as [1] or [2] refer to footnotes located at the bottom of the page in which they occur.

definition of democracy. This is the key. I do not share the same definition of democracy as State Department bureaucrats when it comes to the situation in Colombia.

Simón Bolívar's Army was the laughingstock of the Spanish Court. Made up of peasants and humble country people, it lacked everything from uniforms to food to ammunition. The soldiers were dressed in rags and ponchos, and many died while crossing the Andes in an epic march that was the result of a brilliant strategy, which was to attack the Spanish Army from behind. What Bolivar's Army lacked in material things it overcame with a strong desire for freedom and democracy. That gave it its fuel to fight. Bolívar had been given a crown with golden leaves when he triumphantly entered the city of Bogotá. For the Voltígeros Battalion's role in the battle, Bolívar threw the crown to the soldiers saying: "Those soldiers are the ones who deserve this crown."

Simón Bolívar was allegedly the richest man in the Americas at the time. He was born to nobility and when the time came to educate him, his family hired a private tutor who, unknown to the family, educated the child with the best ideas of the Enlightenment. To help matters, the child was brilliant. He was sent to France and Spain where he became a playmate of the future King Ferdinand VII. Many years later, Ferdinand would set a price for the head of his former playmate for rebellion and insurgency.

Bolívar gave himself totally to the cause of freedom. His hacienda, San Mateo, was used as headquarters in the early days of the struggle. He was completely different from his equivalent, General Washington, in the Northern Hemisphere. He liberated his slaves, and he died in absolute poverty. "I will die as I was born: naked," he said many times. And he did. Simón Bolívar wanted education, freedom and democracy in the most basic sense for all the people of Latin America. He even talked about education for women.

A general cannot fight a war alone. There were other generals, activists and intellectuals in the struggle. And women, who in contrast to the struggle in the Northern Hemisphere, were indispensable actors in the drama for the liberation of Spanish America. Many such players, the best of the crop, were shot ceremoniously by the Spaniards. Ceremony is important in the Spanish culture because of its reverence for symbols. This fact should be kept in mind because of what happened many years later. When this long and bloody war was over, General Bolívar ended up being considered too much a product of the Enlightenment.

The internal opposition to Bolívar was led by General Francisco de Paula Santander. He headed the government in Bogotá while Bolívar fought against the Spanish forces. To quote Gerhard Mansur's biography on Bolívar, when he returned from Perú, "Bolívar brought to Santander's attention the ruinous state of finances and pointed out to [sic] the unnecessary number of public employees and that the crumbling of the nation was notorious." In one of his letters, Bolívar says "the picture of the republic is a spectacle of great misery because there are no public or private funds. Trust, love of law and respect for magistrates do not exist. Unhappiness is everywhere." Santander, consummate master in the art of hypocrisy, pretended publicly to have kept his admiration for the Liberator, but with his friends in Bogotá his attitude was different...he condemned Bolívar's "constitutional ideas."[2)]

Bolívar was forced to leave and died going into exile. The descendants of the Conquistadores did not fight the Spanish for freedom and democracy in this war. This war was fought to keep the vast wealth of the country for themselves. No more gold sent to Spain. "Let us enjoy our riches, and let's look for good business partners abroad" seems to have been the view of the small, petty, provincial and narrow-minded elite of the time—that same elite whose children are today's leaders of Colombia. Still with the same last names, still with the same ideology, still with the same vicious methods.

After expelling the Spaniards, the local elite went on to the business of establishing a democracy. What they established was a "cynical democracy." Father Javier Giraldo, the highly respected Jesuit and Executive Director of Justicia y Paz, calls it a "genocidal democracy."[3)] Actually, it is both. The elites organized the cynical democracy, then and now, as a façade to the international community. Embracing a formal democracy was a condition for opening new markets, investment possibilities and access to raw materials from other countries.

Colombia fulfills all of the formal requisites of a democracy. There are three branches of government which function in beautiful buildings. The Colombian elites are refined, gracious, educated, urbane and possess exquisite manners. They speak the most beautiful Spanish. Do not touch their interests, however, because by a sort of Pavlovian reflex, they become uncivilized killers.

Although the three branches of government in this modern "democracy" exist both on paper and in buildings; in reality, they function as one branch. For 40 years until 1991, Colombia was governed almost continuously under a "State of Siege." The President held almost dictatorial powers, and the lines between the Executive and the Legislative branches tended to be almost nonexistent.

Curiously in this unique "democracy," the Judiciary was able to keep some independence. This ended when the military reclaimed the Palace of

Justice from M-19 guerrillas in 1985 under the pretext that it was protecting the "democratic institutions" from guerrillas. Many of the most independent Supreme Court justices, including the President of the Court, were killed. When the Constitutional Court recently entered a judgment against some of President Samper's decrees, Cabinet ministers and the Congressmen protested strongly, not only denying the Court its jurisdiction but pronouncing it responsible for the problems of the country!

The current President of the Court, José Gregorio Hernández, has admitted publicly that he received threats after the Court declared President Samper's decrees invalid and has accused politicians and members of Congress of responsibility for provoking these threats.[4)]

A fundamental right in a true democracy is the right to life.[2] Colombian "democracy" has failed to protect this fundamental right. The current cycle of violence began in the 1940s when 300,000 people were killed in 10 years.[5)] As the following chart shows, the number of political killings in Colombia in the last decade has far outstripped that of other Latin American countries in recent years.[6)]

Country	Number of Years Under Military Dictatorship	Number of Political Killings
Uruguay	16	220
Argentina	8	9,000
Brazil	15	125
Bolivia	17	243
Chile	17	2,666
Columbian "democracy" under:		
President Barco (1986-1990)		13,635
President Gaviria (1990-1994)		14,856
Victims of political violence in Colombia, January 1988 to December 1995		28,332[7)]
Total victims, including Obscure Assassinations, January-December 1995		67,378[3]

When César Gaviria turned over the Presidency to Ernesto Samper in 1994, he was elected Secretary General of the Organization of American States

2. Editor's note: 'Right to life' here does not refer to opposition to legalized abortion as in the United States. It refers to the rights of citizens to food, security, shelter, healthcare, a life free of violence and state or social intimidation.

3. Editor's note: The figures for "Political Killings" in the chart as presented by the author do not appear to add up to the figure of 67,378 victims. Exactly how the author made the calculations she presents could not be determined by the editor. The editor assumes that "Obscure Assassinations" refers to killings for which assignation of responsibility could not be clearly placed.

largely as a result of U.S. pressure in his favor. The Mexican writer Jorge Castañeda summarizes the Colombia situation in his book *Utopia Unarmed*: "Over 30,000 left-wing militants, activists and sympathizers were killed, more than the organized left lost in El Salvador, and far more than in Argentina, Chile, or Uruguay during the dirty wars of the seventies. The repression of the Colombian left, and the magnitude of its losses are unparalleled in modern Latin American history."[8)]

According to the Andean Commission of Jurists, Colombia Section, on average, there are at least 10 political killings each day in Colombia.[9)] This occurs in a country that has constitutionally forbidden the death penalty for the last 85 years! Even in tragedy, Colombians' lively sense of humor comes through. When a peasant in the Middle Magdalena region was asked what his opinion was about the death penalty, which was being debated by some politicians, his answer was: "Get rid of it."

Colombia does not have "ethnic cleansings" as in Bosnia. Instead, it has "social cleansings" and "political cleansings." Both are based on the same concept as that in Bosnia: to eliminate those different from the eliminator, either by class or by political ideology.

According to Juan Pablo Ordoñez's recently published book on social cleansing: "Throughout the Spanish-speaking world, people use the word desechable (disposable) to refer to items that are used once and then disposed of, thrown in the trash; something that is of no use and consequently that no one will miss, such as a used diaper or a plastic cup. In Colombia, the term has other special connotations. It is used to refer not only to objects without feelings or consciousness, but also human beings, people who are considered disposable from the day of their birth."[10)]

Among those who have been considered disposable by Colombian society are: beggars, street children, prostitutes, homeless, poor people with mental health problems, drug addicts, transvestites and homosexuals. The term was first used in Colombia by the National Police, who claimed that "social cleansing" was of benefit to society because it eliminated "leftovers" whom nobody wants. Their crime is to be poor. In Orwellian logic, these people who above everything deserve compassion and love are considered the source of society's problems rather than a consequence of the failures of Colombian "democracy."

Any self-respecting democracy must permit freedom of association, including the right to choose a political party. Historically the Colombian "democracy" has featured two political parties: the Liberals and the Conservatives. These two entities might as well be considered one party with two heads. There is absolutely no ideological difference between the two parties. They have the same position on social and economic issues, the same interests and same defense of the institutions of Colombia's brand of "democracy."

A challenge to this two-party hegemony came with the formation of the Patriotic Union party in 1985. The Patriotic Union was formed in response to a call by then President Belisario Betancur to guerrillas to take advantage of an amnesty and to enter into peaceful political competition. Formed by former guerrillas who accepted the truce, the Patriotic Union organized at a grassroots level. The party appealed to a broad range of Colombian citizens, both those who had taken up arms against the government and others who believed that the Liberal and Conservative parties had done nothing to represent their interests. The Patriotic Union was formed as a legitimate party and registered with the government in order to be able to compete in elections.

Elections came, and Patriotic Union candidates enjoyed extensive success. Many were elected mayors, city council members and even members of the national Congress and state assemblies. The two traditional parties saw this success as a real threat to their power. Frustrated by their failure to stop Patriotic Union success at the ballot box, persons linked to the Liberal and Conservative parties promoted violent acts to dissuade or eliminate Patriotic Union candidates.

The only two Presidential candidates of the Patriotic Union, who ran in 1986 and 1990, were assassinated, as were more than 2,500 members of this party. To show to what levels the opposition has gone to repress the Patriotic Union, consider what happened in a little town in Antioquia called Segovia. A woman Patriotic Union candidate was elected Mayor, defeating the Liberal Party candidate. A short while later as people strolled through the open market on a Sunday, two jeeps with masked men armed with machine guns suddenly appeared, and the occupants killed people at random. This to punish the town for electing a Patriotic Union member as Mayor.

Likewise, in Tolima province, a woman city council member for the Patriotic Union was killed by a paramilitary group[11)] which also killed her husband and five children between 3 and 28 years old and "disappeared" a two-year-old boy. Although radio reports quickly attributed the killings to FARC guerrillas, in fact a paramilitary group, which had threatened the family on several occasions with the knowledge of the Army and the Police, was responsible for the massacre for political reasons. This is a shining example of "democracy" Colombian style, of respect for institutions and tolerance.

Political killings have taken the lives of labor leaders, religious leaders (nuns, priests, base community activists), lawyers, political activists, cooperativists, teachers, human rights monitors, peasants, actors, journalists and intellectuals. Anybody who thinks may be viewed as a threat to be eliminated.

Remember that during the war for independence, patriots fighting for their freedom were shot ceremoniously in public. At least they had the consolation of dying with their heads up, with the company of the people who prayed for them during the execution and priests who administered the sacraments during their hours of agony. At least they had the consolation of knowing who killed them and why! The modern killings are anonymous, secret, often with the viciousness that is reserved for mad dogs in the streets.

Consider the case of Father Jaime León Restrepo-López.[12)] Ordained a priest in 1971, Father Restrepo had as his first parish Cristales in the northeast part of Antioquia where for eight years he dedicated his life to the poor, promoting participation from the community and creating a sense of community and solidarity. The centerpiece of his ministry was to organize base communities, as the Liberation Theology grassroots groups are called throughout Latin America. Some rich people from the town disapproved of his work and criticized him several times to the Archbishop. In 1980, he was transferred to Medellín. In Medellín he taught philosophy at the Universidad Pontificia Bolivariana and administered a parish.

Later, he decided to go through a personal evaluation and spiritual search for the meaning of his priesthood and went to live with a peasant family. He worked as a peasant in the morning and in the afternoon dedicated his time to reflection, study and prayer. In November 1987, Jaime ended his period of reflection and was assigned again to a parish near Cristales, called Nus. Once again, he confronted oppression, conflict and suffering. For this, on January 17, 1988, at 3:35 p.m., as he was about to celebrate mass, he was killed by a paid assassin.

The truth behind the killing of Father Restrepo surfaced in May 1990. A man came to the Archbishop's office in Medellín and asked for help. According to his account, after he had completed military service, several Army officials obligated him to work for them, saying that if he refused they would put him in jail. He killed for the Army for 20 years. In testimony to the Attorney General's office, the former Army man said Father Jaime Restrepo was assassinated because of accusations made by rich families of the region of Nus. "Señor Humberto Moreno, the Villegas family, the Sierra family, a lady named Ana, a gentleman called William" had complained to the XIV Army Brigade located in Puerto Berrío. Father Restrepo was accused of preaching against the rich and being on the side of the poor.

The witness said that the brigade had at its service groups of civilian collaborators (paramilitary groups) to one of which he belonged. On January 16, 1988, a rumor spread that a "job" was needed in Nus and that Colonel Navas, Commander of the Intelligence Service of the Army, had authorized the "job." Father Restrepo was killed the next day. After this testimony in June, 1990, the witness was killed the following December. No one was charged with the crime or convicted of it.

This rather lengthy example is a typical one because it shows clearly the actors in the Colombian drama: the activist, the rich, the military, the paramilitary and impunity. Especially impunity.

Amazingly in Colombia only 3 percent of killings result in convictions.[10)] Dr. Jaime Córdoba Triviño is the Ombudsman of the Colombian Government, a figure created by the new Constitution of 1991 with the title "Defender of the People." In his keynote speech at a peace conference in Bogotá on September 7, 1995, he said that Colombians not only suffer "subversive violence," they suffer "violence from the state."[13)] Córdoba Triviño said that since the 1991 Constitution was implemented, no diminution has been seen in the violence coming from agents of the state. Government agents abuse power and make war with total lack of regard for human rights, and private people commit crimes at the instigation and with the complicity of public servants. "Thousands of Colombians are terrorized by the action of paramilitary groups that act with total freedom in zones that are controlled by the Army."[13)]

Córdoba Triviño called particular attention to pervasive impunity. "Impunity is the gravest of the injustices that has corrupted the soul of the nation. Impunity in Colombia is the first cause of the flourishing of violence ... In Colombia to our own disgrace, the violators of human rights know that they can kill, disappear and torture with no fear because impunity has become part of their modus operandi."[13)]

There are several different mechanisms that produce impunity. Sometimes the military denies responsibility and characterizes the victims as "guerrillas killed in combat." Sometimes the military obstructs judicial investigations by not cooperating, by harassing witnesses or tampering with or falsifying evidence. Remarkably, in one case, the Colombian military even sent a suspected human rights violator abroad to study at the School of the Americas.

Colonel Luis Felipe Becerra-Bohórquez was the object of both disciplinary and criminal investigations for his participation in the 1980 massacres of 20 banana workers from plantations "Honduras" and "La Negra" in the municipality of Turbo in the Urabá region. Despite the existence of a warrant for his arrest, Becerra was sent to Fort Benning, Georgia, for additional officer training. When he returned to Colombia, he was promoted to Lieutenant Colonel and appointed commander of the Palace Battalion.[14)]

On October 5, 1993, he was involved in a massacre of 13 peasants in the municipality of Riofrío in the Cauca Valley department. Col. Becerra told the news media that 13 well-known ELN (Ejército de Liberación Nacional) guerrillas had been killed in a fierce combat with troops he commanded. Further investigation by journalists showed that the persons reported by Becerra as guerrillas killed in combat were actually poor peasants summarily executed on Becerra's orders. Was he applying at Riofrío lessons learned at the School of the Americas?

Another example of the way in which Colombia's system of military justice protects human rights abusers is the case of Brigadier General Álvaro Velandia-Hurtado. He was the subject of a punitive order issued by the Procurador General's (Inspector General's) Office in July 1995, which removed him from office on the grounds that he was found responsible for the forced disappearance and execution of a young woman whose lifeless body was found with signs of torture in July 1990. The Samper administration's response to the Procurador General's order was to award Velandia by presidential decree one of its highest orders. Meanwhile, the brave Procurador, Hernándo Valencia Villa was forced by threats upon his life to flee the country.[15)] [Editor's note: Colombia Support Network later invited Valencia Villa to speak at the CSN Conference on Faceless Justice, which he did in March 1997.]

This is another common mechanism of impunity: to threaten and murder, if necessary, witnesses, relatives and friends of victims, lawyers and human rights workers. And remarkably under the 1991 Constitution, the concept of "due obedience" was introduced, implying a soldier is not responsible for his acts if he follows a superior officer's orders. In addition, military privilege was extended to include the Police also, meaning that military courts, not civilian courts, try cases of alleged misconduct by soldiers, policemen and their commanders.[16)]

Since Colombia is highly centralized in terms of its political structure,[17] there are areas where the presence of the state is minimal, almost non-existent. These are areas where the insurgent movement has control. The Army has labeled them "red zones." In these zones, the military has a free hand "fighting against subversion." This means anything is allowed, including the formation of alliances with drug trafficking organizations and paramilitary groups, which on many occasions are set up by the Armed Forces themselves.[17] So it is easy to see how human rights violations are frequent in the context of operations against guerrillas or drug traffickers.

Two phenomena arise from the actions of the Army and the Police under impunity: the creation of refugees and the formation of paramilitary groups. At this moment, there are more than 600,000 Colombians who are internal refugees. They are mostly displaced peasants fleeing from terror in the countryside. When they come to the cities, many of them become "desechables" (disposables) because in their desperation many have no other recourse but to become prostitutes, criminals or beggars, the victims of social cleansing.

Displacement happens in the context of counter-insurgency operations. Usually these are transitory operations staged by the Mobile Brigades of the Army which come to a given location for three to five weeks. They typically announce their presence by setting off a bomb to drive out or divide the population. Many flee. Then they start visiting residents house by house. Where the houses are found empty, they destroy the home furnishings. Where there are people, they gather information—especially names of community leaders or members of unions or peasants' organizations. They give this information to paramilitary groups which then search these people out and kill them. The Army also confiscates the land to use for its own purposes.[10]

Drug traffickers buy land everywhere. According to former CINEP director Francisco de Roux at a lecture in Madison, Wisconsin, in 1995: "In the last five years, the drug traffickers have taken between four and five million hectares of the best Colombian land. They are not interested in growing anything, they are not interested in making a profit from agriculture. They are just interested in money laundering. And at the very moment they buy the land, they drive out the peasants and they introduce private armies in order to protect themselves."[18]

Father Javier Giraldo has sketched the role of the paramilitary groups: "Paramilitarism becomes, then, the keystone of a strategy of 'dirty war,' where the dirty actions cannot be attributed to persons on behalf of the state through their visible actions, but are instead delegated, passed along or projected upon bodies of armed civilians, anonymous and easily defined as common delinquents who act and then disappear into the fog. The objective is to cover up responsibility for acts which have no legal justification nor legitimacy ... with the result that they intermesh: 1) Actions of military officers camouflaged as civilians and 2) Military actions of civilians protected in a clandestine way by military personnel. Both types of proceedings have the same objective: covering up to protect impunity." Reportedly, there are more than 130 paramilitary groups in the country.[19)]

The alliance between drug lords and Army personnel here is very clear. For instance, Colonel Luis Alfonso Plazas-Vega was directly implicated in the creation and leadership of a paramilitary group known as MAS (Muerte a Secuestradores, Death to Kidnappers) by an investigation in 1982 by the Procurador General's office. MAS carried out many assassinations of members of the political opposition. The study showed Plazas-Vega had worked very closely with the military head of the Medellín Cartel, Gonzalo Rodríguez-Gacha.[20)] Here the U.S. government funds the Colombian military to fight a "War on Drugs" and winds up being used to help pay for the activities of one of Colombia's biggest drug lords!

Another less publicized consequence of the War on Drugs is the Faceless Justice System. Ostensibly this system was set up with U.S. government assistance in order to protect judges, prosecutors and witnesses in prosecution of drug traffickers.

The U.S. government provided at least $36 million in money and equipment to Colombia to establish this Faceless Justice System, in which judges, witnesses and prosecutors are not identified by name to the defense and thus remain "faceless." Under "faceless justice" there are no court appearances and no jury nor does the accused get to face his accusers or even learn their identities. All evidence is submitted in written form, in briefs, affidavits and depositions taken by officers of the prosecutor at the Fiscalía (Attorney General's Office). If the official in charge finds sufficient evidence to warrant a trial, he submits the case to the judge, and only then does he convert from objective investigator to adversarial prosecutor. At the end of the Twentieth Century, the proceedings of the Inquisition, with all its secrecy, are once again in vogue.

Remarkably, this system has been applied not only in drug cases but in cases of supposed "terrorism." The system is used to prosecute Colombian citizens engaged in social protest or who are leaders of opposition parties. Thus, when Patriotic Union members are not eliminated, they are put in jail and tried in the

Faceless Justice System. Take the case of José Antonio López-Bula and Nelson Campo. López, a lawyer and member of the Patriotic Union, was elected Mayor of the town of Apartadó. He has been one of the most outspoken persons for promoting political change through peaceful means. His administration had many accomplishments. Among them a new school, new public market, main bus station and new streets. López was running for Congress on the Patriotic Union ticket, when a massacre in the La Chinita neighborhood of Apartadó took place on January 23, 1994. In that massacre, 35 people died. The Mayor at that time was Nelson Campo, another Patriotic Union member. He opened his office to investigation and condemned the massacre.

Through the Faceless Justice System, witnesses came forward who had been detained by the Army as guerrillas or who had deserted the FARC guerrilla forces, and who were living on the military base which happens to be near Apartadó, the Voltígeros Battalion's base. There persons were instructed to testify against the Mayor and received payment for their accusations. One witness, Héctor Guisao, stated in a sworn affidavit that deserters were paid 50,000 to 200,000 pesos to testify against López, Campo and Patriotic Union politicians and activists.[21)]

The witnesses were humble country people. The Bishop of Apartadó at the time, Monsignor Isaías Duarte Cancino, today Archbishop of Cali, told me that he is convinced of López's innocence. He urged serious consideration of Guisao's declarations. But the government has to date shown no inclination to take Guisao's testimony seriously.

Meanwhile, there are approximately 16,000 guerrillas of FARC (Fuerzas Armadas Revolucionarias de Colombia), ELN (Ejército de Liberación Nacional), and a dissident faction of the EPL (Ejército Popular de Liberación) in arms. They are active on more than 60 "fronts" in different regions of the country.[17)]

These guerrillas bear a lot of responsibility for the overall violence in Colombia. A guerrilla movement by its very nature must win power quickly—within about 10 years. If it does not, it degenerates, loses its momentum and the war then becomes a war of attrition. The Colombian guerrillas proclaim the combination of all forms of struggle to obtain power. The consequence of this is devastating for non-violent grassroots and civic movements. The human rights statistics cited earlier in this article speak for themselves. This ideology combined with the ideology of National Security from the Army would create an explosive bomb for any country.

Many paramilitary groups formed when enraged cattlemen joined forces with drug traffickers against kidnappings which many guerrillas used as a primary tactic to finance their activities. These kidnappings are also highly violatory of international humanitarian law. Colombian guerrillas are responsible for placing land mines in areas where they are active, with horrifying consequences for the civilian population living there. Lately they have been rivaling the Army by committing acts of torture.[22)]

The U.S. Embassy in Bogotá has frequently accused the guerrillas of being "narco-guerrillas". But in so doing, as Francisco de Roux has shown: "They have tried to put together two things that are totally different: problems with drugs and problems with the guerrillas ... The guerrillas in Colombia are political fighters while the drug traffickers fight for money. They are criminals fighting for money. They are not interested in political power."[18)] While "it is true that some groups of Colombian guerrillas impose taxes on peasants who are coca growers in exchange for their watching the plantations ... this is a way of financing the war."[23)]

Drug trafficking in Colombia is also a result of the highly unequal distribution of wealth in the country. As Dr. de Roux has shown, it is the exclusion of most Colombians from access to wealth which is responsible: "When you have a creative population who are being excluded from the mainstream of the economy, they will enter the economy, but they probably will enter by the back door to the mainstream ... and back door means for us drug trafficking, smuggling, money laundering."[18)]

The most serious consequence of drug trafficking is the way it has affected the ethical values of the country. These are the core of any society. Solidarity and care for each other are replaced by a morality which gives more value to property than to human beings. It has become a society which blurs the fine lines between what is good and what is bad and erases the collective conscience of belonging to a nation. That is Colombia's tragedy.

Colombia is by no means a poor country. It has oil, coal, gold, emeralds and platinum. It is blessed with rivers and a variety of climates where crops can be grown year-round to feed the country's people and have everybody happy. It certainly has the means to give its citizens at least their basic needs. Yet, there is hunger in Colombia.

Malnutrition from birth on affects a substantial percentage of Colombians. Thus 8.7 percent have low weight at birth due to maternal malnutrition, 15 percent of preschoolers are malnourished and 20 percent of Colombians experience chronic malnutrition.[24)] The Food and Agriculture Organization from the U.N. put Colombia in the list of ill-fed countries.[24] There is land and there are people to produce food, but neo-liberal policies do not favor food production for domestic consumption. In 1990, Colombia imported 876,000 tons of food. In 1994, the number was 3 million tons. What a shame in a country with such a rich potential!

Colombia's tragedy is also a result of an absolute lack of political will to implement a deep transformation in the social and economic structures of the country. From the very beginning of the nation, the die was cast. That is why Bolívar was an impediment. As a United Nations report states: "The persistent economic and social differences and the high level of poverty continue to be an underlying cause of violence and crime. Several observers have pointed out that the benefits derived from steady economic growth and stability have not been employed to resolve the most basic problems of poverty and social exclusion. While 75 percent of the population are said to fall below the level of poverty and 13 percent are completely illiterate, public investment in education, health, housing, food and other social programs is said to be very low. Very high administrative costs and the amount of money spent on military activities are said to reduce public investment in social areas even more. In addition, land continues to be concentrated in the hands of a small number of landowners."[17]

The high "administrative costs" that the report describes could be the same corruption that General Bolívar saw when he came back from the wars of independence, and that he brought to Santander's attention as "the crumbling of the nation."

Violence in Colombia is the result of these deep inequalities. What the Colombian elites cannot understand is the meaning of the words stability and security. Stability and security cannot be bought in the arms market. Stability and security cannot be bought by setting up an Army of "300,000 private bodyguards protecting people against people."[18] A nation has stability and security only when its people have food, clothes, shelter, health and education. Those are the things that give security. Only when the great majority of Colombians have these needs fulfilled will the country reach peace.

Colombia's investment in its Army is totally irrational because an army does not produce anything except death, destruction and tears. Like the black holes in the universe which absorb light never to release it again, the Army takes money and never returns it to society. It also eliminates vast human resources that could contribute greatly to the country.

The government cannot keep up perennial peace talks with the guerrillas just to pretend they are doing something for peace. The real challenge is to give basic needs to the homeless, the children, the refugees, the elderly, the women and the mentally ill. If these people have their basic needs met, there will be no guerrilla movement. There are no guerrillas in Norway or Sweden.

The Colombian elites behave like cheap actors in the world theatre. They only care for what people abroad think of them. If it is not too positive, they will buy their opinion. The Colombian government attempted to improve its badly soiled image abroad by paying $3.1 million to the public relations firm Sawyers and Mill in 1991. The propaganda campaign turned the "victim" into "hero" and then into "leader" in the War on Drugs.[25] If only those millions of dollars had been invested in food or education!

The Colombian elite has powerful friends in the U.S. government. If Colombia's current levels of violence and human rights violations had been happening in Cuba or in Nicaragua in the 80s, they would have been on the front page of the New York Times every day. Instead, a Times editorial entitled "Colombia in Crisis" on January 30, 1996, urges President Samper to resign but does not say one word about the human rights crisis.

Ana Carrigan, a journalist who writes about Colombia, aptly stated, "In the past, wherever Latin America's 'dirty wars' have flourished on a scale comparable to the Colombian experience of the last decade ... at the very least the democratic opposition could count on the informed solidarity of an alerted international community."[26] Instead, "the official script that attributes political violence in Colombia to an all-powerful drug mafia has shielded the true identity of the killers of Colombian citizens from public scrutiny and juridical accountability."[26]

The Army in Colombia has all the power it wants. Power was given to the military by the elites to protect their peculiar version of Colombian democracy. There is no need to stage a coup d'état. In Urabá last September, I pondered how General Bolívar must be rolling over in his grave. His beloved Voltígeros Battalion is now one of the most feared battalions in its own country for its cruelty and inhumanity to the Colombian citizens it is supposed to protect.

Two questions can be drawn from the Colombian case which are pertinent to the United States. One question is: Should the United States promote the Colombian version of "democracy" as a foreign policy tool in other countries in the Third World, such as the nations of Eastern Europe or, closer to home, the promotion of civilian governments in Guatemala and El Salvador? In the last case I ask if they would not start killing the ex-guerrillas as Colombia killed the Patriotic Union? Of course, all of these under "democracy."

United States' acceptance of Colombia's "democracy" satisfies its goal of stability and friendship with businessmen and merchants, the centerpieces of U.S. foreign policy in Colombia and Latin America. Living with Colombia's "democracy" is cheaper for the U.S. than seeking to promote a real democracy. Profits are produced for U.S. traders and by using the Colombian Army as a proxy, the U.S. government need not send the Marines to protect its investments there.

The second question to ask: Is the United States itself becoming like Colombia? With its increased concentration of wealth, with the cutting of its "safety net" for the poor, with its growing number of homeless, with its right-wing militias and its violence on the streets, it could be that by looking at Colombia you are looking at your own future. Maintaining vigilance of your democracy would be a way to prevent the darkness of state-condoned violations of human rights.

BIBLIOGRAPHY

1) Anonymous. Lawyer's Committee for Human Rights. The Americas Critique Review of the United States Department of State Country Reports on Human Rights Practices, Colombia, July, 1995.

2) Mansur, Gerhard. "Simón Bolívar," Editorial Grijalbo, Caracas, 1987.

3) Giraldo, S.J., Javier. "Colombia: The Genocidal Democracy," Common Courage Press, Monroe, Maine, 1996.

4) Torres, Héctor. "Samper termina el año amarrado por los militares y los Estados Unidos". Utopías, Vol. III, #30, pagina 12, diciembre, 1995.

5) LaFranchi, Howard. "Disgusted by Drug-fed graft, Colombians seek new image," *The Christian Science Monitor*, page 1, February 20, 1996.

6) Anonymous. Comisión Interinstitucional de Justicia y Paz, "Colombia Bulletin," Vol. 2, #13, pages 14-15, August, 1994.

7) Comisión Interinstitucional de Justicia y Paz. "Víctimas de la Violencia Política," Banco de Datos, September 25, 1995.

8) Castañeda, Jorge. "Utopia Unarmed. The Latin American Left after the Cold War," page 116, Vintage Books, Random House, August, 1994.

9) Comisión Andina de Juristas, Seccional Colombia. "Una situación que no mejora," page 1, Panorama, Primer semestre, 1995.

10) Ordoñez, Juan Pablo. "No human being is disposable," International Gay and Lesbian Human Rights Commission, Colombia Human Rights Committee and Proyecto Dignidad, page 36, 1995.

11) Unión Patriótica. Comunicado de Prensa, #29, febrero 23, 1991.

12) Anonymous. "Aquellas muertes que hicieron resplandecer la vida," paginas 183-197, Bogotá, octubre, 1992.

13) Córdoba Triviño, Jaime. "La crisis de Derechos Humanos no es una ficción," Documentos Su Defensor, páginas 19-22, Vol. 3, #27, octubre de 1995.

14) Commission of Non-Governmental Organizations Report, "Massacre in Riofrío," October 5, 1993.

15) Gallón Giraldo, Gustavo. Carta al presidente de la Comisión Interamericana de Derechos Humanos, Organización de los Estados Americanos (Organization of American States, OAS), Bogotá, paginas 2-3, septiembre 6, 1995.

16) Inter-American Commission on Human Rights. Second Report on Human Rights in Colombia, pages 9-10, January, 1994.

17) United Nations, Economic and Social Council, Commission on Human Rights. Joint Report of the Special Rapporteur on the question of torture and the Special Rapporteur on Extrajudicial, Summary or Arbitrary Executions E/CN.4/1995/111, January 16, 1995.

18) De Roux, Francisco. "Exploring new avenues for peace in Colombia". Lecture at the University of Wisconsin, Madison, April 24, 1995.

19) Giraldo, Javier. "Paramilitarism: A criminal policy of the state which devours the country," Boletín Informativo de Justicia y Paz, Vol. 8, #2, April-June, 1995.

20) Anonymous. "El Terrorismo de Estado en Colombia," pages 250-251, NCOs Brussels, 1992.

21) Laun, John I. Compilation from original sources, November, 1995.

22) Declaración del Comité de Búsqueda de la Paz. Utopías, Vol. 3, #29, página 21, octubre, 1995.

23) De Roux, Francisco. Letter to Senator Russ Feingold, May 24, 1995.

24) Comisión Andina de Juristas. "Colombia: Globalización, Pobreza y Desigualdad," Informe ante el Comité de Derechos Económicos, Sociales y Culturales de la Organización de las Naciones Unidas, diciembre, 1995.

25) Stauber, John and Rampton, Sheldon. "Toxic Sludge is Good for You: Lies, Damn Lies and the Public Relations Industry," pages 143-148, Common Courage Press, Maine, 1995.

26) Carrigan, Ana. "A Chronicle of Death Foretold: State-Sponsored Violence in Colombia," NACLA Report on the Americas, Vol. 28, Issue 5, pages 6-10, March/April, 1996.

2001

Closing the Circle of Violence[1]

Colombia's Paramilitaries in Historical Perspective

On July 16, 2001, Carlos Arturo Marulanda-Ramirez, former Colombian Ambassador to the European Union, was detained by INTERPOL in Madrid under international orders from the Colombian Prosecutor General. He accused Marulanda of crimes against humanity, among them organizing paramilitary groups to torture, assassinate and displace peasants.

Ariel Toscano, a 31-year-old peasant and a former leader of ANUC (National Association of Peasants) living in exile, declared his willingness to testify against Marulanda since four of his brothers were killed by paramilitaries working under his orders. Toscano told the newspaper, *El Espectador*, on July 19, "It is fitting to accuse him of crimes against mankind because he followed the steps of his father, Carlos Arturo Marulanda-Grillo, who during the *La Violencia* period, assassinated and displaced many peasants in order to take their land."

Paramilitarism has a long history in Colombia. In order to understand this phenomenon, one must first understand that Colombia is an exclusionary society—it excludes the majority of its inhabitants from their economic, social,

1. This article was published by the journal *Against the Current* in its November/December 2001 issue, pages 25-30, and is being reproduced in this book with permission of *Against the Current*.

political, cultural and human rights. This exclusion occurs in a country of great natural wealth yet one of sharp inequality, where the wealthiest 10 percent hold eighty times the value of the poorest 10 percent. Colombia also defines itself as the oldest democracy in Latin America.

UNLEASHING VIOLENCE

From 1900-1930, Colombia was governed by the Conservative Party, a party which characterized itself by defending religious fanaticism, protecting the most traditional values of Colombian society and isolating the country from all modern currents of thought. During this time period, the big coffee plantations consolidated lands taken from indigenous peoples and poor peasants, using armed bands which were precursors of paramilitary bands.

In 1930, Enrique Olaya Herrera of the Liberal Party was elected president. This change brought violent local upheavals because some Liberals, oppressed for a very long time, decided to persecute the recently defeated Conservatives. According to the classic book, *La Violencia en Colombia*, duly armed and salaried bandits were created. Their mission was to attack, persecute and kill, if necessary, all persons who would not agree with their politics. Power was concentrated in the figure of the presidency; thus the party in power also monopolized access to power in departments (states) and municipalities. Presidents appointed governors and governors appointed mayors. The stakes were high when the parties went to elections.

In 1945, Gabriel Turbay and Jorge Eliecér Gaitán both ran as Liberal Party candidates for president while a united Conservative Party nominated Mariano Ospina Pérez. With the Liberal candidates splitting their vote, Ospina was elected. Two months after Ospina took office, the first Liberals were killed. When Liberals obtained a majority in the midterm congressional elections, the Conservatives unleashed the apparatus of the state to assure their continued hold.

In May 1947, the government declared a general transportation workers' strike illegal. That July, police in Moniquirá, Boyacá, attacked a Liberal Party fundraiser, killing two and wounding twelve. With the level of violence expanding, a local political boss in the state of Caldas organized a group of armed, violent men called *pájaros* (birds). Strikes, including one by the Magdalena River workers, multiplied—and so did the repression. Telegraph stations, bridges and trains were destroyed, and the Tropical Oil Company's site in Barrancabermeja was dynamited.

On February 7, 1948, more than 200,000 persons who identified as Liberals participated in the Demonstration of Silence. Carrying mourning flags, thousands from all over the country marched silently through the streets of Bogotá. They filled the immense Bolívar Square to hear Gaitán beg President Ospina to exercise his authority and preserve order. Workers, peasants and the poor were drawn to Gaitán's political platform, which melded Liberalism to a program of radical reform.

Barely two months later, on April 9, Gaitán was assassinated. The rage of a people whose leader had just been assassinated almost destroyed the city of Bogotá. This eruption, called the *Bogotazo*, has become a symbol of popular fury in Latin America. It is also a symbol of what can become of a revolution without leadership. Provincial politicians from the Liberal Party called for vengeance over Gaitán's assassination, while their Conservative counterparts called for action to protect their church. The masses were called upon to hate and destroy the enemy.

This was the beginning of a systematic trend of assassinations and terror throughout Colombia and is known as the period of *La Violencia*. Hate, fanaticism, ambition for power, irreconcilable ideas and clashing economic perspectives dominated the countryside, seeking either to bring down the Conservative government or to defend it. Properties were abandoned, people displaced and land tenure forcibly altered. The Conservative government used the police to persecute Liberals. The Liberal Party responded by forming armed groups. The Communist Party, which had existed since the 1930s, decided to form self-defense groups of peasants in regions such as Tolima and Cundinamarca.

Ospina dispersed Congress in 1949, and the Liberals boycotted the 1950 elections, resulting in the election of Conservative Laureano Gómez as President. President Gómez announced that his policies were "pro-United States, pro-United Nations, anti-Communist and against violence." In reality, the highest levels of violence occurred during his presidency, with frequent Army massacres—such as the one in the town of Belalcázar, Cauca, where 112 persons were killed in one day. Many Liberals were killed on the pretext that the Liberal Party, in Gómez's view, was "synonymous with Communism."

By the early 1950s there were four different kinds of private armed groups in Colombia:

1. Political guerrillas, organized by the political parties whose members were deceived and exploited by the political leaders.

2. Bandit groups whose creation was unavoidable when children grew up watching atrocities. An example is Teófilo Rojas (aka Chispas) who, after being a bandit for ten years, at 22 was accused of killing 400 people. When asked what he wanted in life he answered, "I want to learn how to read."
3. Self-Defense groups organized by the Communist Party, which had as one of their leaders Pedro Antonio Marín (aka Tirofijo—Sureshot, aka Manuel Marulanda Vélez), present commander of the *Fuerzas Armadas Revolucionarias de Colombia* (FARC). These groups encouraged peasant communities to share the land and created mechanisms for collective work.
4. The *pájaros*, apparently created by policemen, local officers and political bosses with the idea of "conservatizing" Liberal areas, especially the followers of Gaitán. *Pájaros* were armed private groups and hitmen financed by landowners, industrialists and cattle ranchers. They were mobile, decentralized and trained in surprise attacks.

   At first, the pájaros specialized in killing local political leaders or coffee hacienda owners whose harvests would be useful to finance the organization. Later honest judges and political leaders were targeted, taken from their homes or even in the streets or while in churches and placed in jail. There they were tortured, killed and, at night, their bodies thrown into rivers. There were virtually no killings among the elite, either Liberal or Conservative. In all, around 200,000 people were killed in Colombia during *La Violencia* (1946-1958).

In this situation of violence and chaos the military came to power through a coup d'état on June 13, 1953. Except for the Communist Party and the ultra-Conservatives, most people welcomed coup leader General Gustavo Rojas Pinilla. Rojas immediately addressed the violence by offering political amnesty to the guerrillas. On September 8, 1953, the document for surrender of arms was signed by Guadalupe Salcedo, Commander of the Liberal guerrillas. The following year he was assassinated in the streets of Bogotá.

But at the same time, Rojas declared the Communist Party illegal and initiated a campaign against the peasant self-defense groups that had not accepted official amnesty. With the cooperation of the Pentagon and the CIA-developed Plan LASO (Latin America Security Operation), the Army launched an economic and military blockade. In this degraded way, an Army founded by Simón Bolívar adopted National Security as its ideology and "low intensity warfare" as its *modus operandi*.

But Rojas wanted to govern independently of the political and economic elites, who then became disenchanted with him and sought a different political solution. The solution was a nationwide bipartisan agreement called the National Front, to share rule between Liberals and Conservatives as if nothing had happened.

This agreement limited the functioning of the democratic system and the two parties alternated power from 1958 to 1974, sharing administrative functions. Their ideology was fundamentally the same: The National Front functioned as one party with two separate flags. The military was assigned the task to repress all attempts to introduce any alternative to the Conservative-Liberal National Front Alliance, thus defining the Army's role as targeting an internal enemy.

The National Front leadership mouthed support for reforms but effectively undermined structural change in practice. Thus political movements were created in opposition to bipartisanship, among them ANAPO, General Rojas' party, and the Movimiento Revolucionario Liberal (MRL), a dissident faction within the Liberal Party.

After 1959 the formidable influence of the Cuban Revolution stormed Latin America like a cyclone, and most of the current Colombian guerrilla movements were born during this time. The National Front was seen as an expression of the landowners' interests.

During the late 1960s, it was obvious to President Carlos Lleras, a Liberal, that the social problems in the countryside had to be addressed in order to achieve peace "because this cannot be achieved through the military and the police but through justice."

With the Cuban Revolution hanging like a sword over its head, the Lleras government supported land distribution to poor peasants. However, as sociologist Mauricio Romero says, "As the best lands were concentrated in *latifundios* (large estates), the government's policy of land redistribution aroused vociferous opposition from the powerful landed elites and their congressional allies." (Romero, Mauricio. "Changing Identities and Contested Settings: Regional Elites and the Paramilitaries in Colombia." *International Journal of Politics, Culture, and Society*, vol. 14, no. 1, Springer, 2000, pp. 51–69, http://www.jstor.org/stable/20020064.)

Lleras' support for land reform opened new opportunities for peasants to participate in politics, and they developed their own organizations and their own vision of land reform. Given that the traditional politicians were blocking reform, peasants resorted to invading vacant lands and settling them.

Michael McClintock, researching declassified papers in the Pentagon, found that in early 1962, Washington pressured the Colombian government to adopt a paramilitary strategy toward those challenging capitalism's right to assert economic and political hegemony.[2] This matched well with the already developed native system of *pájaros*.

In 1965, a presidential decree empowered the Ministry of Defense to allow military officers to support private use of arms and authorized the government to utilize the civilian population "in activities and works by which they contribute to the reestablishment of normality." This decree became Law 48 (1968).

Then in 1969, Resolution 5 authorized the military to "organize in military form the civilian population, so that it will protect against the actions of the guerrillas and will support the carrying out of combat operations." This same resolution establishes self-defense boards, which are defined as organizations of a military type made up of civilian personnel selected from the combat zone, trained and equipped to develop actions against groups of guerrillas appearing in the area or to operate in coordination with troops in actions of combat. These same boards would be used to prevent the formation of armed groups.

Father Javier Giraldo, S.J., in his book, *Colombia: The Genocidal Democracy*, (pgs. 81-82, Common Courage Press, 1996) suggests that by being clandestine, paramilitaries achieve the secret objective of hiding the identity of state agents:

> Paramilitarism becomes, then, the keystone of a strategy of "Dirty War," where the dirty actions cannot be attributed to persons on behalf of the State because they have been delegated, passed along or projected upon confused bodies of armed civilians. Those committing the crimes are anonymous and easily defined as common delinquents who act and thereafter disappear into the fog. This covers up responsibility for acts which have no legal justification or legitimacy, not even during times of warlike confrontations. The result is that they confound and complement two types of events:

2. Editor's note: See Michael McClintock, *Instruments of Statecraft: U.S. Guerrilla Warfare, Counterinsurgency, and Counterterrorism*, 1940-1990, Pantheon Books, March 31, 1992.

> actions of military officers camouflaged as civilians and military actions of civilians protected in a clandestine way by military personnel. Both types of procedures have the same objective: to provide impunity through cover ups.[3]

In 1970, Misael Pastrana (father of the current president, Andres Pastrana) was elected President in a fraudulent election contest with General Rojas, who, according to many accounts, won. This delegitimized even more the National Front agreement.

Pastrana reversed land reform and instead supported large-scale agriculture. During the Pastrana administration and the one following, of Alfonso López Michelsen, there was a flourishing of strikes, work stoppages, union demands and student demonstrations. Kidnappings substantially increased. An "illegal" economy, based on marijuana and cocaine, developed, along with smuggling coffee and emeralds. In this climate, the Army became sort of a jack-of-all-trades to "keep order;" Colombian society was greatly militarized.

During the 1980s when the social and political crisis forced the elites to confront the situation, the process of military autonomy was difficult to reverse. The presence of guerrillas, the paramilitaries, self-defense groups, drug dealers and common delinquency led to confrontation with the military and filled the country with a spiral of violence. Although formally accepting the peace proposals, the military rejected them. They knew they had the backing of powerful economic segments and regional forces, and these worked together to put public resources in the service of private parties.

Julio Cesar Turbay's administration (1978-1982) sought to banish communism forever from Colombia. This included not only Communist guerrillas, but any expression of thought considered "subversive"—a term which encompassed many teachers, journalists, intellectuals, even nuns and priests. Turbay's Minister of Defense[4] talked about "cultural subversion" hiding among poets, playwrights, writers, novelists and intellectuals. On September 6, 1978, Decree 1923, a security statute, was promulgated. It struck at the most elementary rights of citizens and launched a witch hunt. Activists began to be "disappeared;" civilians were judged in military courts.

---

3. Editor's note: This quote can also be found in "Paramilitarism: A Criminal Policy of the State Which Devours the Country" from *Desde los márgenes*, página oficial de Javier Giraldo, http://www.javiergiraldo.org/spip.php?article131
4. Editor's note: The Minister of Defense under President Julio César Turbay was General Luis Carlos Camacho Leiva.

On December 3, 1981, a helicopter spread fliers over the city of Cali, announcing the creation of the group MAS (Muerte a Secuestradores/Death to Kidnappers). The fliers explained that, motivated by the kidnapping of a girl in the Ochoa family, part of the Medellín drug Cartel, 223 mafia chiefs had put up money to create a squadron of 2,230 men that would execute without compunction any person linked to kidnapping. Through 1982, the MAS were linked to disappearances, murders and threats.

Campaigning on a promise of finding a political solution to the "guerrilla problem," Belisario Betancur, a Conservative, was elected president in 1982 by a wide margin. Betancur's proposed peace negotiations with democratic openings, amnesty for the rebels and a national rehabilitation plan were combined with a commitment to social programs, including an agrarian reform. Powerful economic groups, the military, the political class (and even his own party) then torpedoed his efforts. These private groups initiated counter-insurgency actions to counterbalance his conversations with the guerrillas.

The guerrillas did not capture the moment either. Weak and divided, they overestimated their own capacity and allowed their military approach to predominate. Paradoxically, the FARC, reluctant at the beginning to participate in any peace negotiation, created the Patriotic Union (Unión Patriótica, UP) as an alternative political party. When the UP elected large numbers of mayors and municipal councilmen as well as departmental deputies and a few members of Congress, paramilitary groups, often in league with military officers, killed more than 3,000 UP activists. By the mid 1990s, the UP was virtually eliminated.

A CASE STUDY IN PARAMILITARISM

To better explain the formation of paramilitary groups on the local level I will use as an example the "Vatican" of paramilitarism, the small town of Puerto Boyacá. Located on the banks of the Magdalena River, Puerto Boyacá is a town with a Liberal tradition. It organized Liberal guerrillas during *La Violencia*.

In the National Front period, the town supported a dissident Liberal faction (the MRL), which had links to the Communist Party. Little by little, the Communist Party became the most important local political force in the region, eventually coming to win elections and dominate the municipal councils. The FARC, a guerrilla group, existed in these areas where, besides indoctrinating peasants, they acted as a "rural civil guard" and controlled cattle theft, earning them the support and sympathy of the region's cattlemen. The FARC grew so much that they developed along several fronts. One of these began to tax both cattlemen and large landowners. Several of those pressured fled but protection taxes—called "vaccinations"—and kidnappings continued.

After Julio Cesar Turbay became president in 1978, the Army decided to militarize the region. First came the murder of seven Communist city council members from Cimitarra, a nearby town. Torture and assassination became common. The Army imposed a curfew. Stores were closed and livestock slaughter was prohibited. As a result, the peasant population—especially the children—were dying of hunger.

The government assigned Puerto Boyacá a military mayor and stationed the Army's Barbula Battalion there. The Fourteenth Brigade was created to control the area, and soon extreme right organizations arrived, the most famous of which was the Colombian Society for the Defense of Tradition, Family and Property (TFP), linked to a fascist movement throughout Latin America.

When President Belisario Betancur's government took office in 1982, with its policy of reconciliation, the Army changed its tactics and adopted the slogan that he who has the civilian population with him is he who will win the war. Army units began to build roads, to support public health campaigns and to work on cemetery beautification. The Army organized a circus that traveled from town to town with the objective of getting orphan children to laugh. And the cattlemen began to see the Army as a strong institution that could defend them.

A meeting was called, attended by the Mayor, cattlemen, businessmen, local political chiefs, victims of kidnapping and representatives of the Texas Petroleum Company (TEXACO), which had oil fields in the region and had been involved in land disputes with peasants since 1928. The meeting created a group to provide defense against the "subversion." They patrolled with the Army and "fumigated" the guerrillas as one fumigates insects. The group focused its attention on breaking up the political organization of the Communist Party and the FARC by means of selective, systematic murder of union members, schoolteachers, peasant and civic leaders in a ferocious campaign of annihilation, killing about 800 people.

The founders of the group consolidated into an innocent-sounding organization *Asociación Campesina de Ganaderos y Agricultores del Magdalena Medio* (ACDEGAM), which published in its newsletter of August 1987 that whoever wanted arms could obtain them from the Army's Fourteenth Brigade. ACDEGAM also organized health clinics, a network of thirty grade schools with teachers it paid, community stores and cooperatives. It built highways and bridges and installed communications networks. All of these had as a goal to win and control the civilian population.

All of this activity required money, and the contributions of the cattlemen and merchants were not sufficient. So at this time, a new actor was incorporated into the group's struggle: drug traffickers. In its haste to launder its illegal earnings the Medellín Cartel began to buy land in the region where it established cocaine laboratories and trained its private armies. Soon the Medellín Cartel drug traffickers joined the group, and from then on the members of ACDEGAM lost no more sleep worrying about lack of funds. With the collaboration of the Army, mercenaries were brought from Israel, Australia, England and the United States to train hitmen and modernize the tactics of the war.

The entry of the drug traffickers gave a new twist to the paramilitary phenomenon because they were not interested in the doctrine of National Security nor in anti-communism; but this would help them justify any action to benefit their earnings and investments. In addition, it helped them win favor with the military and the Colombian elites.

The success of the paramilitary model in Puerto Boyacá led to its being reproduced and perfected throughout Colombia—adapted of course to regional characteristics. One of the most successful paramilitary leaders was Fidel Castaño, who belonged to the leadership of the Medellín Cartel. Following the model of the *Autodefensas Campesinas de Córdoba y Urabá* (ACCU), which succeeded in eliminating literally all the peasant activists in Colombia's northeast, Castaño began building his paramilitary group, the Foundation for Peace in Córdoba, in 1980. Following Fidel's death under mysterious circumstances, his brother Carlos Castaño took over.

The guerrillas, who out of principle did not seek vengeance on the paramilitaries after Puerto Boyacá, decided in response to Castaño's paramilitary force that they would fight back with the same cruelty. From that point on the conflict descended into greater barbarity.

THE RECENT EVOLUTION OF PARAMILITARISM

- During the government of Virgilio Barco (1986-90), an attempt was made to technify the peace process by removing the social foundation of the guerrillas, creating the National Rehabilitation Plan to reincorporate guerrillas into society. A rather humorous incident occurred during this process of peace negotiations when the Movement 19th of April (M-19) guerrillas sought to use Article 33 of Law 48. They requested permission to use arms for their own "self-defense" forces similar to those supported, promoted and protected by the Army. In response, President Barco was pressured to suspend Law 48. It was then declared "unconstitutional" by the Supreme Court—twenty-one years after its passage!

Thus paramilitarism became illegal. But driving it underground did not contain it. By 1989, the Minister of Interior himself declared in Congress that there were 140 paramilitary groups. New models of paramilitary action began, including mass terror. Residents of a community would be brought together in the town squares of small rural communities and some would be selected to be cut up by chainsaws as an effective method to force the population to abandon the area.

- President Cesar Gaviria (1990-94) implemented a constitutional reform to give greater authority to the regions. Governors and mayors became elected by popular vote instead of by appointment, and this reform set loose fierce competition to control local mayoral offices. Besides increasing the interest in participation in politics, this reform increased the fears of the Army and the regional elites that they were going to lose control.

  This in turn led to an increase in military force by both the guerrillas and the paramilitaries. Before he left office, Gaviria left in place Decree 356 of 1994, by which the Convivir "cooperatives" were created. These provided special private watch services which operated in high-risk regions supposedly to return peace to these areas. They were allied to the military and Police in the sense that they would lodge complaints about disturbances of public order and could employ long-range firearms. Ultimately, the Colombian government itself was compelled to restructure the Convivir after it was found that many operated in close association with paramilitaries.

- President Samper (1994-98) was accused of having been elected with drug trafficking money and almost all the energy of his administration was spent on defending itself against these allegations. The paramilitaries took advantage of the power vacuum under the Samper presidency by holding a national meeting and consolidating into one organization, called AUC (*Autodefensas Unidas de Colombia*), with Carlos Castaño as commander-in-chief. Its presence was also expanded during this time period.

  AUC's web page explains how cattlemen, farmers and small businessmen had to organize themselves spontaneously because of guerrillas. The AUC has approximately 8,000 armed men. It defines itself as "a political-military movement which uses the same irregular methods as the guerrillas. Its members are not terrorists, nor common criminals but rather persons who have found it necessary to violate the law because the Colombian state penalizes the legitimate right of self-defense even though it is incapable of providing that defense." Its principal political demand is that it be included in the peace process.

- Andres Pastrana, elected in 1998, has introduced a new element with respect to paramilitaries: globalization and the Free Trade Agreement of the Americas (FTAA). The Colombian conflict is the only armed conflict in the Western Hemisphere that impedes plans to expand the FTAA rapidly. The only South American country with coasts on two oceans, Colombia as an actor in the global drama is a key element in understanding the most recent paramilitary actions. The paramilitaries penetrate into zones desired for investment by international capital, and in these areas the AUC commit atrocities for the purpose of displacing the residents and taking their lands. Today there are more than two million internally displaced persons, many of whom can survive only by cutting the rain forest to grow coca.

The AUC have taken over regions such as Chocó, where megaprojects are planned. These include a possible alternative canal to the Panama Canal as well as oil pipelines, new roads and even sweatshops. AUC paramilitaries told the area residents openly that they must leave because of the canal's construction.

Meanwhile in the southern part of Bolívar Department, an area where a very rich gold mine with high quality gold is located, the AUC paramilitaries decapitated a leader of the miners' union and announced that the multinationals are coming and would provide jobs for many residents. They are also active in Arauca and Putumayo, where there is oil, and the Middle Magdalena, site of the main oil refinery.

Recently, the AUC has decided to form a political directorate. In a ghoulish note, on July 17, 2001, the AUC published a column using the words which Jorge Eliécer Gaitán spoke on February 7, 1948, in his famous Prayer for Peace to justify their right to self-defense. The circle has closed.

CONCLUSIONS TO BE DRAWN

1. The paramilitaries are a national counter-insurgency project of a political nature. They are professional mercenaries who carry out coordinated and strategic actions. They should not be permitted to participate as actors in a peace process because they in fact participate through the Army which formed them.
2. The paramilitaries rely upon support given to them by cattlemen, businessmen, agricultural exporters, industrialists, traditional large landowners, the military and multinational businesses that believe negotiating a peace proposal with the guerrillas would give credibility to the idea that armed rebellion reflects the necessity for economic, political and social reforms. From their point of view, the guerrillas are the result of communism. The case of Ambassador Marulanda is being watched with a great deal of attention by the large capitalists who have helped promote, finance, equip and sustain the paramilitaries.
3. It is undeniable that the guerrillas and paramilitaries obtain large sums of money from the coca business. The FARC tax the growing and processing of the coca, which gives them about 50 percent of their income. Carlos Castaño, on the other hand, has admitted in several published interviews that the AUC receives about 70 percent of its finances from the drug trade.
4. The weakness of the Colombian state is not an accident. From the earliest days of the republic, institutions were designed on paper with the purpose of fortifying local and regional elites. A nation has never been constructed in Colombia.
5. The term “self-defense forces” in Colombia has been used with a sense of possession indiscriminately as much by the guerrillas as by the paramilitaries. Both believe they are legitimate self-defense forces that practice the right of rebellion.
6. The human cost of the terror, the massacres and the genocide against the Colombian civilian population has still not been measured. The paramilitaries give the peasants only three alternatives: You leave, you join us or you die. The directed and selective repopulation of regions appears to be part of a well-planned strategy and the fight involves killing of civilians by both the guerrillas and the paramilitaries.

7. The main hope lies within the vitality of the Colombian people, who in spite of so much pain continue risking their lives and searching for peace with justice. A people with less vitality would by now have been destroyed.
8. It is necessary for the international community to enter into solidarity with the Colombian people. Marulanda's detention resulted from intense pressure by the European Union. The only thing which the Colombian elites fear is rejection by the international community.

1998

The War on Drugs from the Supply Side[1]

REPORT FROM THE FRONT

Last October 25, 1997, a paramilitary patrol landed at the small town of El Aro in Colombia's northern Antioquia province with the intention of "doing away with the guerrillas." For five days the town was converted into a concentration camp. First, they killed Andrés Mendoza, Wilmar Restrepo, Rosa María Barrera and Dora Angela Areiza in front of everybody. The people of El Aro accuse the Colombian Army of complicity because there were people who tried to escape when the paras were not watching, but couldn't get away because the Colombian Army was nearby and the soldiers brought them back.

Before leaving El Aro, the paras assassinated 64-year-old Marco Aurelio Areiza, who owned the town's store. Prior to killing him, they tied him to a tree in the plaza, tortured him, pulled out his eyes and heart and rubbed salt all over his body. His wife and children were forcibly taken to see his remains. On leaving, the paramilitaries burned the town and killed the pigs and chickens. The final result of the paramilitary presence in El Aro was 51 of the town's 68

1. Editor's note: This article was published by *Z Magazine* in its July/August 1998 issue, pages 21–24, and is being reproduced in this book with the permission of *Z Magazine*. Section titles and some commentary not included in the *Z Magazine* article have been included by the author.

houses destroyed and 10 small farms looted and burned. Another 5 peasants were killed, and the paras took with them 1,300 head of cattle and 130 mules and horses.

After the paramilitaries left, the 250 survivors buried the bodies of their friends and relatives and fled to nearby towns, joining some 1,500 other refugees from the region, adding to the one and one-half million refugees in the country.

This is daily life in the Colombian countryside. Colombia's brutal war goes on and on amidst the silence of the world. Has human decency gone away? Is the silence of the world's press complicity? What better way to make these horrors non-newsworthy than to paint them with the brush "on Colombia—that drug mess." Welcome to the "war on drugs"—from the supply side!

THE FAÇADE CALLED DEMOCRACY

Colombia has been for many years the window case democracy which the U.S. State Department loves to show off as Latin America's oldest and most durable democracy. Yes, Colombia fulfills all the formal requisites of a democracy: Presidential elections are held every four years, the three branches of the government function in beautiful buildings, even though in reality their powers are not separate. A string of civilian presidents sign all kinds of international treaties on human rights, women's rights, environmental rights and children's rights. Colombia holds its place at the United Nations, the Organization of American States (OAS), and the International Labor Organization (ILO), where it has no moral problems with the fact that more labor leaders are killed in Colombia than in any other country in the world. This "democracy" only means misery for the majority of its people.

Colombia has always had two political parties, Liberals and Conservatives, whose power struggles have caused many wars. The last one, La Violencia, from 1948 to 1953, left more than 300,000 dead. Killings continued on a lower scale through the 1960s and 1970s. These two political entities might as well be considered one party with two heads because there is no ideological difference between them, and they hold the same position on social and economic issues.

Colombia is by no means a poor country. It has abundant resources such as oil, coal, gold, emeralds, platinum, and uranium. It exports coffee, flowers, sugar, and bananas. An article in the *Wall Street Journal* published last year said that "Colombia boasts continuous economic growth, by far the best in Latin America and perhaps in the world." Yet there is much hunger in Colombia.

Colombia's tragedy is the result of deep inequalities: 3 percent of the people own 70 percent of the arable land, and there is a lack of political will to implement social, political and economic reforms.

PEOPLE REBEL

Because of these deep inequalities and violence, guerrilla movements started forming in the late 1930s. Today there are two major guerrilla forces, FARC (Fuerzas Armadas Revolucionarias de Colombia, Revolutionary Armed Forces of Colombia) and ELN (Ejército de Liberación Nacional, National Liberation Army).

In 1985 a challenge to the two political parties came about when the government, in one of its periodic peace processes, offered amnesty to those guerrillas who would give up their arms and become a political party competing in elections. Created by former guerrillas, the Unión Patriótica Party (UP) organized at the grass roots level and appealed to a broad range of Colombian citizens who believed Liberals and Conservatives had done nothing to represent their interests. Elections came, and the UP enjoyed extensive electoral success: City council members, mayors, state assembly and national Congress members were elected. There was a sense of being a democracy at last! Except that...one by one, hunted down like animals, virtually all of the UP's elected officials and the party's only two presidential candidates were killed. About 4,000 of them at last count. The real number of UP grass-roots activists and sympathizers killed has been lost. No party in the Americas has been wiped out like Colombia's UP. The silence of Colombia's democratic partners and allies in the hemisphere about these killings speaks volumes about commitment to real democracy for all of us in the Americas.

Colombia's violence is well entrenched in its injustices and the peculiar "division of labor" that its sophisticated elites and the military concocted. The Army has all the power to repress while they enjoy the wealth derived from the plentiful resources of the country. The Colombian elite presents a democratic façade to the outside world in order to keep foreign investment coming. The power the Colombian Army enjoys has been given to it willingly. The military does not need to stage a coup d'état. Like pathological lovers, the Colombian elites and the Colombian Army need each other to survive.

A BLESSING OR A CURSE

Colombia has a privileged geographical location as the only country in South America with coasts on both the Atlantic and Pacific oceans. This particular geographic location was the main reason why, in the 1970s, Colombia became a key stop in the trade of cocaine brought from Peru and Bolivia. This stopover for drug trade was initially made by Miami Cubans who wanted to profit from drugs after the American troops came home hooked from Vietnam. Contacts were made with the underworld in Colombia and with shady characters from the emerald trade. Soon the Colombians outdid their Cuban partners and became the main middlemen in the drug trade.

Initially Bolivia and Peru produced coca leaves and paste and the paste was brought to Colombia where it would be processed and refined to cocaine and distributed to the always-hungry U.S. market. So in a Felliniesque reality, we find two contradictory illegal forces, FARC and drug traffickers, cohabiting the vast rain forests of Colombia's Amazon basin. In this way the drug trade with all its money and corruptive power became another factor in the old and vicious Colombian war.

THE PLAYERS

The displaced peasants: The peasants, who have fled from terror during all of these 50 years of war in the countryside, have two options: to go to the big cities and become beggars and prostitutes or to go to the rainforest to colonize the land. If they choose the latter, they till the land and plant crops such as corn or plantains. Since these areas were never developed, they lack transportation routes. Only by using the big rivers and crossing hundreds of miles can the crop reach Bogotá or other markets. By the time it gets there, the crop is rotten or has become so costly that all the profit is practically lost. There is only one alternative open to the peasant farmer who wishes to subsist: growing coca leaves. They do not have to worry about transportation because the drug lords' economic machinery picks up the harvested coca at the farm. Coca is more profitable than corn in the "free market." So Colombian peasants growing coca are the result of social, political and economic problems that cannot and will not be solved by military means.

The guerrillas: The FARC and the ELN have a political agenda that calls for agrarian reform, democratization and protection of natural resources from multinational corporations. But the Conservative and Liberal parties have never allowed for third party or grass-roots opposition.

Colombian politics is very exclusionary. Guerrillas have used kidnappings of rich people to finance their activities. They also place land mines in areas where they are active; and the ELN, especially, has a penchant for bombing oil pipelines, causing untold ecological damage.

In the 1980s, paramilitary groups such as MAS (Death to Kidnappers) were formed when enraged cattlemen joined forces with drug traffickers against guerrilla kidnappings. Recently, guerrillas announced that they would also start attacking civilians they believe are friends or relatives of paramilitaries, which means further spreading of the conflict to the civilian population. This violates international humanitarian law. Today the guerrillas hold virtual control of vast regions of the countryside where for most of this century the only presence of the state has been the Army. Since guerrillas and drug traffickers generally operate in the same areas, many guerrilla fronts tax drug-trafficking operations while protecting plantations of coca; they tax the processing and shipping of drugs, just as they tax any area that comes under their control, and in this way they benefit from the drug trade. But to say that guerrillas are "narco-guerrillas" is a simplification of this labyrinthine world of Colombian politics.

The drug traffickers: Colombia's rigidly stratified class system does not give much opportunity for people to advance socially. In Medellín, for example, the textile capital of Latin America, many people were left unemployed when factories closed during the 1970s economic recession. Unemployed people plus refugees fleeing from terror make an easy breeding ground for drug trafficking.

The underworld and the ruthless emerald-trade mafia in the state of Boyacá quickly took advantage of the new promising drug trade. Fortunes were made quickly by this new class, which became wealthier than the traditional elites. They saw themselves just as much entrepreneurs as the coffee or sugar barons and demanded their share of power. Money talks, and soon those who did not sell themselves were eliminated, among them the incorruptible leaders of the UP party. Here the drug people figured out how to kill two birds with one stone: Since the UP represented the left, and since the drug traffickers sought to win grace from the viscerally anti-communist Colombian elites and military, they proceeded to go after UP people and kill them, as well as non-combatant peasants suspected of guerrilla sympathies, such as the ones in El Aro. In this way, the drug traffickers also started to get land. In the last seven years drug traffickers have taken between four to five million hectares of the best Colombian land. They are not interested in growing anything; they just want to gain social status, and owning land gives status. In taking the land, they drive the peasants out and introduce private armies to protect themselves.

The Army: Keep in mind that Colombia's Army is Simón Bolívar's Army which crossed the Andes in an epic march and gave the first defeat to the

Spanish empire. Made up of peasants, that Army and its aristocratic and enlightened leader sought to found a republic where democracy, freedom and human rights would prevail. That Army later became the private Army of the ruling elites and a proxy Army for a foreign power. Fighting a guerrilla war in the tropics for 50 years has made it the most seasoned and most brutal army in this hemisphere. Lately, as documented by the BBC, this Army has been renting itself out to protect multinational corporations' properties, be they the oil fields in Casanare or the gold mines in Segovia. Colombia's list of graduates from the School of the Americas (SOA) is the longest of any Latin American country. Colombians started training in 1947 and have continued to the present. Colombians will proudly tell anybody that they are not only students but teachers at the SOA.

The Paramilitary: In November 1996 Human Rights Watch released a report called "Colombia's Killer Networks: The Military-Paramilitary Partnership and the U.S.," which documents the historical links between U.S. Cold War strategies, political violence in Colombia and the nurturing of paramilitaries by the CIA and the Pentagon since the 1950s. Paramilitaries are a creation of the Colombian state. They represent an attempt to cover up the brutalities of the Army which are continually reported by reputable human rights organizations. Amnesty International, Human Rights Watch and the myriad of Colombian NGOs, at tremendous risk and despite the numerous killings they suffer, keep reporting atrocities such as the one in El Aro.

These paramilitary groups act together with the military but carry out irregular actions in order to blur the borders between what is civilian and what is military. It is a perverted mechanism because it resorts to secrecy and makes a mockery of democracy and its institutions. When paramilitaries are created, a state's responsibility ceases to exist.

Father Javier Giraldo, in *Colombia: The Genocidal Democracy*, reveals some of the characteristics of Colombia's paramilitaries. The paras receive support from trade organizations and powerful businesses, such as export agriculture, cattlemen, oil companies and drug traffickers. They get political support from the military and leaders of the traditional parties. They receive military support from the Army's local battalion and brigade. The judicial system protects them by absolving the responsible parties and discontinuing the criminal proceedings. Or if the courts condemn someone, they refuse to investigate the lines of command. The executive and the legislative powers provide the military officers who organize and direct this criminal structure with all kinds of promotions in rank and honors.

More insidious is the military-paramilitary modus operandi of the last 10 years. The strategy has been to declare as military objectives, not only FARC and ELN militants, but also members of dissident political parties. They target people who have lived in regions where guerrillas have been present and members of any community organization, such as cooperatives, which represent alternative models to the accumulation of capital different from neoliberalism. For local peasants, geographical territories stop being seen as lands where you feel emotionally attached but become "conquered territories" with armed groups. They are forced to relate to the combined action of the Army and the paramilitaries as those who exercise power. A brutally cynical counterinsurgency tactic of former guerrillas joining paramilitary units is being tried now with young men fighting for the highest payer.

This strategy responds to the "development" plans with a new conception of social and family relations. These relations are based on irrational use of force and loyalties where the most important thing is private property and profitability. A new society is created within the free market model where only those people who have money and property (be it cattle, contraband, or cocaine) can compete. The rest have to beg to be included in the paramilitary scheme or are excluded. The creation of the parastate has arrived.

Paramilitary structures have multiple alliances with important sectors of drug-trafficking in coordination with military units, as the massacres of Trujillo and Riofrío have shown. A typical example is that of Colonel Luis Felipe Becerra, who coordinated the death squad massacres in March 1988 of 22 workers from banana plantations in Urabá. When an honest judge announced preliminary results of her probe against two drug traffickers and three military officials, she received death threats and had to flee. Seven months later, in retaliation, her father was slain. When Colonel Becerra was going to be served with legal papers, he was in the United States where he was taking a course to be promoted to lieutenant colonel. When he returned, he was involved in a second massacre in Riofrío in 1993. A known drug lord wanted the land around Riofrío, so 13 peasant owners were killed through Army-paramilitary cooperation.

The Church and the NGOs: After being one of the most conservative churches in Latin America for centuries, the Colombian Catholic Church has become one of the few institutions left to help the poor. Many priests and nuns have died working for justice and the poor. Many of the internal 1,500,000 refugees have come to the Church's door. The Bishop's Conference has raised its voice in favor of the poor. And the Colombian Jesuits, with their prestigious think tank, CINEP, and their Program for Peace, have taken leadership in struggling for the rights of the poor. Colombian NGOs have led a courageous battle to assist and represent the poor. Many activists have been killed or "disappeared" as a result.

The U.S: The U.S. support for the "war on drugs" does not strengthen democracy or respect human rights. The Colombian Army has a long and close relationship with the U.S. military. From World War II on they collaborated against "communist subversion." Now it is drugs. The State Department has issued reports about human rights violations, but these are not taken seriously by the Colombian elites because the U.S. government keeps giving military aid to the Colombian Army. Human Rights Watch reports that in 1990 a team of CIA and U.S. strategists gathered to assist Colombian military intelligence. The document produced at this meeting does not mention narcotics at all but rather emphasizes combating "terrorism by armed subversion."[2]

So one must question the real goal of the "War on Drugs." Is the "War on Drugs" a pseudo-ethical argument for perpetuating violence for the economic benefit of the elites in both countries? The facts contradict the speeches by U.S. politicians in their moralistic appeals to the U.S. public. Drug czar General Barry McCaffrey announced on a recent visit to Bogotá that the U.S. is willing to help Colombia combat not only "drug traffickers" but also the "guerrillas." It would be interesting to know if he considers the brutally murdered CINEP researchers Mario Calderón (a former Jesuit) and Elsa Alvarado as guerrillas, or the millions of Colombians who desire social change.

REALITY

The reality is that the United States is becoming more and more involved in the region's most brutal war—a war in which the Army, allied with drug traffickers and paramilitary death squads, combats not only guerrillas but anyone committed to political or social change. The victims of this war have been lawyers, priests, nuns, political activists, labor leaders, peasant leaders, university professors, journalists, cooperative members, women leaders, anyone who thinks! Some 4,300 Colombians are killed each year for political reasons out of a total annual death toll of 30,000. This carnage is in a country with a population of 33 million people. According to the Colombian Commission

2. *Colombia's Killer Networks: The Military-Paramilitary Partnership and the United States*, Human Rights Watch/America, Human Rights Watch Arms Project, November, 1996, pgs. 43, 172; https://www.hrw.org/reports/pdfs/c/colombia/colombia96n.pdf

of Jurists only 2 percent of these political killings are drug related, while 28 percent of the deaths are at the hands of the guerrillas and 70 percent are caused by the paramilitary/military alliance.

1999

Globalization & Instability[1]

The Case of Colombia

Edward S. Herman & Cecilia Zarate-Laun

It has been an important ideological premise of the U.S.-organized New World Order that globalization is a very positive thing that "brings us all together," whereas ethnic strife and "balkanization" are regressive tendencies that conflict with globalization. A recent expression of this view was President Clinton's April 7 pronouncement that the bombing of Yugoslavia was to advance this benevolent globalization process by fighting off the ugly forces of separatism and ethnic violence.

GLOBALIZATION GENERATES CONFLICT

But this counterpoising of globalization and ethnic strife is extremely misleading, as globalization has been a primary cause of fragmentation, ethnic strife and other forms of violence. (In his April 7 address, Clinton acknowledged that globalization has created problems that call for U.S. "leadership" in straightening things out, as in Kosovo.) Globalization has been "bringing us together," but under the rule of transnational capital and the governments

1. This article was published by *Z Magazine* in its September 1999 issue, pages 30-34, and is being reproduced in this book with the permission of *Z Magazine*.

and international institutions that serve it in a highly undemocratic manner. Where that rule is resisted, violence occurs, frequently with the active support of the leaders of the globalization process. Globalization has been notorious for its income polarization effects, with vast numbers mired in poverty even as the world's rich become much richer; and as Oxfam noted in a 1995 report on poverty, "deepening poverty is one of the main driving forces behind the civil conflicts which are creating unprecedented numbers of refugees."

The ethnic strife in the most recent focus of attention, the Balkans, is in large measure a derivative of the forces of globalization, to whose account we may include: the integration of Yugoslavia into the global market in the 1970s and 1980s; its weakened economic condition from the recession of the early 1980s and then the brutal IMF structural adjustment plan imposed on it; and its active dismantlement encouraged by Germany, Austria, and the U.S. in the 1990s in pursuit of their regional and global geopolitical interests. The breakup of the Soviet Union, the West's encouragement of rapid privatization and shock therapy in Russia and the integration of China into the global market have resulted in catastrophic conditions in the former and increasing chaos in the latter.

The devastating effects on Africa of its global economic links and the IMF and World Bank policies has also been an important illustration of the close connection between globalization and instability. Peruvian analyst Oswaldo De Rivero even argues that globalization and IMF-World Bank policies have virtually created an important national category that he labels "chaotic ungovernable entities," with some 23 of them extending from Angola to Bolivia to Tajikistan now identifiable and their rapid proliferation and regressive tendencies making a mockery of the phrase "emerging economies" ("States in Ruin, Conflicts Without End," Le Monde Diplomatique, April 1999).

VIOLENCE TO FACILITATE GLOBALIZATION

As regards the active support of violence by the globalizing leaders and institutions, we may recall the U.S. sponsorship of the National Security States in Latin America, Suharto in Indonesia, Mobutu in Zaire, and Marcos in the Philippines. These regimes not only killed and terrorized on a large scale, they also generated an enormous flow of mainly internal refugees, pushed off the land for the benefit of foreign as well as domestic agro-export, oil, mining, and timber interests. In Brazil alone, church sources estimated some seven million peasants were evicted from the land in the years of military rule, and large numbers were similarly treated (with many killed) in other parts of the empire (including pre-Sandinista Nicaragua) to make way for the important, increasingly global interests. These victimized people sometimes resisted and caused "instability" and "ethnic conflict" that had to be dealt with by the globalizing forces of law and order. "Stability" for the globalizers means no obstacle or resistance to their own radical destabilizing operations; the victims should accept their displacement, removal and other injuries without complaint.

This same process goes on today, even in the nominally "democratic" provinces. In many cases, years of class cleansing by U.S.-supported rulers such as Pinochet have left the countries with democracies in complete thrall to the powerful—labor weakened and fearful, concentrated control of business and the media, dependence on foreign capital, global financial markets and the IMF—and thus servants of neoliberal policies and interests. And very often the victims respond, calling for state and global action in the interest of "stability."

For example, Bolivia, often portrayed as a model of reform under Jeffrey Sachs's tutelage and IMF Structural Adjustment Programs (SAPs) beginning in 1985, illustrates a commonly encountered sequence of policy actions, resultant devastating human conditions, conflict and responsive repression (assisted by the United States). Privatization of the tin mines and other public assets, cutbacks in subsidies to the poor and small farmers, restrictive macro policies, a shift to agro-exports under IMF-U.S. pressure and need to service a growing external debt, generated serious unemployment, a fall in the real incomes of a large majority and the familiar spurt of malnutrition and growth of the informal market. Many small farmers unable to compete in traditional crops without subsidies or protection in a global market moved into coca leaf cultivation. This rational economic choice has been increasingly attacked under U.S.-sponsored anti-drug programs that have used chemical warfare and military campaigns.

Thus, having destroyed the livelihoods of large numbers of Bolivians and afforded them no survival alternative to coca leaf cultivation, the United States is now spending large sums directly and through a militarized Bolivian state to crush the coca leaf producers by violence. A Banzer government plan for the Chapare area of coca leaf cultivation calls for the relocation of 20,000 families, many of whom moved there after the 1985 SAP closed the tin mines. The hope is that agro-businesses like Chiquita can be induced into the area to replace the peasants. But the peasant families are refusing to move in a conflict clearly related to the interests of a tiny local elite and the United States and its globalizing program, surely not those of the Bolivian people (see the interview on Bolivia with George Ann Potter, Council on Hemispheric Affairs, Washington Report on the Hemisphere, July 1, 1999).

As another example, in the case of Mexico's corrupt democracy, a Salinas and Zedillo can privatize everything in sight, alter Article 27 of the Mexican constitution to end protection of community land rights, terminate subsidies to small farmers and increase them to agro-farmers and open up timber areas that were a commons of indigenous communities (and protection against flooding) to timber giants like Boise Cascade. These anti-people actions, along with the effects of NAFTA, have produced another burst of refugees from the land into Mexico City and across the U.S. border. It has also led to a series of outbreaks of indigenous violence, including but by no means limited to the Zapatista revolt. These conflicts have been closely and directly related to the annexation and globalization of Mexico (see John Ross, *The Annexation of Mexico*, Common Courage, 1997).

Of course, both Mexican globalization and the Mexican government's steady deployment of state violence have been actively aided by the United States. Clinton has more closely embraced Zedillo in the face of new evidence of corruption and fraud and a more aggressive Mexican counterinsurgency policy in dealing with rural grievances. This U.S. support of both a globalization process that generates revolt and the instruments of state terror that are designed to keep that response in check recalls an important Brazilian church document of the 1960s, which noted that the National Security State was needed because the merciless economic policies being carried out by the Brazilian military government (with enthusiastic transnational corporate participation and U.S. political support) were "generating a revolution that did not previously exist." State terror was needed to cope with the "instability" produced by the already operative "growth with injustice" model. Then, and as regards Mexican state terror and its role today, the U.S. mainstream media avert their eyes.

TERROR AND GLOBALIZATION IN COLOMBIA

Even more dramatic than Bolivia or Mexico today is the case of Colombia, where political killings of peasant and labor leaders, teachers, journalists, priests, nuns, lawyers, women rights leaders, human rights workers, and citizens, carried out mainly by the government and its affiliated paramilitary arms, were estimated by human rights watchers at over 3,800 in 1998. (Over half the trade union leaders murdered in the entire world in 1997 were located in Colombia.) This is a far larger figure than the number of Albanians killed in Kosovo prior to the beginning of NATO bombings in March. The number of internal refugees in Colombia is reckoned at some 1.5 million, also vastly greater than the pre-NATO bombing refugee numbers in Kosovo.

UNWORTHY VICTIMS

But, like Turkey and Suharto's Indonesia, as well as Bolivia and Mexico, Colombia is an increasingly important part of the global economic order, its oil and mineral wealth have attracted the interest of important global economic players, and its government, Army and paramilitary forces are allied with and kill in the interest of those important players. These victims therefore fall into the "unworthy" category, attract little international attention and can be killed and dispossessed on a large scale without indignant outcries from Susan Sontag or platitudes on the importance of each individual by Vaclav Havel. These moralists reserve their preachings for worthy victims.

The unworthiness of Colombia's ordinary citizens can also be read from the fact that, as with Mexico, Turkey, and Suharto's Indonesia, the Colombian government is actively aided by the United States; in this case, with several hundred military advisers, joint training exercises, a strong CIA and DEA presence and $290 million in military aid, making Colombia the third largest recipient of such aid (after Israel and Egypt). This funding is about to be sharply increased as the Clinton administration further militarizes the "drug war," the press reporting a proposed one billion dollars allocation to the Colombia struggle against "narco-terrorism." In fact, this will go to an Army that is itself tied to the drug trade, and that directly or indirectly has been guilty of human rights violations which will bear comparison with any in the world.

OBSTACLES TO "PROGRESS"

Throughout Colombia, indigenous tribes, peasants, and small miners stand in the way of oil drilling, agro-business and large-scale mining which cause their dispossession and severe environmental damage. Occidental Petroleum has had a long-standing dispute with the U'wa Indian tribe that opposes their drilling on Indian lands. Exxon's giant El Cerrejon coal mine and other nearby mines in Venezuela have had injurious effect on a half-dozen local Indian tribes that have opposed their operations. The Chocó area in the Northwest part of Colombia below Panamá is rich in minerals and oil and contains one of the world's last pristine rain forests. It is being rapidly opened to mining, oil and timber exploitation, and pipelines, ports, railroads, a canal and the last 65 miles of the Pan American Highway are being pushed forward to bring this region into the global market. Free trade zones are in the planning stage for the Chocó area. The local peasants are resisting, and the paramilitaries, the Army and other drug warriors have been quietly pushing them out, often by extreme terror (a preferred paramilitary method is cutting people alive in pieces with chainsaws, impelling a flight in which everything is left behind).

In Southern Bolívar there is a gold mine long coveted by the transnational mining companies as it produces first-quality gold in an open pit location. Local peasants have been exploiting this mine for 40 years, along with miners organized in a union and working for a local company. The peasant and union leaders in this area have been murdered, and in 1998, some 10,000 farmers and peasants were driven out by paramilitaries, who were funded by gold mining companies and protected by the Colombian Army.

These Colombian conflicts and "instability" are closely tied to the new global economic order. Colombia, like Bolivia and other Latin American countries, has been subjected to a SAP that called for enlarged exports of primary goods to generate hard currency. This program helped force privatization and liberalization of trade and investment, encouraging an influx of foreign capital. The United States enthusiastically backed these "reforms," which benefited their transnationals. But these policies have threatened and damaged indigenous communities and their ecological systems and helped produce terrorist responses; the main oil pipeline in Colombia has been bombed over 500 times, and the regions of oil development are notorious for death squads and other human-rights abuses.

ANTI-NARCO-TERRORIST DEATH SQUADS

The situation in Colombia is somewhat reminiscent of that in El Salvador and Guatemala in the 1980s, where the U.S.-aided armies killed and produced refugees on a truly massive scale, with the help of paramilitaries (death squads) closely affiliated with those armies. It is recognized by all human rights groups, and has even been acknowledged in the State Department's own human rights reports, that most of the killing in Colombia is done by Army-affiliated and protected rightwing paramilitaries. As in El Salvador and Guatemala, the use of death squads allows the Army to do much of its dirty work by proxy, making it appear that the Army and government are not in the business of mass murder.

It is also widely recognized that the Colombian paramilitaries and Army are heavily involved in the drug trade; the conservative London *Economist* even alleged that the drug traffickers protected by the paramilitaries "are far deeper into drugs [than the guerrillas]—and the DEA knows it." (February 20, 1999) But this has not prevented the United States from aiding the Colombian Army in the name of fighting a drug war.

In effect, the United States supports a "narco-army" and "narco-guerrillas." The guerrillas do receive enormous amounts of money from the drug trade, and they kill on a large scale; some 14 percent of total human rights violations reported by Colombian NGOs are attributed to the guerrillas. But that leaves 84 percent to the paramilitaries and two percent to the Army. Nevertheless, the United States has aligned itself completely with the dominant killers and dominant participants in the drug trade and leaves their drug terrain alone.

U.S. aid to Colombia has been earmarked for specific regions of the country such as the Amazon and Orinoco basins that happen to be the areas of influence of the rebel Revolutionary Armed Forces of Colombia (FARC), while largely avoiding the northern areas of the country where the drug trade routes are protected by paramilitaries closely allied with drug-traffickers and members of the Colombian Army. Exempting and supplying arms to an important segment of the drug trade suggests that, as with anticommunism in the past, the drug war rationale covers over the pursuit of larger objectives that can be read from what the Army and paramilitaries do—remove, kill and silence the large segments of the rural population that stand in the way of exploitation of Colombia's resources.

U.S.- AND TNC-SPONSORED MILITARIZATION

The Colombian Army and Police have long been trained and supplied arms and intelligence by the United States, and that close cooperation has been enhanced recently, including "a series of electronic surveillance and radar stations built and staffed by American technicians ... maintained around Colombia as part of the enhanced cooperation strategy." (*NYT*, July 14, 1999) The Colombian Army is proud of its close connection with the U.S. army; one of its leaders, General Manuel José Bonett, stating recently that "we're fighting this war on behalf of the United States." (*Washington Post*, May 25, 1998) It is also the transnational corporations' (TNCs') Army. On September 11, 1996, the London *Guardian* disclosed that British Petroleum (BP), the largest investor in Colombia, had secretly rented 150 officers and 500 soldiers of the Colombian Army to serve its "security" interests and had brought in British counterinsurgency professionals to train the Colombians. BP also exchanged intelligence information with them, some of which was used in tracking and killing local "subversives." The other oil companies in Colombia have also cultivated the Army and Police and hired paramilitaries and foreign mercenaries to protect their oil pipelines.

The United States has a long and terrible history of supporting military governments and regimes of terror in Latin America. This used to be rationalized on the grounds of a Soviet-communist threat, as in Guatemala in 1954, Brazil in 1964 and El Salvador and Nicaragua in the 1980s. Although this was a fraud and cover for the desire to assure a completely amenable and investor-friendly environment, it was effective in making active U.S. backing of the institutionalization of state terror acceptable to mainstream intellectuals and media. It was even claimed that we supported and trained military personnel in the interest of democracy and human rights, an Orwellian claim that was not challenged in the mainstream press even as 10 democratic governments were displaced by our military trainees in the 1960s, with our tacit or open support, and even after Amnesty International reported in the 1970s that Latin America—the U.S. backyard—had become the world's focal point of torture and "disappearances."

NORMALIZING U.S. AID TO COLOMBIAN STATE TERROR

It is a testimonial to the power of rationalization and to the willingness of the mainstream media to suppress information on—and normalize—U.S.-supported terror, that the United States can once again escalate aid to a military regime that is committing Guatemala-type and scale human-rights atrocities and do this at the same time as it engages in "humanitarian intervention" in the Balkans, and while Clinton humbly apologizes for the U.S. connivance in earlier military violence in Guatemala and comes off with a halo of virtue. Drug czar Barry McCaffrey can assert without contradiction that it is the guerrillas that are making "a criminal attack on Colombian democracy" and pretend that U.S. support of the Colombian Army and paramilitaries is favorable to democracy, without eliciting any mainstream critical analyses or references to the scandalous contrary record of history.

Colombian human rights workers documented 1,332 killed in 201 separate massacres in 1998, in addition to another 2,500 more individual assassinations. Many of these massacres were extremely dramatic and immensely newsworthy, with heads cut off and hung on poles and numerous flights of hundreds of terrorized women and children. It would have been possible to arouse a great deal of public indignation if reported here, but these were people standing in the way of progress, killed by agents supported by the U.S. government. Accordingly, the media have been busy elsewhere.

The flurry of articles on Colombia in the *New York Times* in July focused mainly on fights between rebels and the Army and U.S. "concern" and involvement in the interest of controlling the drug trade (July 12, 14, 17-19, 27, 29). Larry Rohter's apologetic frame is "Colombia's war against the twin plagues of drugs and guerrillas," ("With U.S. training, Colombia Melds War on Rebels and Drugs," *NYT*, July 29, 1999) which downgrades and even legitimizes the mass killing by the paramilitary death squads, who are allies and agents of the U.S.-supported Colombian Army. The problematic of this attack on drugs, such as Army involvement in the business, the discriminatory locus of attacks on drug cultivation and the possibility that the narco-terrorism focus is misdirected and even a cover for other ends, are not raised. Neither this nor any other article in the recent series mentioned the penetration of Colombia by the oil companies and their conflicts with the indigenous peoples.

Although paramilitaries and Army have carried out the great bulk of Colombian killings, the *Times* had no article (or paragraph) on the organization, funding and death-dealing activities of these forces. It did, however, devote a full article to "A Guerrilla's Half Century in Colombia's Mountains," (*NYT*, July 19, 1999) which quoted an unnamed diplomat on guerrilla leader Tirofijo's "Pol Pot" qualities and gave numbers supplied by the Colombian government on people he executed or who were missing to Tirofijo's account. The paper did not mention, nor did it cover in 1998, any of the 201 massacres listed by human rights groups.

There is also no account in this *Times* series of the history of U.S. military aid and its consequences for democracy and human rights. By ignoring this history, giving unwarranted credence to the drug war rationale, demonizing the narco-guerrillas while gently treating the U.S.-supported mass killers, and reserving its attention and indignation for worthy victims (e.g., Kosovo Albanians, people executed by Tirofijo's forces), the *Times* once again serves as a propaganda agent of the state. At this historical juncture, it helps engineer consent to U.S. support of another round of very serious state terror aimed at crushing any resistance to the ongoing process of globalization without justice.

At the time this article was written, Edward Herman was an economist and media analyst; Cecilia Zarate-Laun was co-founder and program director of the Colombia Support Network.

AUGUST 31, 2000

Colombia Owes Its People and the United States Some Straight Answers

Article by Cecilia Zarate-Laun
Capital Times, Madison, WI

Dear President Clinton,

You have just visited Colombia.[1] I read that you visited the beautiful, walled city of Cartagena. I am sure you enjoyed its beauty and admired its history.

Since you have declared your commitment to a negotiated solution to the conflict in Colombia and to respect human rights, I would like to suggest several questions that need answers from President Andrés Pastrana. I hope in his answers he will give these questions the serious attention they require.

Ask President Pastrana why the Seventeenth Brigade of the Colombian Army did not protect residents of the small hamlet of La Unión, a part of the Peace Community of San José de Apartadó in northern Colombia. Why did soldiers and an Army helicopter protect paramilitary forces as they killed unarmed peasants?

1. Editor's note: President Clinton visited Cartagena on August 30, 2000 with his daughter Chelsea. He was met on the Cartagena airport tarmac by Colombian President Andrés Pastrana. Cecilia received no response to her letter from President Clinton or anyone on his behalf.

Why did the office of Colombia's vice-president, Gustavo Bell, tell peasants, who fled in terror after the massacre, that his office would help them as long as they were refugees but not if they were to remain in La Unión advancing their self-sufficient projects? Does the Colombian government's response to the massacre have anything to do with the coal deposits in the nearby Abibe Mountains?

Raise questions with President Pastrana about who ordered the killings of six schoolchildren in Pueblo Rico. Have all of those responsible for this incident, including the commander of the Fourth Brigade, been identified and prosecuted?

Mention to President Pastrana your concern that in just the last seven months, there have been 366 assassinations in the city of Barrancabermeja, showing a systematic plan of extermination of residents of that unfortunate city. Why have grass-roots social organizations been targeted for killing? Should not these organizations and labor unions be protected as expressions of democracy? Paramilitary forces have declared that by the end of this year, they will control the city. Why does the Fifth Brigade of the Colombian Army not stop these killings? Does the reaction have anything to do with the fact that the city is the center of Colombia's oil drilling and refining?

To achieve the negotiated solution that you say you support, will you advise President Pastrana to fully support the concept of declaring Barrancabermeja a "Peace Territory?"

Inquire why the Colombian Army did not stop the massacre of El Salado in northern Colombia, where 39 peasants were beheaded in the town square by paramilitaries, where they later danced, drank and had sex while the townspeople cried out in pain and despair? Does this have anything to do with territorial control of the nearby San Lucas Mountains, which contain significant gold deposits?

You probably enjoyed Cartagena and admired its beauty more because all of the beggars, street children and poor street vendors were forced out of the city so that you would not see them. I hope you enjoyed the colonial city. You are fortunate that President Pastrana did not schedule a visit to Chambacú, where the sights, smells and tales of horror by thousands of refugees from the war might have been upsetting.[2]

Do not forget who you represent—the generous people of the United States,

2. Editor's note: Chambacú was a neighborhood of Cartagena, outside the city's historic center, inhabited mostly by Afro-descendants, where many of the poor residents did not have potable water, a sewage treatment facility or electricity. The Colombian government carried out a slum eradication project there in 1971, but the relocated residents' economic condition had not changed substantially thereafter, according to a report at https://second.wiki/wiki/chambcc3ba_barrio.

with their respect for human dignity and their tremendous sense of democracy. Ask these questions in their name.

Do not let memories of the merrymaking during your celebration of Plan Colombia distract you. As you watched the beautiful sunset at the end of your visit to Colombia, I hope you were mindful of history. Remember that the walls of the fortressed city of Cartagena were built a long time ago to protect the city against Anglo-Saxon pirates who came to sack my country.

2002

How the FTAA Is Being Implemented in Colombia

The Free Trade Agreement of the Americas (FTAA) purports to be a hemisphere-wide arrangement for free movement of goods, services and capital throughout the hemisphere in order to implement globalization. Its guiding principles include elimination of tariffs, removing environmental restraints on transnational business, undermining the labor movement, opening all of the Americas to copyright and product protection, imposing a culture of mass consumption whose focus is the individual and the satisfaction of his needs as prompted by commercialization of the media. Plan Colombia is the military-focused program to implement the FTAA in Colombia.

Colombia, the northernmost country in South America and Latin America's third most populous country with 44 million people, has been for decades the scene of civil conflict pitting the Colombian Army and allied paramilitary forces against two guerrilla organizations.

The conflict originated in deep social, economic and political inequalities. In the 1970s this conflict was exacerbated by the involvement of excluded sectors of the population in drug-trafficking, which brought new actors and the combined effect of new money concentrated in landholdings and more corruption at all levels of government. The new developing trends for globalization created an even more desperate situation for Colombia and had devastating consequences, particularly for the poorest sectors of the population.

Plan Colombia is designed to eliminate the conflict that has delayed the establishment of multinational structures, and seeks to remove people from lands thought necessary for mining, energy or large infrastructural projects. A remarkable thing about Plan Colombia is that it foresees the forced displacement of people, and the U.S. government provides money for services to people displaced by policies it is implementing through its vassal Colombian government.

Colombia is an indispensable area to be cleaned up for the FTAA, due not only to its natural wealth and resources but to its privileged strategic location. It is the only country in mainland South America that has coasts on the Atlantic and the Pacific Oceans, and in this way it is the corner and crossroads for new trade passages.

New ways for routes (such as the construction of the Atrato-Truandó canal), new accessible sweatshops and new pipelines connecting to the Pacific that will facilitate the supply of oil to countries such as Japan are planned. Besides all of these, Colombia has a leadership that would happily initiate and facilitate the selling of the country to whoever pays more and will share the enormous profits with them, ignoring the rest of the inhabitants.

Violations against human rights, massacres, displacements, selective assassinations and terrorist methods are reported constantly from territories that have been considered frontier territories in Colombia, such as the Putumayo, the Chocó, Arauca and others. However, we should always keep in mind that the low- intensity war in Colombia has as its ultimate goal the imposition of an economic, political and cultural system that is authoritarian and exclusionary. This system is devised in order to facilitate the implementation of the FTAA in all the territory of the country, including areas that have long been considered very much part of the traditional Andean region, some of them untouched by the war until now.

I am going to focus here on the coffee region, particularly the states of Caldas, Huila and Santander. The area around Bucaramanga and its port on the Magdalena River, Barrancabermeja, was the object of a bloody dispute between the guerrillas and the paramilitaries. Barranca, as it is affectionately called, is the largest city controlled by the paramilitaries and a source of pride for them, since the city was for many years the cradle of protest movements in the country.

Before I describe incidents in each area, I would like to explain the "methodology" that is generally followed in order to achieve the control of a specific area. Jorge Gómez Lizarazo, Defender of the People in the Magdalena Medio region, has identified four specific steps that are used in order to eventually tailor the targeted region to Plan Colombia's goals. He describes them in an article entitled "Trabajemos en el Proyecto de Nación" published in a CREDHOS report made public in June, 2002. These same methods are standardized countrywide, with small changes according to the situation and the region. The steps are:[1]

1. Annihilation of the existing community and social organizations that worked together trying to create a democratic and participatory society. Terror is an essential part of this stage and the most barbaric and savage acts are committed in order to destroy the leadership of persons that have dreamed of constructing a democratic Colombia. Leaders are exiled if they are lucky. Usually they are killed and tortured: The first targets are social leaders, religious persons, politicians, human-rights activists, journalists, labor leaders, lawyers, teachers and peasants. A few regional examples follow.

   In its report for the first six months of 2002, the Permanent Committee for Human Rights of the department of Caldas in the coffee-growing region states that the armed conflict which had not been seen in this region at all, now is all over Caldas. Their report accurately describes the above mentioned first step. It painfully details the assassination of several indigenous leaders, such as María Fabiola Largo Cano, who had run for Mayor of the city of Riosucio. In February, the writer and journalist Orlando Sierra was killed. Mr. Sierra was denouncing cases of political and administrative corruption. On April 12, 2002, Hernán Ortiz, a union leader, was executed. The Permanent Committee was able to get a list with names, addresses and telephone numbers of targeted activists, some of them already killed.

   As a part of the same paramilitary advance strategy, the local Manizales newspaper describes daily the victims of "social cleansing," such as beggars, petty thieves, drug addicts and alcoholics, usually in the sector of the market place where there is a school for hit men. The authorities

1. Editor's note: The following 4 numbered points on this and the following three pages are Cecilia's paraphrasing/discussion of the four points made by Jorge Gómez Lizarazo in his article just mentioned, "Trabajemos en el Proyecto de Nación."

cynically justify these killings, which are especially celebrated by businessmen in the area.

Children and young and unemployed persons are recruited to be part of their armies. The Department of Huila, near the demilitarized zone that was the site of the dialogues between the government of Andrés Pastrana and the FARC, experiences not only the arrival of displaced persons at its capital Neiva, but the increased number of disappeared persons, especially young people in areas controlled by the military and the paramilitary. The guerrillas have been using the infamous method of recruiting children as soldiers.

Another particularly despicable method of disappearing persons is by forced recruitment, such as was the case of 19 young men from Neiva who were taken to Meta Department, allegedly contracted to work in agriculture and construction, but were forced to become part of a paramilitary group. Several persons believed to have been disappeared seem to have been recruited by the illegal groups, including the guerrillas.

Even more dramatic is the case in the department of Santander. From January to June of 2002, 160 persons were disappeared (105 men and 55 women) according to several human rights groups, such as FUNPROCEP (Fund for the Protection of Culture and Education) and CREDHOS (The Regional Corporation for the Defense of Human Rights). Several disappeared persons are businessmen, but the majority are young people forced to work in illegal crops, prostitution, transportation of chemicals for processing illegal substances or stolen vehicles. The desperate families go to Police stations, Defensoría, NGOs or the mass media to denounce the disappearance of their children, most of them minors. After six months, the children show up again with large sums of money for their families, but under a cloak of silence due to death threats if they do not return or if they go to the authorities.

Intimidation and extortion are the usual tools to start the control of a specific area. All of these start under the cover of darkness and secrecy at night, with the tacit collaboration of state agents, like a fungus that grows dark and rotten, and then little by little they start to act openly to show up their evil ways at midday under the full tropical sunshine, without shame. No force stops them since the "democratic" elements of the state look the other way or ignore what is happening under their very own noses.

2. Controlling all of the activities of these groups and of the communal activities during this stage, the paramilitaries act as an organization that complements or substitutes for the Army and the Police or both; they freely patrol the streets, have operational centers and take over private security organizations such as community watchmen, etc.

   At this point they feel the ownership of the place and start to restrict individual freedoms, such as freedom of movement, freedom of association and freedom of expression. And they establish checkpoints. They approve or disapprove candidates for public positions and tell the community for whom to vote. They establish rules for daily life and mobilize the population to generate political actions that make their position more solid. During this stage they consolidate illegal economies and illegally tax businessmen. If they see the need, they establish food and medicine blockades in order to show they are the authority.

   More examples: I personally witnessed a large mobilization of the population in poor neighborhoods in Barranca, forced to demonstrate opposition to the establishment of a demilitarized zone in the Middle Magdalena for conversations with the ELN (Ejército de Liberación Nacional, National Liberation Army). The paramilitaries went house by house forcing one or two members to be at the demonstration...or else. The terrorized population did not have the right to say no.

   In the city of Manizales, particularly in popular neighborhoods, there were graffiti saying: "We arrived. AUC" and "Good boys go to bed at 8 p.m.; the others, we put them to sleep. AUC". In Barrancabermeja, the AUC feel they have to scold the parents of boys wearing long hair or earrings, or daughters with mini-skirts. They patrol the streets and mediate between neighbors or couples. Pets should stay within the owners' property. Bars selling liquor must close at 2 a.m. or are "taxed." If they sell alcoholic drinks to members of the AUC in service, they are also taxed. If a peasant does not maintain his farm well, it is given to a needier person as defined by them. Husband and wife should not fight.

   In a well-known case the AUC called 460 Barranca workers hired by the local office of Plan Colombia and informed them that they should "collaborate" with 10 percent of their salary if they did not want problems. Some workers denounced this, but most of them kept silent since they did not want to lose their jobs or their lives. Two couples had to leave the city because the women were threatened with death by their former lovers who had become part of the AUC; the former lovers did not accept that they were living with someone else.

A very lucrative business for the AUC is the control of stolen gasoline and other petroleum products from the Colombian oil company ECOPETROL. In 2002 about 800 million pesos were lost by the city in local taxes on gasoline. It is calculated that the AUC makes 150 million pesos daily from stealing gasoline.

In Aguadas in the state of Caldas, the AUC imposed the election of the Mayor, and associating with drug traffickers, they exercise authority in the region. A natural consequence of this situation is the high number of displaced persons all over the country. The leaders of displaced people are a favorite target of the AUC. Just in Bucaramanga 18 leaders of displaced groups have been threatened by the AUC in the first six months of this year, 2002.

3. The next step is reorganization of the society. The paramilitaries create many political, economic, social, cultural and security organizations that replace the ones that were destroyed in the first stage. These new organizations direct and orientate the civilian population on the rules of the new society and do not have as a goal the struggle to obtain social, economic or political rights.

4. Step four is one of legitimation and legalization: The paramilitaries become the "para-state," condition public servants to the point that they weaken the state that they say they defend and become a de facto government facilitated by an almost total impunity. They do not confront the Armed Forces militarily but establish territorial borders for each other and share the authority.

All of the activities described above are part of a strategy to eliminate vibrant grassroots organizations and movements and replace them with a society of zombies ready to produce in the sweatshops being built for foreign consumption. The systematic killing of labor leaders and the destruction of the unions to form a docile workforce at the behest of multinational businesses is part of the recipe to implement the FTAA.

Cultural events are their favorite method to get to the people in order to articulate their social base and legitimate their totalitarian project. This is to present an image of prosperity and peace with the purpose of attracting capital investment.

There is something very important to keep in mind with respect to the FTAA. It is not only in material matters but also, what is more dangerous, through control of the mass media where those who promote the FTAA can control ideology and culture, and even the human spirit. Almost without perceiving it, we are little by little losing the soul of Latin America, that soul which is so rich in inheritances: Indigenous, Black, Hispanic with its variants of Moorish, Jewish, Basque and Catalán. We will be forced to adore Walt Disney, who was a man who despised and humiliated Mexicans and through them all of us.... and all of our children will grow up with his merchandise of individualism and exclusion.

What is finally established is highly authoritarian government, totally divorced from human rights, dignity or respect for International Humanitarian Law. Apparently these have to be restricted in order to save "democracy and its institutions." Only then can the FTAA be implemented.

BIBLIOGRAPHY

1. "Situación de los Derechos Humanos en el Departamento del Huila," Comité Permanente por la Defensa de los Derechos Humanos, Capitulo Huila, Junio 2002
2. "Situación Regional de DDHH y DIH," Coordinación Colombia-Europa Regional Nororiente. Primer Semestre 2002, Bucaramanga Julio 2002
3. Informe Comité Permanente por la Defensa de los Derechos Humanos, Comité Regional de Caldas. Primer Semestre del año 2002
4. Normas de Convivencia Autodefensas y Población Civil. Obtained by a CSN delegation to the Putumayo, July 2002
5. "Crisis humanitario y de DDHH," Corporación Regional por la Defensa de los DDHH (CREDHOS), Informe, Agosto-Diciembre 2001. Barrancabermeja, Diciembre 2001
6. "Situación Regional DDHH y DIH," Magdalena Medio Colombia. Corporación Regional por la Defensa de los Derechos Humanos CREDHOS. Barrancabermeja, Diciembre 2001—Junio 2002

MARCH 2001

Speech on Implementation of the Free Trade Area of the Americas

Rosario washes her hands several times a day. "They smell bad," says the 11-year-old girl and runs to the bathroom to wash them again. The teacher in her school tries to convince her that her hands are clean and there is no need to put them in water and scrub them again. Nowadays she gives Rosario creams and perfumes. But the smell does not go away. The smell of burning and rotting flesh has been fixed firmly in her mind ever since a few months ago when she saw some paramilitary forces torture a young man from her town and set fire to him as he lay dying and was already being picked at by buzzards.

Early this year I read in a Colombian press article how on a January morning, paramilitary forces entered a little town in Antioquia in the northern part of the country and at random took a displaced peasant who was accompanied by his five-year-old son. They cut off the father's head and it fell at the feet of the horrified child. Last Wednesday, March 28, 2001, the number of selective assassinations this year in the oil-producing city of Barrancabermeja reached 300, in a city of 250,000 population. That same day five peasant members of a regional committee were killed in the Colombian headwater region in the south of Colombia by members of the infamous AUC (Autodefensas Unidas de

Colombia) paramilitary. These paramilitary forces carry lists and take the listed persons out of their homes.

All these barbarous actions have some things in common: First, they eliminate the limits which set apart civilians as non-combatants and, in fact, treat civilians as military targets. Second, all these paramilitary actions take place under the watchful eye of the Colombian Army, which has been converted into a frozen Army that does not protect the civilian population and arrives late upon the scenes of crimes or does not come at all to those places. And on other occasions, the Army surrounds small towns, as happened in the case of El Aro in Antioquia, while paramilitary forces carry out massacres; in El Aro the Army even forced those terrified peasants who tried to flee to return to the town where the massacre was underway.

But this Army is always useful for multinational corporations (MNCs), a number of which have hired the Colombian Army to protect their installations against guerrilla attacks or civilian demonstrations. For example, the Colombian Army forced U'wa indigenous protesters off their own lands in order to allow Occidental Petroleum to drill on them. For many years, British Petroleum protected its rich oil installations in Caño Limón with Colombian Army troops, and the BBC (British Broadcasting Company) has documented abuses of the civilian population in the vicinity by these troops.

The War on Drugs, which is an excuse to implement Plan Colombia, is a smokescreen to obscure the real cause of this endless war: globalization. Although the origin of the war in Colombia is the result of a society which excludes the majority of its members from their social, political, economic and human rights, this class war has never been resolved. The production of coca is the result of the despair and poverty of peasants displaced from their lands. In the wars of Central America, many of the displaced peasants traveled to the United States. In Colombia they go to the country's last frontier: the tropical rainforest.

The United States government is anxious to resolve this war with a peace at any cost because this, the last war in the hemisphere, makes difficult and impedes the achievement of treaties such as that for the proposed Free Trade Area of the Americas. That is the reason why the strategy is to use paramilitary forces to impose by force a new society where economics and policies predominate, which assures the territorial control of the dominant classes. This is what lies behind the pacification by force by means of massacres and selective murder of peasants and labor union leaders who are assassinated without remorse.

Just since January 1 of this year, 2001, 25 labor union leaders have been murdered. In this corner of South America, protests, critical thinking, opposition and analysis are silenced so that there will be order and security ("stability") for investors. Through arrangements between large landowners, politicians, cattlemen and others, the paramilitaries are financed so that they may kill, massacre and threaten the population. They also finance their activities by trafficking in drugs.

The alternatives for threatened peasants are to flee, to die or to be quiet and cooperate. If we look at Colombia's geography, we see that the paramilitary forces focus their activities on places where investors and transnational companies wish access to natural resources. For example, they have terrorized the Chocó, where a sea-level canal-railroad-highway crossing from Atlantic to Pacific is proposed. Likewise, in the south of Bolívar Department where there are gold mines, in the Guajira Peninsula with its coal mines which have been worked by Exxon and Drummond, and in territories rich in oil, where Occidental Petroleum, Amoco or Harken (a company in which President George W. Bush was an investor) wish to drill.

For the rest of the world it might be a "War on Drugs." For us it is the implementation, by whatever force may be necessary, of the treaties of the Free Trade Area of the Americas. As Colombia's ambassador to the United States, Luis Alberto Moreno, said in a speech at Notre Dame University this past Monday, March 26: "We wish to work for a broader agreement, an area of Free Trade of the Americas for 2003. It is a secret to no one that economic prosperity has an impact upon political stability," even if it means peace without justice.

2004

The Comic Tragedy of the "Peace Negotiations" with the Paramilitaries

On Wednesday, July 15, 2003, at 4:45 pm, in a place called Santa Fé de Ralito in Northern Colombia, an agreement was signed between the Colombian government and the major paramilitary group, the Autodefensas Unidas de Colombia (AUC, Self-Defense Forces of Colombia). After a period of months of highly confidential discussions, and with the mediation of members of the Catholic Church, the AUC made a commitment to cease hostilities and to demobilize its members in a gradual process that will end in 2005, as the beginning of a peace process. The government, on the other hand, commits itself to creating conditions that guarantee security through the concentration of troops in previously defined places. All of this was done in the name of achieving peace, strengthening democracy and reestablishing the monopoly of force in the hands of the Colombian state.

With unusual efficiency, Fernando Londoño, the Minister of Interior and Justice, drafted a Bill that gives the Colombian president discretionary powers to commute prison terms for alternative punishment such as reparation to the victims, ending the conflict, or helping to achieve peace, to members of illegal groups that declare a stop to hostilities and participate in a peace process. Mr. Londoño explains that it is evident that depriving people of their freedom as the only answer to crime fails on many occasions to resocialize the delinquents and that contemporary law has evolved a lot on the issue of alternative sanctions.

The High Commissioner for Peace, the psychiatrist Luis Carlos Restrepo, alleges that in a negotiated solution it does not make sense to offer jail as the only alternative to negotiation. The beneficiaries must commit themselves not to engage in crimes in the future, not to leave the country, not to occupy or run for government offices for 10 years, not to carry arms and not to contact their victims. And they should restrict themselves from going to certain parts of the country. The government will create a Verification Commission to supervise the beneficiaries, who must sign a document with all the specifications. Supervising judges would establish probationary periods of one to five years, at the end of which the judge can declare total freedom for the criminals.

The Bill would be hilarious if it were not immoral, painful and tragic. First, from the beginning of the secret conversations, one of the goals was to find a recipe to forgive atrocious crimes committed by the paramilitary groups. According to highly respected organizations such as the United Nations, Amnesty International, Human Rights Watch and others, Colombian paramilitaries have committed the majority of the crimes against mankind that have been committed in Colombia in the last years. AUC paramilitaries have selectively and indiscriminately assassinated defenseless populations, have massacred people using methods as cruel as cutting persons alive with chainsaws, have disappeared thousands, kidnapped many, sexually abused women and children and contributed to the displacement of millions of defenseless Colombian peasants. All of these have been done in order to control strategic territories that will be useful for future mega projects; projects that will benefit multinational corporations or territories that are going to be used to plant coca.

Their crimes have been committed with the direct support, the complicity or the tolerance of the Colombian Armed Forces, as has been demonstrated in innumerable cases. Human Rights Watch has called the paramilitaries "The Sixth Division of the Colombian Army."[1] From their luxurious residences, cattlemen, businessmen, large landowners, entrepreneurs, drug dealers and

1. Editor's note: For a detailed treatment of the paramilitaries and the Colombian military see Human Rights Watch, "Colombia's Killer Networks: The Military-Paramilitary Partnership and the United States," November 1996.

members of the Colombian elite have secretly supported and sponsored these thugs in order to eliminate social protest in Colombia. Both the military and the AUC have as a common enemy: the guerrilla or whomever they perceive as guerrilla.

Traditionally a peace process is carried out with groups that rebel against a government. The Santa Fé de Ralito agreement is interesting since it is a negotiation among friends. The Colombian paramilitaries have never said that they are against the state. On the contrary, they have always said that they defend the institutions and what these represent. A negotiation with oneself cannot be called a peace negotiation. The AUC are accused of sedition, which is defined by them as "transitory interference with the normal functioning of the state." The AUC can keep their arms, their uniforms and their internal structure while they are concentrated in previously defined areas which, in marked difference with President Andres Pastrana's negotiation with the FARC, will not be demilitarized but will have a belt of the Armed Forces protecting them.[2]

There are many obstacles to this peace process. First, economical. It is calculated that there are about 13,000 AUC members which will cost 208 million U.S. dollars or 16,000 U.S. dollars for each member for two years. Who is going to pay for all of this? The Colombian government says it has no money because corruption, the cost of the war and the foreign debt have devastated the country's budget. The U.S. government said through its former Ambassador Anne Patterson that they will give two to three million dollars during the first two years.[3] The State Department has declared the AUC to be a terrorist organization, but according to the newspaper *El Tiempo*, on July 20, 2003, functionaries from the U.S. government said that once they lay down their arms, the AUC members cease being terrorists. The Europeans meanwhile

2. Editor's note: In fact, many of the paramilitary soldiers who entered the so-called demobilization process kept their weapons, or obtained others, and returned to paramilitary units. The Colombian Government's High Commissioner for Peace, Luis Carlos Restrepo, who was in charge of the demobilization for the government of President Álvaro Uribe Vélez at the town of Santa Fé de Ralito in Córdoba Province, did not keep careful records of who had surrendered their weapons. After the supposed paramilitary demobilization, Restrepo disappeared for several years before reappearing, having reportedly relocated to the United States. For an excellent, detailed and very critical analysis of the paramilitary "demobilization" see a July 31, 2005 report by Human Rights Watch, "Smoke and Mirrors: Colombia's Demobilization of Paramilitary Groups." For the Agreement between the Colombian Government and the AUC paramilitaries, see https://peacemaker.un.org.
3. Editor's note: See Ambassador Patterson's assessment of U.S. policy toward Colombia in "U.S. Department of State Archive, Ask the State Department," questions to and answers by Anne W. Patterson, 2001-2006.

have not said anything about money.

Another difficulty is security. To prevent the guerrillas from taking back territories under paramilitary control, it will be necessary to have at least 3 soldiers for each paramilitary, according to declarations by the Minister of Defense [Ed. note: Jorge Uribe]. Thirty-nine thousand soldiers will be necessary to control the territories since many of the paramilitary supporters created the paramilitaries—hereafter paras—to fill the vacuum left by the state. The peasant soldiers created by President Uribe could be used for these areas.

The close relationship between the paras and drug-trafficking is a further serious problem. A confidential report that was leaked to the media in Bogotá reveals that the AUC franchises its name to drug traffickers for millions of dollars. A notorious thug called "Don Berna" or Diego Murillo Bejarano, regrouped what was left from the Medellín and Cali cartels and is now the Inspector General of the AUC (whatever this means). The paras are responsible for about 40 percent of the total drug trade according to the analysis published by *El Tiempo* on July 20, 2005. Several of their leaders, particularly Carlos Castaño and Salvatore Mancuso, have extradition orders from the United States pending. In a humorous if not cynical idea, some of the AUC legal advisors requested that drug trafficking be considered also sedition or a political crime! Even Castaño rejected this suggestion. The United States government must watch these developments carefully.

Both the United States and the European Union together have been outspoken on the issue of impunity for atrocious crimes. Neither the proposed Bill nor the Santa Fé de Ralito agreement mention the thousands of deaths "extra-judicially executed." These include many labor leaders, teachers, journalists, priests, human rights defenders, political activists and university professors. Not a word! It seems that the more serious the crime the less punishment the culprits get. Clearly, the Bill is the definition of impunity.

Besides the AUC, there are several other paramilitary groups that are still active and not included in the negotiations. They are located in areas where they are still needed for counter-insurgency, such as the regions of Urabá and Chocó, the Magdalena Medio and Southern Bolívar. What is going to happen to them?

The Office of the High Commissioner for Human Rights of the United Nations issued a press release reminding the government that actions related to ending the internal armed conflict should abide by International Law respecting truth, justice and reparations. Any negotiating initiative must combine reconciliation with deep respect for the rights of the victims. It is the duty of the state to avoid giving benefits to the authors of atrocious crimes. Doing so gives the perception that people can commit all kinds of crimes with the security that they will not be punished. This in itself might stimulate the continuation of the armed conflict. The United Nations (UN) office criticizes the lack of the principle of 'proportionality' or punishment appropriate to the gravity of the crimes. Another problem that the UN office sees in the Bill is that it suspends the privation of freedom to persons who have not even started to pay punishment for atrocious crimes.

The issue of reparations is another concern. Are the paramilitaries going to return the lands taken from the nearly three million peasants who are displaced? Is the collection of lands taken with blood and chainsaws going to be the basis for a real agrarian reform?

Eduardo Cifuentes, the highly respected and recently retired Ombudsman, called the Bill a "given calamity" that favors impunity and would create a horrible precedent for the country because the peace that it will produce will be fragile, since it will not bring reconciliation. This will only be obtained with justice and true reparation for the victims. Journalist Salud Hernández advocates the right of the victims to know at least where their loved ones are buried and how they were killed.

A final consideration is that impunity is inconsistent with justice, and democracy can only be strengthened with justice. Without these two elements, democracy and justice, seeking peace will be just an illusion.

2003

The Insecurity of Democratic Security

On January 28, 2003, Colombia Support Network (CSN) launched an Urgent Action Message about our sister community (CSN Syracuse) of Cajibio in Cauca state protesting the arbitrary detention of many peasants, truck drivers, young people, housewives, school teachers, aldermen, members of medical missions, etc., since December of 2002. All of them are accused of being either collaborators or informants of the guerrillas as a result of the policy of Democratic Security of President Álvaro Uribe Vélez.

The Uribe administration does not have a policy of peace but prefers a military solution to the Colombian conflict. President Uribe's goal is the defeat of the guerrillas and the creation of conditions that will allow the imposition of a peace agreement without the deep changes in the social, political and economic structures that Colombia urgently needs. Democratic Security, defined below, does not contemplate stopping violations of human rights or International Humanitarian Law.

It is obvious that the majority of the Colombian population pleads for security, given the multiple attempts against life, unemployment, low salaries, impunity and the control of the brutal paramilitaries. All of these reflect an enormous lack of protection for the citizens. The same applies to the lack of guarantees for social and political organizations in the opposition, which limit even more the freedoms of the population. The question then is: For whom is the security of President Uribe's model? At the service of whom is this policy of Democratic Security? If we add to this situation the global policy of the United States in its fight against terrorism after September 11, it is clear that insecurity is being used as a political tool to legitimize the defense of a political, cultural and economic model that excludes the majority of the inhabitants of this planet from their minimal rights.

The policy of Democratic Security of President Uribe combines in a very peculiar way two wars: the old counter-insurgency war trying to stop the advance into the cities of the rural fronts of the FARC and the ELN and the new counter-terrorist war trying to neutralize the urban networks of the same guerrillas. The paramilitaries do not seem to be targeted by this new war. Neither are the drug dealers. In this way the policy of Democratic Security justifies the detention of thousands of citizens accused of being militias, collaborators or informants of the guerrilla movements.

Uribe's Democratic Security is based on the principle that to obtain the dreamed-of security, Colombian civil society must be allied with its state and become active with its Army and its Police. In other words, it militarizes daily life through "voluntary cooperation," which I assume will become obligatory as time passes by. Neighbors must inform when they see people bringing suspicious boxes to nearby homes. Eventually we will see networks of bakers, nurses, retired people or drivers spying on each other. Security has become a commodity to be traded, and spying is instituted as a profession to solve unemployment. This is the principle behind the millions of informants and of the 20,000 "peasant soldiers."

On August 8, 2002, the day after taking his oath as President, Mr. Uribe traveled to the city of Valledupar to inaugurate his first group of citizen informers. A journalist from *El Tiempo* spoke to informant #1477. He was a young man in his 30s wearing blue jeans and tennis shoes who started to work with the informants' network set up by the Police in his town to report "suspicious persons." When asked what he considered suspicious, he said "people who is [*sic*] not from the town, I look at his waist to see if he carries a gun, and I look at his eyes, and if he avoids to look at me directly, it means he hides something." When asked if he has made mistakes, he said "Yes, I reported a suspicious individual who ended up being a counter-insurgency soldier doing intelligence."

The highly respected Data Bank of CINEP, in its Bulletin #10 in the May-June/03 edition, considers that the government of Álvaro Uribe, associated with the political and economic classes and the mass media, are legitimizing the paramilitaries as a component of Democratic Security and that control of the civilian population is the central goal of military operations. General Gallego, the commander of the Police in Medellin during the Orion military operation, guided his units with these words: "... everyone has to be detained ... then we will see who has no charges ... everything that moves has to be detained ..." Daily life is militarized: military checkpoints, house searches, detentions, census, military occupation of schools, parks, cultural and recreational centers and so on. Political opposition has no space. People who do not share the official policies are traitors, guerillas and terrorists. When a territory is recovered by the Army, paramilitaries come to take control of it.

Other elements of Uribe's Democratic Security are to increase the number of soldiers, to acquire modern military equipment and create more Mobile Brigades, anti-terrorist groups and seven high mountain Battalions in areas controlled by the FARC. Because of his government's policies of austerity and sacrifice, Uribe established a tax on patrimony so the war and the economy became intertwined. From this idea of saving money, Uribe decided to create peasant soldiers. Young peasants will be recruited and trained at their nearby brigades. They will be part of the military in their own communities and will sleep at home at night. They can take their arms home, and they can use them in case there is a guerrilla attack. Needless to say, these soldiers and their families will automatically become military targets of the guerrillas and in this way more members of civilian society will be incorporated into the conflict. Who can stop the soldiers from using their arms for other purposes than defending the country from terrorists? Without doubt, the United States will use its aid to exercise pressure on the Colombian government for advancing its own agenda.

Another worrisome element of this policy is the assignment of judiciary duties to the Army and the elimination of search warrants when searching homes or human rights organizations such as the case of the Permanent Assembly of Civil Society for Peace. No need for judiciary orders to detain individuals or entire communities. This was the case in Saravena in Arauca province where thousands of persons were concentrated in the Coliseum and branded with ink in a clear reminder of the stadium detentions during the dictatorship in Chile. Uribe's attempts to eliminate the Defensoría del Pueblo (Ombudsman's office) and the Constitutional Court, two of the most celebrated achievements of the 1991 Constitution, do not honor his pledges of respecting the Constitution.

In the meantime, the Data Bank keeps reporting thousands of selective killings, arbitrary detentions, displaced persons and an alarming increase in the use of torture.

More worrisome seems the fact that the official statistics offer a panorama of more insecurity. According to the Ministry of Defense, in the year 2000 there were 21,585 insurgents, and between 2000 and 2003 the number of neutralized insurgents was 18,114 by death, desertion or capture. Subtracting numbers there must be only 3,471 total guerrillas left in Colombia. Using the data from the same Minister of Defense, between 2000 and 2003 the guerrilla numbers have grown by 25 percent. Are the official statistics reflecting reality? Would it be possible that what these statistics are showing is extrajudicial executions and arbitrary detentions of the civilian population in areas of conflict? Such as the housewives, truck drivers, teachers and so on of Cajibio? There is too much democratic authoritarianism and much less security.

1997

Who Cares About the Butterflies?

I want to demonstrate at a micro level the devastating consequences the globalization process has for countries outside the centers of economic decision-making.

The Colombian Pacific Coast is generically known as the Chocó, although it touches four provinces: Chocó, Cauca Valley, Cauca and Nariño. It lies between Colombia's borders with Panamá on the North and Ecuador on the South. On the East it is bounded by the western side of the Andes mountain range. The Pacific Coast stretches 1,300 km in length. Of a population of 900,000, 40 percent live in urban centers and the rest in small communities dispersed along the rivers and the Coast. Ninety percent are Afro-Colombians, 5 percent indigenous (the Emberá-Catio, Tule and Cuna nations) and 5 percent mestizos.

The region of Chocó has the highest concentration of endemic species in the world. This makes it one of the richest reserves of biodiversity on the planet. The Chocó is cut off from the rest of Colombia by the Western Andes range and by the impenetrability of its territory. This isolation has helped to protect its biodiversity with tropical rainforests, swamps and rivers covering 80 percent of the area. The Chocó contains 7,000 to 8,000 species of plants, many of them not botanically classified yet, and at least 600 species of birds, more than are found in all of North America. Forty-seven percent of the reptile population is endemic and just in the region of Anchicaya alone there have been 525 species of butterflies reported, 37 percent of them endemic.

For the past 500 years the Chocó has been used as a dispensary from which natural resources are taken away, always to integrate them into the mercantilist international system. The Spanish invaded the Chocó at the beginning of the Sixteenth Century. From the mountain ridges of Darién—a region in the Chocó—Balboa "discovered" the Pacific Ocean. Soon the Chocó became one of the traditional sources of gold for the Spanish Crown. Before the mining in the Chocó, platinum was an element unknown to humanity. In 1740, the first samples were sent to Spain.

The manpower provided by the indigenous people diminished, as the population declined to one-tenth of its size before the Spanish Conquest due to mistreatment and epidemics of smallpox, measles and typhoid. The Spanish Crown decided in the middle of the Sixteenth Century to introduce black slaves from Guinea, the Congo, Sudan and Angola to provide the labor needed for continuing the pillage of natural resources. Soon the slaves also rebelled, fleeing from the mines and forming settlements in inaccessible areas called "palenques." These former slaves, called "cimarrones," kept attacking production and harming the economic interests of the European colonizers. In the Nineteenth Century, independence was won from Spain, and the Viceroyalty of New Granada became the Republic of Colombia. Ownership changed hands because the aristocratic creoles (descendants of Spaniards born in America) wanted to take power and control of the national territory. The structures of the mining economy continued. Slavery was abolished in Colombia on January 1, 1852.

The Afro-Colombian communities lived in urban and rural centers along the river banks, surviving by agriculture, fishing and small-scale mining. They developed a deep sense of community, kinship and oral tradition, keeping alive generation after generation, almost untouched, the traditions of their African ancestors to this day. The indigenous communities are less visible in small settlements located in clearings in the forests. They also hunt, fish and grow crops or harvest plants from the jungle.

Recently the Pacific Coast has been the object of an ambitious plan of development by the Colombian government called "Plan Pacífico." The objective is very simple: to exploit the vast natural resources of the Chocó (gold, platinum, uranium, oil, precious woods, etc.) to obtain wealth to pay Colombia's foreign debt. The plan seeks to open and modernize the production system for the world markets. In other words, to implement globalization.

Plan Pacífico includes the construction of at least 11 roads, most of them to permit more access to the Pacific from the Andean region, and to improve North-South communication. The most conspicuous example is the finishing of the Pan-American Highway, completing the 108 km of the famous Darién Gap which remains unbuilt between Panamá and Colombia. This highway represents the ultimate dream of the promoters of NAFTA, neo-liberalism and free trade, because it will unite the Americas from Alaska to Chile. The Darién Gap is one of the most fragile and important ecological reserves in the world because its swamps and rivers have kept a great variety of plants and animals and it provides important evidence for the study of biological links between North and South America. All these highways will guarantee to big capital the permanent flow of goods and natural resources throughout the Americas.

Plan Pacífico also calls for pipelines, hydroelectric projects, ports, a complex railroad system and the spectacular project of the construction of an inter-oceanic canal to connect Colombia's Pacific and Atlantic coasts. A naval base in the Bay of Málaga will serve to protect projects from civilian or guerrilla protests. All these plans include mining and deforestation on a commercial scale. Although Plan Pacífico has an ecological component and speaks of "sustainable development," the region is being prepared for the opening of markets recommended by the International Monetary Fund (IMF) and international banking.

IMPLEMENTING PLAN PACÍFICO

Since February of 1997, the civilian population of the Chocó has been intimidated, kidnapped and threatened by groups which identify themselves as paramilitary or "self-defense" groups. They force the people to get out, leaving behind their lands, crops and cattle. As a method of intimidation, persons taken at random are executed in front of their community. Pax Christi International cited the case of the small settlement of Vijao, where the youth Marino López was decapitated and dismembered to terrorize the population and cause them to leave. Simultaneously the area was bombarded by the Armed Forces of Colombia.

Once abandoned, the small towns are occupied by the Army and paramilitaries, who have no attachment to the land, creating a concentration of land in the hands of owners whose identities remain unknown to the public. The refugees, mainly women and children, live in camps. (For more information see the website of the Colombia Support Network, https://colombiasupport.net).

CONSEQUENCES OF GLOBALIZATION

There are several consequences of globalization which affect people at the individual level. Let us look at the Chocó refugees, for example.

1. The people are required or forced to participate in the market economy. The Chocó refugees who were self-sufficient now have to sell their labor in the overcrowded labor market or become prostitutes or beggars.
2. Globalization creates a "mutation" in people who begin to believe that if one does not participate in the market economy—that is, if one does not have money or a Visa card—one is not a human being.
3. Little by little globalization transforms humanity into a collection of passive consumers alienated by television, captivated by sports as business, who become computer slaves and buyers of useless electric products.
4. With globalization, economic power becomes stronger than political power, or the economic power of the minority is converted into political power serving its interests. Democracy is lost because decisions are centralized in the boardrooms of corporations. Ironically, the much criticized 'central planning' of former socialist countries becomes a reality of western democracies.
5. Globalizing the economy is carried out not to serve the needs of the majority, but to serve the conspicuous consumption of a minority. In other words, goods are produced only to obtain profit and not to serve humanity.
6. Globalization in its anxiety to sell degrades humanity; it converts human activities which have great dignity into objects to be bought and sold. For example, the storytellers of the Chocó will no longer tell stories true to their tradition but rather tell them to obtain money. The subsistence economy has ended and the storyteller needs money to buy Coca-Cola. The children of the Chocó will grow up with Mickey Mouse as entertainment instead of the legends of their elders.

Thus little by little, we arrive at the final objective of globalization: to convert us all into consumers where fraternity, solidarity and human compassion are unknown.

The struggle to regain the soul of humanity, the preservation of nature and of the beautiful, brightly coloured butterflies of the Chocó is carried out in the jungles and shanty towns of Colombia today.

2001

Let's Defend the Defenders

In 1819, during the Congreso de Angostura, Simón Bolívar, speaking about how to organize a state, emphasized the need for a moral authority. He said that the jurisdiction of this holy tribunal must be effective with regard to education and training, while having a voice only regarding punishment and sanction.

Since that time the idea has surfaced at times as part of the legislative branch and at other times as part of the Attorney General's Office, but in general it has been difficult to legislate or execute. Obviously, given the complexities of the Colombian conflict, it is not an easy task. In 1991 after a referendum, the Colombian people decided to change the 1886 Constitution in order to establish a modern constitution that would better fit current times. The government sent several commissions abroad to explore and update ideas for the new document. One of the novel ideas came after visiting Sweden, where they found the figure of the Ombudsman, an office that would fit with Simón Bolívar's original idea of a moral authority. In the Nineteenth Century, the Swedish constitution established the Ombudsman as a representative of the community that takes care of and investigates complaints against abuses by the authorities. It is a symbol of democratic states.

The new Constitution of 1991 (considered by the Inter-American Commission of Human Rights as one of the most advanced in Latin America) created an office called the Defensoría del Pueblo (Defender of the People or Ombudsman's office). It was charged with the responsibility of defending and promoting human rights and the oversight of public policy within the framework of a democratic, participatory and pluralist state. The Ombudsman's office defends the citizens because the citizen is and must be the most important category within a democracy. The citizen is not only the origin of the power of the democratic institutions, but the ultimate recipient of the actions originated from that power.

Article 284 of the Constitution provides that the Ombudsman can request from authorities all the necessary information for exercising his functions without opposition from anyone except in specific exceptional cases mentioned. It is important to say that the Defensor does not carry out judicial or disciplinary functions. His authority comes from the Constitution itself, the legal principles and the support of a democratic society, its moral qualities. The Defensor exercises fundamentally the power of critic. The Defensoría is not only for Colombians but also for foreigners in Colombia.

Besides the Constitution, Colombia has international responsibilities because it has ratified international human rights treaties by which it has made the commitment to apply such international principles internally, as recommended by the different organisms of the United Nations. Particularly since the 1980s, the United Nations has recommended to its member states the creation of national institutions to promote and protect human rights. Therefore, the creation of the Defensoría del Pueblo in the 1991 Constitution meant not only the follow-up of international norms, but also the current trends in modern constitutional tendencies.

The specific tasks of the Defensoría are to educate, promote, defend and protect human rights. I will summarize the concrete activities of the Defensoría in order to clarify both the importance of this office and the urgency to keep it:

1. Promote and publicize the human rights of the Colombian population. Through the publication of educational materials, books, a website, conferences, periodicals, reports, audio-visual material, etc., the Ombudsman's office helps the common citizen to understand, reflect on and respect human rights as a responsibility, for both public servants and private citizens. But the Defensoría goes beyond just simply publishing and educating. It moves forward to point out where the law should be applied in concrete terms in order to set goals to develop a truly democratic Colombia.

The Defensoría strongly believes that an improvement in human rights cannot come only from strengthening the Ombudsman's office because human rights abuses are a structural problem of Colombian society, and to solve this situation it should come from a transformation of the same society. The role of the Defensoría would eventually allow for the citizens themselves to be the engines for a change into a more inclusive society. Besides general education, the Defensoría does special projects for specific cases. I will illustrate with two examples:

a) Development of workshops and educational material in the five municipalities that were selected as part of the Demilitarized Zone (DZ): La Macarena, Uribe, Vistahermosa, Mesetas and San Vicente del Caguán. The Defensoría was the only government office that had a permanent presence in the DZ. The following activities were developed in order to protect and defend human rights in the area: workshops to train vulnerable groups on human rights and International Humanitarian Law; education about the role of the Defensoría and the legal rights of the population in the area; training about reconciliation and mediation by the citizens themselves with the armed actors; mediation with the armed actors; receiving and following complaints from the communities when they believed their rights were violated. Guided by the Defensoría, the communities developed an emergency plan in case the situation became urgent. All these activities were financed thanks to the generosity of the governments of Sweden, Canada, the Low Countries and Switzerland. It is possible to say that the activities initiated a reconstruction of the social fabric in the area and is perhaps the only thing left from the peace conversations. [Editor's note: The peace conversations referenced here took place in the Caguán between the Fuerzas Armadas Revolucionarias de Colombia (FARC), and the government during the administration of President Andrés Pastrana, 1998-2002. A demilitarized zone was established as part of the effort to carry out peace talks between the Colombian government and the FARC guerrillas. (Note that the first year of his administration is 1998).]

Another notable example is the special attention of the Defensoría toward displaced persons. With the financial support of the High Commissioner for Refugees of the United Nations, an office was created in 2000 to focus exclusively on people displaced by political violence.

The office not only coordinated with other offices to help support policies for the benefit of the displaced but developed a compact disk with all the rules and legal regulations about displaced people to be used by mayors, city clerks and governors. It also developed graphic and eloquent material teaching the displaced about their rights, where to go and what to do. A campaign was developed for communities that receive displaced people to promote solidarity as a fundamental pillar for integrating and living together based on principles such as what unites us, what makes us closer and how we can walk together in this emergency. At workshops, people shared, for example, the lives of six persons who were displaced by the same violent act. The cases were analyzed, and studies with local authorities were made not only to look for ways to solve the problems but to develop a long-term agenda and to promote the creation of local municipal committees to help the displaced.

b) Another activity born from the armed conflict is the accompaniment of communities at risk, particularly those which are the target of armed actors because of the weaknesses of the local authorities and the absence of government institutions. The Defensoría has also visited communities that are returning to their places of origin, such as Naya in Cauca, Cacarica, la Belleza, La Reliquia and Ciénaga del Opón. All want to be protected and productive. For two years, the Defensoría has permanently accompanied the communities that have returned to the Cacarica River Basin; this valuable experience has given the Ombudsman's office tools to get closer to the suffering communities.

2. The Defensoría monitors the State's behavior to protect human rights through the behavior of its agents. Likewise the Defensoría monitors and denounces violations of International Humanitarian Law by all the armed actors in the conflict. It uses public denunciations and moral sanctions as its tools. Education of state agents is used to assure that they know their duties. Through its Resolutions and Recommendations, it demands that the state develop legal and constitutional instruments to guarantee the protection of human rights and the definition of policies to ensure their protection.

On September 24, 2001, at an illegal checkpoint, the 59th Front of the FARC kidnapped Señora Consuelo Araujo Noguera, who was totally defenseless, and assassinated her. The Defensoría condemned these acts as violations of International Humanitarian Law because the FARC ignored the immunity of noncombatant persons.

On October 27, 2001, the Defensoría condemned the ELN's (Ejército de Liberación Nacional) bombing of pipelines and classified them as infractions of International Humanitarian Law since they are indiscriminate attacks against civilian/corporate property that have dangerous consequences for health and the environment. This behavior is expressly forbidden in Articles 13, 14 and 15 of Protocol II of the Geneva Conventions of 1949. On September 15, 2001, members of the Autodefensas Unidas de Colombia (AUC) assassinated nine persons in the unincorporated town of Frías in the municipality of Falán. The same day the same group killed two more persons in the town of Paloc and another two in the town of Lérida. The Defensoría qualified these acts as very serious violations of International Humanitarian Law, since attacks against the civilian population violate the Geneva Convention and Article 13 of Protocol II of the same Convention. According to these norms, homicide, mutilations, cruel treatment and torture are forbidden against people who are not directly participating in the hostilities.

3. Research on Human Rights. The Defensoría constantly analyzes, researches and publishes documents related to the respect, protection and enjoyment of freedom, human rights and civil liberties for common citizens and minorities. The Defensoría researched and published reports on displaced people, children and jails in Colombia with the collaboration of the United Nations. They are heartbreaking reports, available on its website both in English and in Spanish (www.defensoría.gov.co).

4. The Defensoría uses constitutional and legal resources and actions to obtain immediate preparation in cases of human rights violations by the state or individual public servants. The Constitution empowers this office to file constitutional injunction actions, called Acción de Tutela in Spanish, compliance suits, popular actions, class actions and unconstitutionality suits. Many of these suits created conditions that make human rights violations less likely, which means these actions also have preventive purposes.

   As an example, the Defensoría insisted on the review of a constitutional injunction against the Consejo Superior de la Judicatura because this tribunal decided that military justice should investigate General Jaime Humberto Uscategui for the killing of 49 persons in Mapiripán. The Attorney General's office had already detained General Uscategui, but on June 2, 1999, the Army presented a petition arguing that military justice should be the one to investigate him. The Attorney General's office declared that the facts in Mapiripán demonstrated that the attack was not improvised but carefully planned in detail for several months with all its logistics and with the support of the Armed Forces under the command of General Uscategui, who was the commander of that region.

The widow of one of the victims presented a constitutional injunction against the decision, alleging her right to equal access to justice. The Supreme Court maintained the decision, but the Defensoría argued that when crimes are of such gravity, as are crimes against mankind, all links between the facts and the military service are broken, and civil justice must investigate the facts. The Constitutional Court ordered the Consejo Superior de la Judicatura to solve the conflict of competence in 10 days. The said Court held that the military have the absolute obligation to stop violations of International Humanitarian Law, and by action or omission they violated their duty by not confronting the aggressors. The case went to civil justice.

In 1991 the Defensoría received 2,113 complaints about the effects of the fumigations as part of Plan Colombia. The Defensoría carefully followed the fumigation strategy and the alternative development programs in order to guarantee human rights and to oversee that their implementation does not violate public health, the environment and the rights of the weakest members of Colombian society. Summarizing its findings, the Defensoría concluded that in reference to fumigations, this strategy does not follow the legal rules established for the use, application and transportation of herbicides. This is obvious when the Defensoría found that the program did not follow indicated parameters to evaluate its impact, and further made use of commercial runways without permits from sanitary or aeronautic authorities. The program is carried out by a U.S. company, Dyn Corp International, based in McLean, Virginia, that does not have the permits, makes use of wrong aircraft that cannot fly at the required altitude for fumigation planes and makes use of chemicals that do not adhere to the safety parameters given by the company that produces the chemicals. [Editors' note: The chemical used was Roundup Ultra®, produced by Monsanto.]

In 1992, the National Council of Narcotics (Consejo Nacional de Estupefacientes) approved the use of chemicals different from glyphosate. Besides glyphosate, Roundup contains another element that, according to a letter sent by the Minister of Health to the Defensoría on October 10, 2001, produces a more acute toxicity than glyphosate. In its visits to the countryside in the Putumayo, the Defensoría found out that the Police added Cosmo-Flux 411F without the needed permits. The Defensoría concluded that the way it was implemented violates rights in the Constitution such as the rights of the environment and the right to use of natural resources. Further, it violates strategic ecosystems, Colombia's biological and cultural diversity and the Declaration of Rio de Janeiro requiring studies to evaluate the negative impact of the fumigations. On many occasions, the Defensoría has demanded the suspension of the fumigations until the eradication strategies are reformed.

5. The Defensoría guarantees legal defense of those not able to procure defense on their own, assuring the right to justice and due process. It provides legal aid for those who lack economic means to hire their own defense in criminal or family law cases.

Several inmates of the jail in the city of Valledupar requested permission from the director to establish a committee for human rights for the prisoners as it is advised by the Defensoría. The director of the institution denied this permission, saying not only that it was not needed but arguing that it was totally at his discretion. The Defensoría, representing the inmates, brought a constitutional injunction, arguing the right of association in the name of the inmates before the Court in Valledupar. The judge ordered the director to allow the organization of the committee in 10 days.

In another case, in the city of Bucaramanga, a father who worked recycling garbage and had been displaced by the political violence came to the Defensoría asking for help for his nine-year-old daughter who was seriously ill with a chronic kidney disease, progressive infection in the kidneys, malnutrition and depression. She was in a hospital for seven months and the doctors warned that the girl needed some medicine for the rest of her life. The Defensoría presented a constitutional injunction arguing the fundamental rights of children. The International Red Cross transferred the girl to Medellín for a kidney transplant, and she is being treated there at the University Hospital Saint Vincent de Paul.

6. Another task of the Defensoría is to mediate between individuals and state agents in cases of omissions or actions by the state that affect enjoyment of rights or the freedom of the individual, in order to stop the violation, repair the damage and prevent future violations. It also mediates between the actors of the armed conflict, urging them to commit to respect International Humanitarian Law.

   On December 15, 2000, Wilson Borja Díaz, president of the union for state workers, was injured in an attempt on his life in a terrorist attack. It left him seriously injured. The same day he was treated at a private hospital. Even there his security was threatened and the family decided to transfer him to the Frank País Hospital in the Republic of Cuba. This was done with the approval of the Colombian government. When representatives of the union requested the Ministry of Health to honor Law 548, which establishes that the Ministry of Health will pay for services given to victims of the armed conflict, the Minister refused even to take the issue to the meeting of the Social Security Council. The Defensoría urged the government to evaluate the urgency of his case, and the government finally paid the government of Cuba the costs of Mr. Borja's treatment.

   Another example is the case of a resolution which ordered the exclusion of about 400,000 persons who did not have proper documents from health insurance. The Defensoría found out that due to lack of organization in the information system, several companies did double billing. Further, by ordering the exclusion of people with no papers, the Defensoría argued that the poorest segments of the population were the punished ones and not the insurance companies that benefited from the situation. Both the Ministries of Budget and Health cooperated with the Defensoría to develop a system that would take care of this matter.

7. The Defensoría promotes citizen participation by educating citizens on the new Constitution and on the importance of their participation in their duties as citizens to make Colombia a real democracy. The Defensoría undertakes the difficult task of forming public opinion on human rights. Public opinion is very important in a democracy, and in this aspect the

Defensoría has the duty to guide public opinion through actions, reports and Ombudsman positions that allow the interpretation of events through the human rights focus. Thus the office educates the citizens, shapes public opinion and guides it to participate not only in the defense of human rights but also in the development of a more democratic nation.

8. It supports and coordinates Personeros Municipales, officials with duties similar to City Clerks, in order to aid them in their function to respect and promote human rights at the local level. It also trains them to use legal and constitutional actions and resources to help guarantee human rights and to educate citizens at the municipal level.

9. One of the most celebrated achievements of the new Constitution was to give the Ombudsman parliamentary functions by assigning him/her legislative initiatives on human rights issues in order to develop legislation to put into practice the new 1991 Carta Magna (Constitution). The Defensoría introduces bills to Congress in matters related to promotion, practice and popularization of human rights. It also presents a yearly report to Congress.

   In 2001, the Defensoría received 43 invitations by Congress to formulate comments and observations on bills introduced. Among the most relevant are to recommend a review of the drug policies; forbid eradication with chemicals; recognize the need to protect the civilian population from the armed conflict; recognize the displacement of the rural population as a humanitarian catastrophe and that the future of the country itself is directly linked to how this social tragedy will be solved; and recommend the creation of an integrated national system to serve the displaced population. On other matters, the Defensoría considers that the recommendations made by the High Commissioner of Human Rights are obligatory to the Colombian state, since they are based on international treaties ratified by the Colombian state. Also, the Defensoría considered that Congress must look for an institutional answer based on the principles of a democratic state and the Constitution in order to preserve legitimacy and ethical superiority over the armed actors. An example of the problems that need addressing is when the Executive, represented by the President, is given extraordinary power to create military operations which violate International Humanitarian Law. Likewise, the Defensoría calls attention to special articles within bills on security and defense that eliminate or restrict controls, punishment or disciplinary actions over the public forces.

The Defensoría worked very hard on the project to make Colombia a member of the International Criminal Court created by the Rome Statute signed on July 17, 1998. According to Article 93 of the Constitution, international treaties ratified by Congress are the law internally and are the framework to interpret the Constitution. The Defensoría recommended that Colombia sign the treaty as the most effective mechanism for the protection of human rights.

10. The Defensoría sues, defends and challenges before the Constitutional Court laws related to constitutional rights and requests from the same Court the review of constitutional injunctions.

11. Another function is to invoke the right of habeas corpus. The Defensoría concentrated efforts to prepare a bill to develop Article 30 of the Constitution by which habeas corpus was regulated. It was proposed to accord with new developments in jurisprudence and comparative law. Previously, habeas corpus contemplated only establishing freedom for persons illegally detained. The Defensoría recommended that habeas corpus have a double aspect: a fundamental right and a constitutional action. Habeas corpus would oppose arbitrary judicial decisions. The new law establishes three kinds of habeas corpus: preventive, restrictive and corrective. The first two protect a person against loss of freedom. The third one avoids illegitimate imposition of forms and conditions of prison. Habeas corpus not only covers exclusive protection of freedom but also rights intimately linked with it, such as the right to life[1], integrity against forced disappearance and against cruel, inhumane or degrading treatment. Habeas corpus cannot be suspended during states of emergency.

The Defensoría is assigned a very small budget compared with other organisms of control such as the Attorney General, the Comptroller and the Procurador General (Inspector General). The Colombian Defensoría has 22 regional offices and 13 sectional offices distributed all over Colombia. The institution has a grand total of 809 employees since its foundation, in spite of the fact that the violations of human rights have increased dramatically in the last years and that more and more people use the Defensoría and

1. Editor's note: 'right to life' here is not used in the way currently used in the United States as referring to abortion, but rather to the right of all citizens to life and well-being.

demand its services. However, in the last five years the budget assigned to the institution is not at all adequate in relation to its function, and every year its budget is diminished. It has different departments each headed by a Delegate Ombudsperson: National Complaints Office (Oficina de Quejas); Attention to Displaced Persons; Public Defender Office; Criminal and Penitentiary Policy; Rights of Children, Women and the Elderly; Collective Rights and the Environment; Social, Cultural and Economic Rights; Indigenous Peoples and Ethnic Minorities; Promotion of Human Rights; Citizen Participation; Legal Resources; Health and Social Security.[2]

There is no doubt that the Colombian Defensoría has demonstrated in its 10 years of existence that the decision made by the 1991 Constitution was the right one. Polls in Colombia show that this is one of the most respected and recognized offices by the Colombian people. In a recent report made by several organizations, among those the Presidential Program Against Corruption, the World Bank and the Comptroller General, the Defensoría appears as one of the three state institutions considered the most honest. In the same report it is expressed that the Defensoría is perceived as one of the institutions most sensitive and close to the needs of the Colombian people, particularly the poorest ones. On several occasions the Office of the High Commissioner of the United Nations for Human Rights has made public statements on the excellent work of the Defensoría.

The Colombian establishment has shown a permanent distaste for the Defensoría since it was established 10 years ago. Recently elected President Álvaro Uribe Vélez and his Minister of Interior have indicated on different occasions the need to reform the Constitution, expressing direct interest in going back to the 1886 Constitution with its clause allowing State of Siege and basically eliminating the Defensoría by fusing it with the Procuraduría (Inspector General's Office).

The 1991 Constitution states that the Inspector General's Office also has the duty of protecting human rights, making sure that they are effective, with the

---

2. Editor's note: The 12 Delegate Ombudsman's Offices, as specified in the Colombian Constitution, are the following: 1) Infancy, Youth, and Older Adults 2) Orientation and Advice to Victims of the Internal Armed Conflict 3) Criminal and Penitentiary Policy 4) Prevention of Risks and System of Early Alerts 5) Right to Health and Social Security 6) Agrarian Matters and Lands 7) Constitutional and Legal Matters 8) Collective Rights and Rights of the Environment 9) Rights of the Population in Human Mobility 10) Rights of Women and Gender Matters 11) Economic, Social and Cultural Rights 12) Ethnic Groups. (Source: Defensoría del Pueblo, https://www.defensoría.gov.co/) This list differs somewhat from Cecilia's list above.

help of the Defensoría. This statement is being used by the Uribe administration to conclude that the work of the Defensoría can be assumed by the Inspector General. This explains why Uribe proposes to combine both Defensoría and Procuraduría as one. This fusion of offices is highly unreasonable, since the Inspector General (Procurador) has as its duty to sanction state workers who commit wrongs. Presently it has many disciplinary proceedings underway, particularly against military and police officers that have not been resolved. This makes it impossible, in practical terms, to assume the promotion of the exercise of human rights without the continued input of the Defensoría.

More importantly, it is highly unreasonable to concentrate in one institution both defending human rights and disciplining state functionaries who violate them. These two functions are of a completely different nature and should be kept separate. In addition, this fusion of entities would take away emphasis on the subject of human rights, a situation that cannot be accepted, given the conditions existing in Colombia today.

Let's defend the Defenders!

PART C

Cecilia's focus on the reasons for creating the Colombia Support Network (CSN), an organization to provide solidarity to Colombian communities in areas of conflict, and how CSN should function.

NOVEMBER 2021

Brief History and General Purpose of the Colombia Support Network

Jack Laun

The Colombia Support Network (CSN) began in September of 1987. A group of people led by Cecilia Zarate-Laun and her husband, Jack Laun, decided to form the organization to focus attention on Colombia, Cecilia's native country. The principal purpose of the organization was, and continues to be, to educate persons in the United States about Colombia in order to have them try to convince elected officials in this country to change U.S. government policy toward Colombia. We were concerned about the very negative aspects of that policy—for example, huge sums of money granted to the Colombian government for military operations and for coca crop spraying with the herbicide glyphosate (Roundup Ultra made by Bayer-Monsanto). We were also very concerned about the damaging activities of U.S. corporations such as Exxon (now Exxon Mobil) and Drummond Coal Company (both of which developed coal mines displacing native communities), which caused great environmental damage; Chiquita Brands, which paired with paramilitary forces to murder banana plantation workers who belonged to or organized unions; and Coca-Cola Corporation, whose local franchise holder hired armed men to kill labor union leaders.

The plan was and continues to be to organize chapters in the U.S. and match them with community organizations in areas of conflict in rural Colombia. These Colombian organizations are dedicated to changing the status quo in the very unequal Colombia by peaceful means. In order to build these relationships, we sponsor delegations from U.S. sister communities to the rural communities we have identified. Under Cecilia's leadership, CSN adopted some fundamental principles which would guide its work and CSN chapters in their relationships with sister communities: 1) CSN works for a negotiated solution to the Colombian conflict, and for peace with justice in Colombia, through strengthening civil society. 2) CSN is not aligned with any of the armed groups in Colombia. 3) CSN seeks to strengthen U.S. democracy by giving U.S. citizens a voice and an opportunity to influence foreign policy toward a key country of our hemisphere.

The Colombia Support Network obtained from Dane County, Wisconsin (which includes the capital city of Madison), official recognition of a sister community relationship with Apartadó, a municipality in Antioquia province in northern Colombia in the primary area for banana production in the country, which has been beset by violence for many years. This sister relationship has functioned since 1991 to provide support to the Peace Community of San José de Apartadó, a community of small-scale farmers who do not allow arms in their town and who have been continuously threatened by paramilitary forces. The CSN chapter in Central New York has similarly formed a sister community relationship with a rural community, Cajibio, in Cauca province, and through a sister organization, the Movimiento Campesino de Cajibio, has helped strengthen the commitment to self-sustaining agricultural programs and peace in an area of substantial violence by paramilitary and guerrilla forces.

Our organization has also developed ties with the Kamentsa indigenous community in Putumayo province, assisting them in their efforts to gain legal protection for their lands and in opposing construction of a major highway which would cause severe damage to their sacred lands and to sources of water for them and others in the Amazon foothills, which form a part of the region known as the "Lungs of the Earth".

Our organization publishes a quarterly newsletter called *Action on Colombia*, which is sent online to CSN members. We have taken delegations to sister communities in Colombia and have invited sister community leaders in

Colombia to come to the United States to visit their U.S. sister communities and to attend an annual meeting held in Madison, Wisconsin. Because of difficulties in travel caused by the Covid-19 pandemic, CSN now holds periodic topical conferences for CSN members and other interested persons by ZOOM.

1992

People-to-People Diplomacy: Reflections About Sister Cities[1]

When human beings wish to begin that series of organized assassinations called "war," before they do so they generally develop a psychological war as part of the ritual—as old as humanity itself—of declaring one another "enemies." Being enemies to one another they describe the other as almost inhuman, "different from us." The others are the devil. They are cruelty. They wish to destroy us and destroy that which we love. They personify violence; we do not. Logically, this image of the enemy arrives at the inescapable conclusion that the other must be destroyed, must be assassinated, and when this happens, an act of purification and salvation is committed.

PSYCHOLOGICAL POISON

The great demagogues of history from Attila to Hitler have been masters in the art of transmitting this psychological poison. In recent years, this stereotype full of hatred has become sophisticated to the extent that the humanity of the enemy is depersonalized to a form totally abstract. It is the enemy who must

1. Editor's note: This article first appeared in Spanish in the Colombian magazine *Apertura*, No. 14, August 1992, pp. 16-17. It was translated into English for this book. Additional material, written by Cecilia Zarate-Laun, has been appended to it beginning with the subheading "Further Reflections on Sister Cities." Minor editorial changes have been made to smooth the transition between the two parts.

be destroyed; for example: the communists, the subversives.

In the *Iliad*, the Greek hero Diomedes is going to attack Glauco, and he asks that he identify himself. When Glauco does so, Diomedes throws down his sword, and with friendly words, he shouts to Glauco that they cannot fight because their grandfathers had been friends. At that time, the tradition of friendship had such cultural power that it prohibited fights, even between two distant descendants.

Although it did not end the Trojan War, this noble gesture exemplifies another profound truth of humanity: In spite of our warlike tradition, we also have the capacity to form positive alliances and strong human ties that cross the frontiers of race, language and nationality and create links capable of curing hatred and ending violence.

CULTURE OF COOPERATION

The use of the culture of cooperation to connect or create sister cities from hostile countries is a recent phenomenon which began at the end of the Second World War when the people on both sides of the border between France and Germany began to consider how to end the profound bitterness caused by the war. In a dramatic gesture, the mayors of two border towns embraced and united their cities with this act of friendship. In that way, the European movement of "jumelage," or sister cities, began. Under this movement of ordinary citizens, they did something which governmental treaties drafted by career diplomats were never able to do: Transform the centuries old hostility between France and Germany into a culture of cooperation.

At the present time, this same process changed relations between the United States and Nicaragua. The irony of the movement consists in the fact that it contributed to a growth of friendship without precedent between the two countries at a time when their governments were at war.

A NEW DIPLOMACY

This new diplomacy called people-to-people, thus had the ability to rehumanize relations and eliminate sources of hostility. The rapid growth of sister cities between the United States and Nicaragua (from 10 in 1985 to 77 in 1987) indeed reflected the concern of the people of the United States faced with the high level of official aggressiveness of their government, and the increase in military activities of the United States in Central America. The movement also reflected a desire to find a positive and constructive form of acting that would include not only political activists but also ordinary citizens.

The method of Sister Cities promotes a spirit of friendship among the citizens of the world in order that there will be comprehension and peace which result in improving economic, cultural and social relations among the peoples of all the world, since only through personal relations is curiosity converted into knowledge, cynicism to confidence and human warmth to goodness. Since sister city projects take place at a local level, they provide opportunities for direct interchange and immediate human contact. For this reason, they offer the average North American citizen the opportunity to have friendly relations with other communities of people and to end the limitations of mutual distrust, apathy and hostility.

The Sister Cities movement in the United States also reflects the tendency of local communities to make themselves independent, and even more, to oppose the foreign relations policies made in Washington. The Sister Cities break the barriers between the peoples of two countries in an unprecedented way, transform distrust into understanding and end stereotypes and suspicions.

FURTHER REFLECTIONS ON SISTER CITIES

The modern concept of sister cities was born in the deep desire of the members of civil society, tired of the bloody wars, to begin a rebuilding that was not only physical but also moral and emotional, between the populations that had been destroyed by the warfare. These peoples had suffered the wounds of wars declared by the governments of their countries, the causes of which the very people affected could never understand clearly.

Recapturing what was stated earlier, that's what happened at the end of World War II on the border between France and Germany. The mayors of two neighboring villages destroyed by the bombing met and walked in the ruins. Weeping, they embraced each other and began to consider: Why if we were living in peace and were neighbors, partners and friends and we helped one another, and suddenly the governments declared war, why, from one moment to another did we turn into enemies? In this moment they decided that the two villages would declare themselves to be brothers, and they would collaborate mutually in the process of reconstruction. That was how the sister cities movement was born in Europe.

The years passed, and a world power, the United States, under President Ronald Reagan, decided to declare war on a tiny nation that wanted to decide its own destiny. Using a counter-insurgency strategy, they began the attacks on cooperatives, schools, churches and small businesses on the Nicaraguan border. Tired of pressuring Washington to cease that unjust war and not being heard, the Peace Movement in the United States decided to revive the concept of sister cities and oppose, in a very active but peaceful way, their government's foreign policy toward Nicaragua.

The North Americans took pacifism very seriously and with great commitment. For them, pacifism is not synonymous with passivity. On the contrary, they developed all the creativity, dynamism and efficiency inherited from their ancestors, the Western pioneers, to challenge the forces of power. At that moment the relationship of sisterhood between North American cities and Nicaraguan villages blossomed. Sisterhood meant more than material solidarity which was also furnished at this time; it was and continues being a sisterhood of solidarity, of accompaniment, of moral uplift and support of those who suffered from the war. Such was the activity and presence of the North American pacifists on this occasion that the United States government had no choice but to resort to an illegal and unconstitutional method, as was the Iran-Contra affair, in order to destabilize Nicaragua; they could not organize a military invasion due to the fixed opposition of the North American people.

Sister cities also reflect a very important concept: Civil society has the obligation to form an integral part in the reconstruction of the social fabric; diplomacy and international relations should not be left solely in the hands of governments because these reflect interests that do not necessarily serve the interests of the majority, and thus diminish democracy. Sister cities reflect a diplomacy of "people-to-people" that expresses the most beautiful qualities of a nation—in this case, the generosity and respect for justice and democracy that are part of the basis on which the North American nation was founded before the development of savage capitalism.

With this idea in mind, years later in 1988, the Colombia Support Network (Red de Solidaridad con el Pueblo de Colombia, Network of Solidarity with the People of Colombia) based in Madison, Wisconsin, sought the collaboration of local authorities to create a sister relationship between Dane County, in which the city of Madison is located, and the city of Apartadó in Antioquia, Colombia. Following Resolution #392 of May 3, 1989, Dane County declared itself sister city to the town of Apartadó. In Resolution #97 on June 2, of the same year, the City Council of Apartadó reciprocated the gesture, declaring itself the sister city of Dane County. By appealing to democratically elected local authorities in both societies, relations of respect and civility that cannot be easily altered were created. Delegations have visited both cities, and the population of Madison has continually demonstrated its solidarity and concern for Apartadó.

School children write letters, they accompany the Peace Community and so on.

The city of Apartadó was chosen as a sister city by Father Francisco de Roux when, as director of CINEP (Centro de Investigación y Educación Popular, Center for Popular Research and Education), we consulted him about which city of Colombia at that time was suffering most from the ravages of violence. In a different position now as director of the Program of Development and Peace of the Middle Magdalena (PDPMM), he continues to play his role as selector of sister cities.

Colombia Support Network decided to expand, creating chapters of its network in other parts of the United States. This network is made up almost completely of American citizens who are more and more concerned about the grave situation of human rights in Colombia, and who view with alarm the growing intervention of their government in Colombia's civil war, using the pretext of a "War on Drugs." They question if this is really a war on drugs or a façade for another war of intervention. They also question if with their money and in their name the government of their country is collaborating in the creation of another Vietnam.

Thanks to the continuous and hard work of Colombia Support Network throughout the United States, the network is in a process of growth. To be a chapter of the network, each group must have a sister city to accompany and help strengthen her civil society and democratic processes. At this time, the following bases for sister cities are being created:

Arenal with Boston, Massachusetts

Puerto Wilches with Champaign-Urbana, Illinois

San Pablo with Minneapolis, Minnesota

Apartadó with Madison, Wisconsin

Cacarica with Chicago, Illinois

During the last decade, the situation, equivalent to a civil war in Colombia, has greatly increased the numbers of internally displaced people from the countryside fleeing the war. Two of the areas most affected by the war, Urabá and the Middle Magdalena, are the areas where Colombia Support Network is working to develop sister cities.

Both the displaced of Urabá, principally from Chocó as well as those of the Campesino Exodus from the Middle Magdalena, have organized into communities that are preparing to return to their places of origin. In both cases, the displaced populations also demand that the Colombian government recognize them and respect their human, civil, political and economic rights.

CSN supports the rights of the displaced and believes that supporting them through their Sister Cities projects not only fulfills its objective to support Colombian civil society but directly questions the counterinsurgency strategy of the Colombian government of displacing the civilian population by means of its Army and paramilitary groups without resolving the problems causing the war.

CSN questions the passivity of the United States government because it removes the civilian population, particularly poor campesinos, from areas where multinational companies have their eyes set on the development of mega-projects that come from their plans for international globalization.

The well-being of the campesinos is not taken into account given that the modern economy offers few alternatives for the poor. Through its war on drugs, the government of the United States emphasizes military aid, while disregarding the most important aspect of the cause of illicit crops, which is the abandonment of the campesino population that is only trying to survive. The participation of ordinary U.S. citizens in the life and struggles of the people of Colombia suffering the effects of the war is a very effective weapon for strengthening a democratic Colombia with social justice and for questioning the activities of the government of our country. Sister cities organize around an alternative of hope and accompaniment in the search for dignity, sense of community and self-sufficiency. The return of the campesinos to their places of origin is a heroic gesture facing enormous difficulties and becomes a manifestation of recognition that the earth is their best hope of survival in a global economy that offers few opportunities.

From the North/South perspective the sister cities respect the dignity and self-determination of our brothers suffering in the South. The projects and strategies are carried out in an atmosphere of accompaniment, dialogue and brotherhood. We of the North learn the significance of the power of union, organization and of shared dreams and hopes for change. Those of the South learn that there are people in the North who are concerned about their fate, who want to work with them and are desirous of working face-to-face with them to examine the unjust relations of the modern world. They also work to help them create strategies for finding constructive relationships that do not foment injustice. Most important of all is that the projects of sisterhood break isolation and offer an opportunity to begin to create global relationships that give priority to the rights of human beings and not to profit. The poor of Colombia need to know they are not alone.

ACTIVITIES

For the Sister Cities project to be effective and have impact we suggest the following activities.

From the United States

1. The participation of ordinary citizens of the United States in the lives and struggles of the Colombian people is a powerful instrument of pressure so that human, cultural, political and economic rights are respected and the counter-insurgency policies of the Pentagon are challenged. Constant communication by telephone, faxes, emails, visits and delegations as well as letter-writing campaigns to the two governments in urgent actions have helped in an effective way to save lives and stop atrocities. This permanent moral accompaniment hopes to leave no community alone in moments of desperation caused by the different armed actors. As an example, the courageous Mayor of Apartadó, Gloria Cuartas, always credits Colombia Support Network for saving her life thanks to the activities of the sister city of Madison, Wisconsin.
2. The sister cities also carry out campaigns and apply pressure to implement accords that the Colombian government has made with communities but has not complied with.
3. Projects of material assistance are small, but they are focused on solidifying the community organizations that help strengthen the community. None of them are made to create a spirit of dependence or charity, but rather are made with a great sense of dignity and respect. A component of such projects should include external help to aid in finding contacts with markets for products that are alternatives to planting coca.
4. Education is a fundamental component in the sister cities relationship. Americans are educated about the realities that confront our brothers and sisters in Colombia and in aiding the people to understand the causes of poverty and of the war in Colombia.
5. CSN supports the novel concept of Peace Communities. This experiment in active neutrality in the midst of war ought to be respected and supported.

From Colombia

1. The most important thing is to maintain the levels of direct communication between each town and its sister community. This information ought to be consistent, clear, honest, balanced and always with the community in mind.

2. Keep the names and addresses of the local and regional civil and military authorities up to date.

What Kinds of Communities Do We Want?

In our search for peace with social justice in Colombia and for a negotiated solution to the conflict, we at Colombia Support Network (CSN) have reached the point at which we will have to define what kind of communities we feel are the most appropriate to complement us in our organizational objectives.

After exploring different regions and going through different experiences, we must consider the characteristics of the communities we want in a clear and defined way. Some considerations follow:

We want communities that are very much aware and clear on the need for a structural change in Colombian society and of the need to have a real and participatory democracy in Colombia. Our communities should have a genuine political clarity on the call for change, yes, but doing so by nonviolent resistance, a total novelty in a country used to violent resistance.

We need communities whose internal organizing is the result of a collective decision and not the result of an external agent who decides "to organize" them and to be their voice. Our communities must have their independence and sovereignty according to the Constitution of 1991. This internal clarity is fundamental in order to make decisions that reflect their perceived needs and desires and not to reflect the voice of regional institutions that appropriate "their needs" without representing their interests but rather the ones of the external agent.

Their political autonomy must be the guide for their relation with CSN. The decision to work with CSN must be decided by the communities. CSN offers them a sisterhood that backs their political project through international support, accompaniment and a voice. To be their voice in the United States in an equally sovereign project of the people of the United States, which is their respective sister chapter. The sister community work of the chapter depends completely on the permanent communication and sharing of the situation by the Colombian sister community. If a community does not inform CSN, after a certain amount of time, let us say six months, the CSN chapter must search for another community which shares its interests.

Our communities must be ones where the care and rights (civic and social rights) of the weaker members of society such as orphans, widows, displaced, the elderly and the sick are attended to. Youth and children have to have priority in the development of educational and social projects. Their care for human rights must be guided by the Universal Declaration of Human Rights as defined by the United Nations.

The communities must be very clear with respect to the political actors in their area, and they must keep their political autonomy from false discourses, especially at the moment of elections, because the traditional elements of Colombian society will try to influence them or force them in the name of "supporting our democracy and our institutions" to support candidates who do not represent their interests but who want to keep the façade of democracy.

With respect to economic projects, the communities must maintain their political autonomy and seek models of participatory economics that will benefit the community and do not stimulate individualism. They must be alert when it comes to their economic projects to avoid economic benefits from outside organizations which may pressure them with conditions which are against their own goals and sovereignty.

These external organizations offer an apparent change, but in reality they want to keep everything the way it has always been. These are siren songs that attempt to divert the communities towards economic projects that traditionally have benefited the old political structures or the international community that has economic interests in Colombia.

Seeing the need to back the political autonomy of the communities, it is necessary to think about the development of a CSN solidarity fund for our sister communities that supports their productive projects without the loss of their political autonomy. I want to quote a sentence from an email from Marylen Sema from our sister community in Cajibio, Cauca: "... we would like to have financial support from organizations that do not oppose our struggle for life, human rights and our autonomy ... organizations that give us financial support but that do not make us change our political views ..."

PART D

Studies by Cecilia of different regions of Colombia and defining developments in these regions.

MAY 2002

An Overview of Cauca

I wrote this little paper a few years ago. The conditions have not changed at all. This is why I decided to send this to you all because I hope it will help you to understand the situation in Cauca better. I am not sure Cajibio and Naya belong to CIMA (Comité de Integración del Macizo Colombiano, The Committee for the Integration of the Colombian Massif) but the general reality is the same.

The Department of Cauca is situated in southwestern Colombia, and it is a Department of large ranches which date back to the colonial era, when concessions of indigenous lands were made by the Spanish Crown to reward the conquerors of this region. Popayán, the capital, was very important in colonial times, and from there expeditions left for the founding of Quito. This very short historical sketch helps us to understand modern Cauca. This state has, on one hand, extensive landholdings which are still being disputed by the same indigenous communities who have been battling for them since the Spanish Conquest. It is also a state of small farms in poor rural communities.

Together with the neighboring department of Nariño to the south and on the border with Ecuador, Cauca shares one of the most mountainous regions of South America. The Andes Mountain Range forms there an enormous massif, or knot, which in geography is called the Colombian Massif, where the three branches of the Andes Mountains which enter Colombia extend and form valleys of the great rivers which originate in this knot of mountains: the Magdalena, the Cauca, the Patía and the Caquetá rivers. The richness in water and biodiversity of this region has made it attractive for numerous development plans now in times of globalization. In spite of being a rich source of water, forests and minerals, the Colombian state has maintained this region in the most complete abandonment, without social investment.

The population of Cauca, reportedly 1,236,420 in 2002,[1] is in its majority indigenous, Afro-Colombian and peasant. Seventy percent of the population lives in rural areas, producing basic food crops: potatoes, corn, plantains, sugar cane, fruits, pasture grasses for beef and dairy cattle, fish and pigs. These communities demand investment of the Colombian state in concrete solutions to serious problems of poverty and abandonment as well as processes of rural integral development, improvement and support for the small-scale producers of the agricultural sector, assistance in marketing their products, potable water service, electrification, communication networks, schools and health services.

The abandonment exhausted the patience of the forgotten rural communities of Cauca, which decided to perform a "diagnosis" or a listing of the most urgent necessities. They organized at the grassroots level to demand their rights beginning in 1980. In 1987 they signed the "Guachicono Accords" with the national government; in 1988 their needs grew, and the government failed to perform its commitments under the pacts. In 1990, after an open town meeting was held, communities coming from several municipalities decided to create an organizing expression of their own which would include the municipal communities of the region of the Colombian Massif. This organization was called CIMA (Comité de Integración del Macizo Colombiano, Committee for the Integration of the Colombian Massif). It has as tasks the integration of the region through multiple cultural activities, the creation of a newspaper and the organization of the first civic general strike of the Colombian Massif region. The strike, in which more than 30,000 peasants participated, paralyzed traffic on the Pan-American Highway for six days from August 20, 1991, obliging the national government to negotiate directly with the strikers. There the abuses and lies of the hack politicians of the region were denounced.

The organizing process of these communities has continued very actively in the last two decades, and they have organized conferences and diagnostic sessions with greater and greater participation of indigenous groups as well as environmental organizations, directors of regional corporations and government functionaries, all of which gave legitimacy to their meetings.

1. Editor's note: Departamento Administrativo Nacional de Estadistica (DANE), estimates of population for 2002.

However, reactionary sectors of Cauca society and of the armed forces sharpened the persecution and the stigmatization of the CIMA leaders, accusing them of being accomplices and supporters of the insurgent movements, making them the object of threats, persecution, home searches, killings and massacres. An example is the massacre of Los Uvos, where 17 defenseless peasants were murdered on March 31, 1991, by members of the José Hilario López Battalion of the Colombian Army.

The Colombian state continued not living up to the terms of the accords. The communities of peasants and indigenous of the Cauca confronting a situation of poverty, unemployment and lack of stimuli for small scale and medium scale production, decided in a heroic form to carry out a Great Mobilization of the Colombian Southwest. For 26 days more than 46,000 persons blocked the Pan-American Highway beginning on November 1, 1999. In a cynical and astonishing form, the government of Andrés Pastrana showed that it would not respond in support of the accords which had been signed by the previous governments, which it cannot avoid doing under the law. The politicians of the traditional parties were absent and did not defend the just demands of the peasants. This absence has never been forgotten by the inhabitants of the region. The magnitude of the mobilization obliged the government of Pastrana to negotiate a set of points of agreement, besides promising to protect the mobilized communities and their leaders.

In May of 2002 we can summarize in the following way the necessities in the Cauca region:

1. The Colombian government seems to be reserving this region for private capital and for foreign investment, giving impetus to the change of the peasant and indigenous economy into an economy at the service of large landowners. The result is seen clearly in a social crisis. For example, extensive production of pine and eucalyptus trees threatens the reserves of water. Near Popayán crops for agricultural export grow, such as asparagus, broccoli, lumber, African palm, fruits and flowers, and there is production of lumber from pine and eucalyptus trees for the transnational Irish company Smurfit, associated with the Colombian company Cartón de Colombia.

2. The valley of the Cauca River, which begins in this Department, is being used for extensive cattle raising and monoculture of sugar cane dominated by large-scale private capital. In this area, industries of the neighboring Department of Valle del Cauca, with their headquarters in

Cali, have moved to Cauca more than 200 factories and five industrial parks with investments in excess of $200,000,000 U.S., making use of the so-called Páez Law. Ten years ago the Páez River overflowed its borders and the national government approved a tax exemption for ten years for the benefit of the communities close to the river. The industrialists of Cali knew how to make good use of this concession and brought in exchange contamination to the waters and pollution of the environment.

3. There exist three proposals for hydroelectric power plants in this region: in the crossing of the Ovejas/Cauca Rivers, the hydroelectric plant of La Salvajina; the dam on the Timba River; and the dam on the Micay River, which will transform the ecosystem and will displace communities living in these zones.
4. The region of the Pacific, which is rich in minerals such as gold and platinum, bases its economy on fishing. The establishment of thermoelectric plants is proposed, using the coal mines in the region and energy from the volcanoes in the region.

The process of changing the ownership of land, eliminating the form of production by peasants and indigenous peoples who rely upon the production of food products, is at the root of the social crisis in the Colombian countryside. To separate the peasant from his land is to separate him from his soul, as was said by a peasant from Cauca: "The soul of men is not in ourselves, the soul of men is the water, air, land; if a moment arrives in which we lose our land, we will have been converted into beings without souls, which is what we now see happening in our territories, day laborers depending upon 'patrones'..."

A peasant without land loses his power to determine his own destiny and his future depends upon those who expropriate his lands. This is very well understood by the peasants of Cauca when they join together to form organizations such as CIMA, because they unite in resistance so that they will not be displaced, so that they will not lose their seeds and so they will be able to maintain their control of the food production. It is a form of resistance to multinational corporations of the food industry so that they do not expropriate their knowledge of plants and medicines, even though these peasants understand that they may be murdered or disappeared. What we see in Cauca is corporate globalization in development and how it obliges isolated rural peasant communities to link themselves of necessity to the great economic centers through what amount to campaigns of extermination.

All of the tradition of social struggle in Cauca is becoming the victim of a destructive campaign on the part of the paramilitaries in a form which evidences complicity with the military forces. A document on the subject from Human Rights Watch, *The "Sixth Division": Military-paramilitary Ties and U.S. Policy in Colombia*," 2001, tells how beginning in January of 2000 the AUC (Autodefensas Unidas de Colombia, United Self-Defense Forces of Colombia)[2] appeared in Cauca, beginning a movement from north to south, putting into practice a strategic plan of dirty war with selective assassinations, massacres and displacement of social organizations, peasants and indigenous peoples of the region.

I will use examples to explain the way of operating of these groups. In February of 2001, just five minutes from Popayán, ten peasants were massacred when they traveled in a public bus to the municipality of Cajibio. Carlos Castaño, the notorious commander of the AUC, publicly recognized his authorship of the killings.[3] Between April and May, paramilitaries appeared taking up checkpoints in the municipality of El Tambo. In June, 80 uniformed men arrived at the small settlement of Pigua, where they gathered together the population and told them that they would remain in the zone to cleanse it of those who were helping the guerrillas. In the municipality of Timbío, they invite themselves to all of the social activities. They extort money from merchants, and they put a limit upon the sale of food of 100,000 pesos (about $50 U.S.D.), or they accuse the people of being guerrilla supporters.

In Popayán, they began to carry out "social cleansing," murdering 170 persons in the neighborhoods at the periphery of the city and controlling meetings, night travel and haircut styles for youths. Girls cannot wear short skirts and cannot form groups of young people at the corners. The paramilitaries use taxis and street vendors, whom they pay to inform them of any unusual movement in the city. The AUC finance themselves with money of the large landowners who produce coffee or who are cattlemen, or other large landowners and politicians. The school teachers are continuously attacked and persecuted by the AUC. On November 15, 2001, at about 2 a.m. the Army entered the municipality of Mercaderes with six heavily-armed men in civilian dress, and they remained in the town identifying themselves as paramilitaries.

---

2. Editor's note: The AUC (United Self-Defense Forces of Colombia) was a paramilitary and drug-trafficking organization.
3. Editor's note: A Colombia Support Network delegation to Cajibio visited the scene of the massacre and was able to speak with family members of persons who had been murdered. Delegation members learned that Carlos Castaño had sent paramilitary forces from his home base in northern Colombia to Cajibio to support the owner of a large ranch nearby at his request. Castaño admitted publicly to doing so.

The Colombian Army has bases and military control posts all along the Pan-American Highway, but in a strange manner the confrontations which they have are only with insurgent groups and not with the AUC, who themselves set up checkpoints next to the military bases and camps.

Another complication is the fumigation of rural areas seeking to destroy coca or poppy fields. During my last visit to Cauca accompanying Professor Noam Chomsky, we heard very moving testimony by a community which brought us to tears when we heard the very sad stories of how fumigations with glyphosate destroyed their organic coffee crops, which were ready to be harvested to sell to Germany. They completely denied that they had planted heroin poppies in their region, but said that rather other communities different from theirs had planted poppies in mountains located a far distance from their fields. Their crops of coffee, sugar cane, corn, fruits such as lulo and mora, and pasture grasses for milk cattle and pigs and even ponds of fish were destroyed by the fumigation. They say that other consequences were diseases such as typhoid fever, chronic diseases and gastrointestinal diseases. They asked that their right to life, health and environment be protected as required by the National Constitution of Colombia and that they be paid restitution for their economic losses through the harmful policies which act against the unprotected rural communities.

The personal stories of these people broke our hearts. Among them was a 72-year-old woman whose children were murdered by the paramilitaries. The small parcel in which she grew her crops was hit and her crops killed and she was now in charge of two granddaughters, ages seven and nine years old. Another man ran a large coffee farm and provided employment to several other people. In order to grow organic coffee he obtained a loan from his neighbors, and now they are demanding that he pay them and he is at the point of losing his land because he has no way of paying them given the loss his farm has sustained as a result of his crops having been fumigated.

A moment of triumph for these communities was the election of an indigenous governor in 2000. What was meaningful here was the act of political rebellion which had no precedent, when the traditional political class of Cauca was defeated and an indigenous leader was elected Governor of Cauca. At the time Floro Tunubala was the only indigenous person elected governor of a state in the Americas. His triumph was symbolic because the previous governors of Cauca left the Cauca government highly indebted to the international banking community.

JUNE 4, 2002

My Travel Companions

This past month of May, my trip to Colombia with Professor Noam Chomsky finally took place. Invited by the Universidad Nacional de Colombia, which had conferred upon him a doctorate Honoris Causa, this solemn occasion had been lovingly and carefully in planning for months. I am going to describe and share with readers this memorable trip.

I arrived in Bogotá two days early and found a range of activities very well coordinated by Professor Carlos Martínez together with Darío Fajardo. I learned the details of the visit and soon felt very welcome as part of the organizing team, which had planned for security, logistics and public relations down to the smallest detail. My role was more that of telling of Noam's specific requirements and continuing with my physical presence to work out the last-minute details of the activities which for the last several months I had coordinated with the team from the United States.

I should not have been surprised, but besides his tremendous intellectual capacities, Noam displays a very rare simplicity and talent with people. He is a delicious travel companion with a great sense of humor which helps him easily overcome any difficulty and alleviate the tensions of an environment which can become sad when speaking with the victims of the war.

He arrived on Saturday night and on the next day, Sunday, he met with prominent Colombian human rights activists. In the afternoon there was a meeting with grassroots organizations in a room of the university. This was a requirement of the teacher who never disdains persons who are politically active, never looking down on them. On the contrary, he listens to them with great attention and affection. Representatives of displaced people, campesinos, of women, of the arts, the Permanent Committee for the Defense of Human Rights, the Bishop of Putumayo, young people, the Communist Party and others came. All of them told details of their situation and of their vision of Colombia. Particularly moving was the testimony of the campesinos, who expressed their desperation facing a future so uncertain, and their spirit to keep struggling.

We left for Cauca very early on Monday. We were received by CIMA (Committee for the Integration of the Colombian Massif), and this first meeting helped us get to know the problems of the region and of Cauca Department especially. After putting our luggage in our hotel, we lazily walked along the very beautiful colonial streets of Popayán, since it was a holiday and our meeting was scheduled for three o'clock in the afternoon. Noam admired the colonial buildings and the churches, and he walked on the path over the Puente del Humilladero (Bridge of Humiliation) from which in epochs long past disobedient slaves were hung. There we pondered the ups and downs of history. Noam went up to the church of Belén (Bethlehem), where he contemplated a panorama of the city.

The meeting began at 3 p.m., and we spoke with grassroots representatives, especially with indigenous of the CRIC (Regional Indigenous Corporation of the Cauca), who have a very clear vision of the situation.[1]

At the end of the day, we met with a rural campesino community, whose testimony caused us to cry on hearing their very sad stories of the crop fumigations and the use of glyphosate, which destroyed their organic coffee crop that was ready to be harvested to sell in Germany. They denied completely having poppies planted in their region, but rather they were grown in the surrounding mountains by communities different from their own. Their crops of coffee, sugar cane, corn, fruits such as lulo and mora, and grasses for feed for their beef cattle and milk cows and pigs, and tanks for their fish were destroyed by the fumigation. They said that other consequences were diseases like typhoid fever and chronic and gastrointestinal diseases. They ask that the right to life, health and the environment be respected according to the National Constitution of Colombia, and that they receive restitution for their economic heritage affected and lost by these harmful policies which

1. Editor's note: Background information that Cecilia compiled in preparation for her trip with Noam Chomsky is set forth in the article "An Overview of Cauca" in this volume.

despoil the unprotected rural communities. The personal histories break one's soul. Like that of the 72-year-old widow whose children were murdered by the paramilitaries, her small parcel fumigated, and who now has two granddaughters in her care. Another man had a large coffee farm and employed several people. In order to grow organic coffee he borrowed money from his neighbors, and now they are demanding repayment and he is on the verge of losing his land.

A moment of triumph for these communities was the election of the Governor a year ago. In an unprecedented act of political rebellion, the Cauca political class was defeated, and the indigenous leader Floro Tunubalá was elected Governor of Cauca, being the only indigenous governor elected in the Americas. Although his triumph was highly symbolic, and Taita Floro received us very cordially, there is not much that he is able to do because the prior governors of Cauca left the government highly indebted to international banks. Floro always supports development projects when the rural communities benefit from them.

Professor Noam Chomsky giving the keynote address at the CSN Conference on the Faceless Justice System in Colombia at the University of Wisconsin in March 1997."

We returned to Bogotá on the following day for the ceremony, which was very emotional and full of affection and admiration for Professor Chomsky.

The university choir embellished the solemn act, and the discourse deepened the significance of the words, such as the word 'terrorism,' which has different meanings depending upon who uses it. Professor Chomsky gave an excellent analysis of contemporary North American foreign policy.

For my return, I had to be at the El Dorado Airport in Bogotá very early, and I was very sleepy. At my side on the plane was a friendly North American gentleman who insisted upon conversing. I fell asleep on takeoff and finally opened my eyes when the plane was already flying. Immediately, my travel companion began to tell me that while I had gone to sleep on takeoff, it was excellent. He said, "I know a great deal about planes because I fly continuously over Colombia since I work for a company from my country, DynCorp." As if in a spell, my sleep dissipated and I began to ask questions about his work.

He told me that his company is formed by employees who previously worked for the American government, so there is almost no cost in training them. He said the owners are the employees themselves, numbering 35,000 and based in Fort Worth, Texas. Their motto is: "We do anything that the government of the United States asks us to do." "We are in the whole world," he continued. The profit is 13.6 percent of each dollar invested in them, and at this time they make passports for the government of the United States. He told me there are two kinds of flights over Colombia: those which have to do with drugs and those which have to do with the military. He works in the drug flights area. They fly at high altitudes in Cessna planes provided with powerful turbines, and the crew is himself as the pilot, the mechanic and a photographer who constantly takes photos with special lenses made for them by Kodak. The military flights as well as the drug flights deliver their information to the offices of DynCorp in Florida so that experts can analyze them. Then they are passed to the American Embassy in Bogotá and finally to the government of Colombia. He adores Plan Colombia and says he hopes it will be increased by millions of dollars more.

I remembered my conversation with Cauca communities for whom Plan Colombia is a plan to worsen the war, to intensify the internal social conflict, the paramilitary advance, indiscriminate fumigations, the development of a dirty war and the systematic destruction of my country. Suddenly I felt a desire to cry, but I decided no...I must continue the struggle for justice. I decided to tell this story so that my unknown readers will decide to collaborate in the struggle for a better world. An example? Noam Chomsky.

2001

Background on the Putumayo

Putumayo Department is located in the southwest region of Colombia, and it takes its name from the majestic river which crosses the department from west to east and serves as a natural border between Colombia, Ecuador and Peru. The capital of Putumayo is Mocoa. The department's population (2001) is 332,434 inhabitants. Most of its territory is located in the rain forest area and it has three natural regions: High Putumayo, Middle Putumayo and Lower Putumayo. Its two main rivers, the Putumayo and the Caquetá, were for many years the main form of transportation. In 1985, Putumayo's indigenous population was calculated at 11,900. The indigenous communities are Ingas, Kofanes, Sionas, Huitotos, Paeces, Embera-Chamí and Kamentsá. These indigenous groups have had the rivers as a geographic and religious reference; the river represents the anaconda from the boa family, the largest serpent found in the Americas.

COLONIZATION

The process of colonization in Putumayo goes back to the Sixteenth Century. Spanish Conquistadors arrived searching for gold and quinine. Catholic missionaries and encomenderos came to the region and established isolated settlements using the indigenous labor force, particularly the Ingas, who were descendants of the Inca Empire. The Jesuits came in the late Sixteenth Century and later on in 1886. Spanish Capuchin monks were assigned the task of introducing Christian civilization to the Putumayo by the Holy See and the

Colombian government. These monks dictated a set of rules giving themselves the right to distribute lands belonging to indigenous communities and founded the town of Puerto Asís. These legal mandates came from the Colombian government, which until 1890 had as a goal to dissolve the communitarian life of indigenous groups. These attitudes began to change in 1958 as a result of indigenous struggles in Colombia and with the establishment of new protections in the new Constitution of 1991.

Putumayo has experienced economies of enclave associated with models of development towards the outside, leaving very little for the local economy. Since the Nineteenth Century there have been six stages of development in the Putumayo, most of them accompanied by a lot of violence.

I. Rubber Economy

Starting at the end of the Nineteenth Century until the 1920s, a process began which incorporated the Amazon region into the world economy. Small settlements of rubber plantations along the river, mainly in the hands of English merchants, characterized this period. The rivers were the main source of transportation, sending raw rubber to the Amazon ports in the Atlantic. In the 1920s, the rubber produced in Malaysia became cheaper, and therefore the Putumayo's rubber production was abandoned. In the process of development of the rubber plantations, thousands of indigenous died working for the Casa Arana Company, on the border between Colombia and Peru. Many died of hunger, beatings and all kinds of oppression. In a book published in Lima by the Peruvian judge Carlos Valcárcel, *El Proceso del Putumayo y sus Secretos Inauditos*, 1913 (*The Putumayo Affair and Its Dark Secrets*), he relates that more than 20,000 indigenous were assassinated in the rubber plantations of the Putumayo in a period of 10 years. Life in the rubber plantations was masterfully described by Colombian writer José Eustasio Rivera in his famous novel *La Voragine*, 1924 (*The Vortex,* Earle K. James, translator, 1928, 2003).

II. Frontier Economy

In 1933, after a war with Peru in which Colombia defended its right to the Amazon, the Colombian government initiated a migratory process to the Putumayo, bringing peasants from neighboring departments of Nariño, Cauca and Huila, with the idea of strengthening the frontier and using its Army to defend it. Colombia started towns such as Puerto Leguízamo and built roads to Florencia and Pasto as a demonstration of sovereignty over its territory. People came attracted by gold in the rivers.

III. Economy of the 1950s

The situation of chaos and institutional disorder in the period known as "La Violencia" (roughly 1946-1957) in the center of the country, when more than 200,000 people were killed, caused violent displacements to remote regions such as the Putumayo. The most fertile lands in the country were concentrated in a few hands near the large urban centers, and the mistaken belief that the land in the Amazon areas was fertile brought many peasants to this area. But the lack of roads, working capital and the low productivity of the land caused many settlers to become disillusioned.

IV. Economy of the 1960s

In the 1960s the development of the Putumayo became strongly associated with the oil boom. This brought the construction of roads. The towns started to grow, and many fortune seekers arrived looking for land and work. In 1963 oil drilling started, and in 1973 Texaco agreed to the reversion of its oil fields to the Colombian government for development by the state-owned oil company, Empresa Colombiana de Petróleos (Ecopetrol). In this period, the population was made up of urban workers in the oil fields and peasants who populated the valleys of the rivers to plant food crops such as corn, cassava and plantains. Unfortunately, this dynamic process of colonization was not supported by the state through constructing utility services and farm-to-market roads or providing security to its citizens.

V. Coca Economy

Since the 1970s, the illegal cultivation of coca has attracted a great number of people, and this economy has brought more money than the oil boom. Even the people who came with the idea of developing agriculture and the indigenous communities were incorporated into this economy out of need. Legal crops did not receive credit or technical assistance from the Colombian government. The Cali and Medellín cartels profited from the desperation of the peasants by stimulating the cultivation of illegal coca crops. In March of 2000, there were more than 120,000 hectares of coca cultivated in Colombia, of which more than 60 percent were in the Putumayo, employing 50,000 peasants. According to the report *Los Cultivos Ilicitos y la Realidad en Colombia*, 2000 (*Illicit Crops and the Reality in Colombia*, 2000), from the Defensoría del Pueblo (Ombudsman's Office), one hectare of coca produces 1,250 kilos of coca leaves every 100 days. To produce one kilo of coca paste, it is necessary to produce 568 kilos of coca leaves, which means that there are an average of 2.2 kilos of paste per hectare in each one of the three harvests in a year. In 1993, a kilo of coca cost $600 in Colombia. That same kilo in the United States could be sold for between $10,500 and $40,000. The largest profits are in the international market on the demand side. *Plante* (*The National Plan for Alternative Development*) which, as the Colombian government's crop substitution office, focused on areas where the incidence of illegal crop cultivation is high, has calculated that for each 1,000 pesos that a buyer of coca paste pays, the Colombian peasant only receives six pesos. Even so, the profit for the peasant is larger than the traditional crops produce.

VI. Current Economy

The current situation in the Putumayo has to do with a combination of several political, economic and strategic factors. The Putumayo's land and resources are being disputed by the guerrillas, the paramilitaries, and the Colombian government, which through Plan Colombia promotes the United States' interests such as market penetration for its products and access to raw materials, particularly minerals and the rainforest canopy.

HUMAN RIGHTS VIOLATIONS

The dirty war in the Putumayo started in the 1980s. The increased number of violent deaths is directly associated with the cultivation of coca and the presence of guerrillas. The fact that the Putumayo borders on Peru and Ecuador made it ideal for the trafficking of cocaine, with the increased presence of bodyguards and hit men. The high prices of the coca leaf gave peasants and the indigenous large amounts of money, which altered their traditional ways of life and increased the use of violence for resolving conflicts.

Local power was in the hands of politicians from two political parties, the Liberals and Conservatives, who kept up their traditional patronage customs, such as offering public jobs in exchange for votes or for working in their electoral campaigns. In this way, they kept control of the towns' budgets and local governments. The same happened at the state government level, where even with the high income from the oil revenues, there was no investment in utilities such as electrification, telephones or water purification for the countryside. If roads were built, they were constructed to connect towns where the oil industry was being developed. In 1984, FARC guerrillas (Fuerzas Armadas Revolucionarias de Colombia) opened up their Thirty-Second Front in the Putumayo. In 1986, in the towns of Orito, Puerto Asís and Valle del Guamuez, there were an increased number of violent deaths. Just in Puerto

Asís 73 persons died violently, not counting the bodies thrown into garbage dumps or into the rivers.

Politically, particularly in Puerto Asís, the UP (Unión Patriótica, Patriotic Union), a legal third political party, became very strong. The UP developed as a political expression of the Communist Party, FARC guerrillas who decided to lay down their arms and become active in politics, activists of other groups and people who were unhappy with the two traditional parties. If anyone was found carrying Voz, the magazine of the Colombian Communist Party, it could cost the person his/her life. Militants of the UP were automatically considered guerrillas or their sympathizers. Motorboat operators working on the Putumayo River were considered FARC members because the Army suspected they transported guerrillas and food for them. On March 4, 1989, the headquarters of the UP in Puerto Asís was searched, and its account books disappeared. Rigoberto Torres, the local UP coordinator, was assassinated by a captain of the National Police who was the head of the political campaign against political opposition groups. That same year, 12 UP activists were assassinated, and the rest had to flee to other parts of the country. This was part of a national campaign to eliminate the UP by paramilitaries with the support of the Armed Forces and the money of the drug dealers. These latter wanted to gain the favor of the rabidly anti-communist Colombian elites. As a consequence, the UP disappeared from the political scene of the Putumayo in 1989.

In the 1980s a second institution developed, the Civic Movement of the Putumayo. It was pluralist, heterogeneous and above suspicion of collaborating with the guerrillas. It acted above the parties and demanded electricity, sewer systems, roads and adequate public services. In 1987 leaders of this group started to be killed. For example, a journalist, Luis Cristóbal Arteaga, was assassinated in Valle del Guamuez on August 20, 1990. In addition, 15 leaders of an indigenous movement, OZIP (Organización Zonal Indígena del Putumayo, Indigenous Zonal Organization of the Putumayo), were killed in its first four years of existence. OZIP promotes the peaceful invasion of government offices to pressure the Colombian government to meet its commitments, such as land titles, technical assistance, credit and promotion of human rights. Indigenous people are seen by the political establishment as potential guerillas. The idea is to weaken the grassroots movements by accusing them of cooperating with the rebels.

In 1987, a paramilitary base was created at El Azul, near Puerto Asís, which was part of the private army of the military leader of the Medellín cartel,

Gonzalo Rodríguez Gacha. He was fleeing from persecution in the center of the country by the Police and the Army. The existence of this base was denounced by the state intelligence services, but in reality the war against drugs in the Putumayo was limited to repressing medium-size drug dealers who were not closely linked to the cartels and whose detention served to show that the government was doing something against drugs. Basically, those were the ones who were not parties to the economic agreements with the public forces which facilitated freedom of movement and trafficking. An example is the case of Edgardo Londoño, whose farm was located near Puerto Asís. He was incarcerated because he refused to pay 25 million pesos to the Police commander of the Department of Putumayo since he already had paid that sum to the local Police commander.

At the beginning, the relationship between the drug traffickers and the FARC was of cooperation, doing business together with no aggression against each other. Two members from the FARC's Thirty-Second Front controlled the airport in El Azul, protecting the airport and charging a tax for this protection. Hit men from Rodríguez Gacha's forces killed them, and the FARC and a small guerrilla group, EPL (Ejército Popular de Liberación, People's Liberation Army), attacked El Azul, losing the battle. In 1990 three FARC fronts captured the place and killed 60 paramilitaries there.

Civilian authorities ignored the emerging problem by doing nothing when the public forces abused citizens. A group called "Los Combos" patrolled a great part of the territory, and the political and economic power of the dealers increased. Liberal and Conservative activists allied themselves with the paramilitaries to persecute the left and other political opponents. Captains of the Police in Puerto Asís were denounced before the Procuraduría as "accomplices of the paramilitaries, by allowing them to operate in the region and by tolerating the existence of paramilitary training centers." British mercenary Peter McAleese was in charge of training the paramilitaries. Another group known as "Los Macetos" came out of this training. There were 200 young men brought from other regions of the country because the idea was to rotate the assassins around the targeted regions. After the killing of Rodríguez Gacha, the paramilitaries came under the leadership of the Castaño brothers, Carlos and Fidel. Carlos Castaño is today, in 2001, the ruthless nationwide commander of the AUC (Autodefensas Unidas de Colombia), the largest paramilitary army in the country. [Editor's note: Carlos Castaño was later killed on April 16, 2004, reportedly at the order of his brother Vicente.]

The human rights situation deteriorated more and more. There was a massacre at Las Palmeras rural school, located five kilometers from Mocoa, on January 23, 1991. Five persons were executed, accused of being guerrillas, by a joint attack by the Army and an Elite Corps of the Police using helicopters. Among the victims was Hernán Cuarán, a 25-year-old school teacher. Cuarán was assassinated in front of his students. When a child said Cuarán was their teacher, an agent answered, "No. All of them are guerrillas." Artemio Pantoja, a plumber who was at the school building and whose daughter was the secretary of the Police headquarters in Mocoa, insisted they respect his life since his daughter worked at the station. An agent called Mocoa and a Colonel Linares ordered all of them killed. Police Colonel Pedro Pablo Linares made a public statement saying, "They were guerrillas killed in combat who were going to dynamite a pipeline." This statement was countered by the interior secretary of the state of Putumayo because he knew the victims and because there was no pipeline in Mocoa. The enraged citizens of Mocoa carried out a public protest against this criminal act.

This situation resulted in displaced people who carried with them fear, uncertainty, distrust, grief and resentment because all their rights as citizens are violated and the Colombian government seems indifferent to their problems.

In 1990, Colombian president Cesar Gaviria ordered the creation of commissions and "mesas de trabajo," (working groups) with the participation of all citizens around the country, to debate the new Constitution. The ones in the Putumayo became open town meetings where people questioned not only the administration of the local government but its cooperation with the drug dealers and paramilitaries and its failure to defend them. At the end of 1990, the Army attacked the FARC's National Secretariat on election day, when the referendum to approve the new constitution was being held. The answer from the FARC was to attack the economic infrastructure around the country. Just in the Putumayo from December 10, 1990, through April 1991, there were 20 dynamite attacks against Ecopetrol oil pipelines, two work stoppages and 10 direct confrontations with the Army.

CURRENT SITUATION IN THE PUTUMAYO

In 1998, the paramilitaries came back to the Putumayo, and they are present in most of the region. There is a paramilitary base in El Placer. The paramilitaries are present in the urban areas and the guerrillas in the rural areas. The situation for the population is very difficult because if they go to the rural areas they are branded as paramilitaries or their helpers. If peasants come to the towns they are immediately accused of being guerrillas. In both cases they are killed. In 1999, there were 13 massacres in the Putumayo, killing 77 persons, according to the document *Luz para la Vida* (*Light for Life*) from the Defensoría del Pueblo and the UN High Commissioner for Refugees Office.

CROP SPRAYING

In general during the 1980s, the market forces were the ones which decided coca prices: supply and demand. It seems that now the coca price is defined by the paramilitaries and the guerrillas, who impose the price. In other words, there is no such thing as free markets in the Putumayo. FARC sets a price for a kilo of coca and only allows the sale to those to whom they authorize the sale. The same with the paramilitaries.

In general, a kilo of cocaine is sold at 1.5—1.7 million pesos (about $6,800 - $7,000), and net profit per hectare is 200,000 pesos ($90). Comparatively speaking, a cargo which is about 100 kilos of corn is sold at 30,000 pesos and after paying the costs, the peasant is left with only 10,000 pesos per cargo (about $4.50). It is said that the guerrillas allow peasants to plant coca as long as they also plant food crops. They absolutely do not allow consumption of drugs.

Since the 1990s, people in the Putumayo have observed the presence of U.S. military alongside Colombian military as part of troops in the coca destroying operations. This has usually happened at the end of the year, when U.S. military personnel used to come to the military base in Puerto Leguízamo to teach courses for training Latin American soldiers.

One should understand that in the Putumayo, colonizers have to plant coca as the only agricultural possibility that can guarantee their maintenance. The root of the problem is a social conflict that has not been solved: As long as there is no technical assistance, no credit, no roads and no marketing strategies, the Putumayo peasant, who is generally a displaced peasant from other regions of the country, has no other alternative than planting coca to survive. A military solution is no solution.

The situation with the crop spraying is alarming in terms of food, since food crops are sprayed simultaneously with the coca plants. Cassava, corn, plantain, rice, rubber and tropical fruits are lost. Waters are contaminated, and people, particularly children, suffer diarrhea, headaches and skin rashes after crop spraying. The soil becomes sterile. Young people do not want to study anymore but want to work as 'raspachines' or pickers of coca leaves. Now with the spraying, many want to join the guerrillas because they say they do not want the government to poison them. They say they prefer to die fighting. Peasants would prefer crop substitution by peaceful means and help with loans and technical and financial assistance.

The ecological consequences of the spraying are extremely serious because they are destroying the Amazon rainforest. They not only affect the soil, the water, botanical and zoological diversity, but they are destroying the planet itself.

CONCLUSION

The Colombian government tries to make us believe that the situation in the Putumayo has nothing to do with the military aspects of Plan Colombia. This Department, whose population is made up of migrants from all over the country plus the indigenous and Afro-Colombian communities, suffered for the last two months the consequences of a work stoppage declared by the FARC, the increased presence of paramilitaries who want to recover control of the territory, restrictions imposed by the Army and the shortage of goods and services indispensable for survival.

The world decided to demonize the Putumayo, and its people are victimized. After being excluded for a long time, finally they are included, but as victims of the war. The only answers they receive to their multiple needs are military, when what is urgently needed is a social solution. All their rights are violated—human, civil, political, social, economic, cultural and ecological rights. This becomes an example of how Plan Colombia will be applied in a cruel society where the poor and humble become pariahs in their own country.

REFERENCES

1. Conclusiones del Seminario-Foro Nacional, "El Desplazamiento Interno en Colombia," ILSA, Justicia y Paz, Instituto Interamericano de Derechos Humanos, Dupligraficas, Bogotá, 1992
2. Andean Commission of Jurists/Colombia Section "PUTUMAYO," Informes Regionales de Derechos Humanos, Editorial Codice, Bogotá, 1993
3. Defensoría del Pueblo, Alto Comisionado para Refugiados de las Naciones Unidas, "Luz para la Vida," Masacres Ocurridas en Colombia, 1999, Impreso Editorial Carrera 7, Bogotá, Febrero, 2000
4. Defensoría del Pueblo, "Los Cultivos Ilícitos en Colombia," Imprenta Nacional de Colombia, Bogotá, Agosto, 2000
5. WOLA and others, "Nos están fumigando como cucarachas," Informe visita Putumayo, Mayo, 2000
6. Vicepresidencia de la República, "Panorama del Putumayo," Boletín Observatorio de Derechos Humanos, Septiembre, 2000
7. CINEP y Justicia y Paz, "Noche y Niebla," Banco de Datos de Derechos Humanos y Violencia Política, Julio—Septiembre, 2000, #17

SEPTEMBER 2-9, 2007

Traveling to the Putumayo

An Account of Cecilia's Visit to Putumayo Communities

Pasto, Sibundoy (Alto Putumayo),
Mocoa (Medio Putumayo), El Tigre Corregimiento

On Sunday September 2, I initiated my trip, which was planned as an exploratory trip to prepare for the delegation of our Kansas City chapter to its sister community. The diocese of Putumayo was the local contact organization, under the leadership of Father Campo Elías de la Cruz, who visited Kansas City last year. The Putumayo diocese organized my appointments and agenda.

When I arrived in Bogotá on Sunday night, my luggage did not arrive with me. I had to improvise my wardrobe since I was leaving the next day at 6 a.m. In Pasto, I was picked up by a trusted driver selected by Father Campo, and off we went on a scenic trip in the beautiful Andes Mountains, going to Sibundoy. After a brief stop in Pasto to buy toiletries and clothes, we drove through parts of Nariño state and parts of Putumayo which are mountainous and cold but extremely beautiful. They are full of forests and waterfalls. After four hours of travel, I saw one of the most beautiful valleys I have ever seen in my life:

el Valle del Río Sibundoy (the Valley of the Sibundoy River), arriving there at 1 p.m. The town is one of the headquarters of the Diocese of Mocoa-Sibundoy. It has a plaza with a unique selection of acacia trees which suffered a disease and were cut, but in the remaining healthy trunks, local artists carved colored sculptures of the history and legends of the Putumayo which you can see in my annexed picture (below).

Father Campo met me, and after lunch, we went to see a garden project by displaced families from the Bajo Putumayo who sell their produce to local families. The garden is located on land belonging to the Diocese. After that we went to the ongoing meeting of the Comisión Vida, Justicia y Paz (Life, Justice and Peace Commission) of the Diocese, where I met its members, among them its president Reverend Mario Toro, a Franciscan priest who formerly was head of the Franciscans in Colombia. I was graciously welcomed at the meeting, where they were discussing having a public debate with the candidates for Governor of Putumayo in the upcoming October elections. One of the subjects of the debate will be the question of what happened to the pacts between the government and the peasants. Late that afternoon we went to a meeting of all the parishes of Alto Putumayo, where the lay people described their participation in different activities in the nearby town of Colón. After that, we visited a hot-water bath with water coming from a nearby volcano. The guide explained that when the weather outside is cold, the water automatically becomes warmer and vice versa. We came back to Sibundoy to a warm dinner and singing session, with Father Campo showing his mastery of the guitar.

Legends of the Putumayo on an acacia tree in the Town Square of Sibundoy (Plaza de Sibundoy)

TUESDAY, SEPTEMBER 4: OFF TO EL TIGRE AND VISITING THE COFANES

On Tuesday, very early in the morning, we took public transportation en route to Mocoa, the capital of Putumayo, to meet the head of Pastoral Social, Father Julio Burban. He is very interested in Colombia Support Network's (CSN's) project and assigned Gildardo Aranzalez from his office to accompany us to El Tigre. We took the bus, a ride of four more hours, to El Tigre, where the indigenous communities we visited are located. Riding the bus, we went on a partly paved road built around the oil pipeline that takes oil to the Pacific coast. We passed next to the military base of Santa Ana. The Colombian Army constantly patrols this area to protect the pipeline from being attacked by the Revolutionary Armed Forces of Colombia (FARC) guerrillas.

We arrived at El Tigre at 2 p.m., just in time to have some lunch and take a canoe (below) to our first appointment with the Cofán nation at their resguardo (reservation), half an hour up the Guamuez River.

We arrived at the resguardo (reservation) of the Cabildo Cofán al Valle del Guamuez/San Miguel (Cofán Council in the Guamuez/San Miguel Valley), where we were received by the authorities of the Cofán people and members of this community.

Cecilia and Father Campo traveling on the Guamúez River en route to the reservation of the Cofán Council

Willington Chaparro spoke in the name of the community. He talked about being in the process of recovering their culture as indigenous people and the reconstruction of the country as a whole, since the current situation is very serious because of the fumigations[1] and attacks by the military. Recently, a military helicopter destroyed their little school. They want access to education and the recovery of their ancestral territory. He said that they have been affected directly or indirectly by the coca industry. He says the indigenous are an ethical voice in the neo-liberal world.

What has affected them the most have been the fumigations, which have caused more than 40,000 persons to be displaced in the Putumayo. The Cofanes told how these fumigations have affected their economic situation. The most important issue for them is to rescue their culture from western world influence and the need to strengthen their identity, their mother tongue and its grammar, their unique vision of the cosmos and their own wisdom because this will give them strength and respect. They want to do this with others to reconstruct society and to share what they have in order to rescue life. They want people of good faith and good will to help them in different areas—technological, professional and economic—so they will have a team accompanying them.

Then another leader, Libardo, talked about developing their own education in Santa Rosa del Guamúez. They are developing their own Plan de Vida del Pueblo Cofán (Life Project of the Cofán People), having a permanent session where they realized that ethno-education must be their priority. In their Department of Putumayo they have the first four centers of ethno-education which strengthens their cultures, which every day become more organized in spite of having enemies opposed to all these processes. The Cofanes want to advance and consolidate this area so they can have more indigenous teachers to prepare and educate children in each community. Many years ago they did not know what an indigenous teacher was, and now they have more than 40 teachers in 18 schools. They need infrastructure and the creation of a special college.

Libardo then spoke about the fumigations. He said that in the indigenous communities they have reflected a lot in order to create consciousness about manual eradication of the coca plant and also thinking about how not to let

1. Editor's note: The reference here is to the Colombian Government's program to reduce the coca crop by aerial spraying of coca fields with the herbicide "Roundup," made by Monsanto and containing glyphosate.

themselves die of hunger. When the coca business came, it brought with it a change in their cosmovision of the world, but this is like a tree that destroys its branches, leaving the roots which are still alive.

Another leader, Julio, spoke about how the fumigations have been a social, political and economic problem and how the armed groups have stopped their development. He mentioned how the government gives a little but does not solve the real problems. He is concerned about the Cofán People losing some of their own territory each day, and with this they lose their cultural identity. He mentioned that they are an original Amazonian tribe dating back to the origins of time. They need to have projects to recover their territory in order to have their culture of hunting and fishing, with productive projects according to the Life Project of the Cofán People. He emphasized the loss of their original territory and with this the loss of their sacred places and their values. Their land is being taken by colonizers who invade their soil. The Cofanes need to recover their territory in order to protect the ecosystem and especially to recover their traditional medicine in order to use it. They are the protectors of the yage[2] plant. He said that they want to protect their traditional medicine, strengthen the cabildos (indigenous community councils) and communicate with other cultures, with their own system of government and their own justice system, rescuing and implementing their ancestral laws. They need alternative development projects because they need food security for the short, medium and long term. Julio accused the Army brigade of eating their chickens.

We were delighted when the indigenous bilingual teacher invited her five-year-old pupils to sing for us old Cofán songs in their own language.

We went back to El Tigre before dark and felt the different voices and noises of the nearby rainforest. I was exhausted after such a long day and went to bed immediately.

WEDNESDAY, SEPTEMBER 5: VISITING THE EMBERÁ-CHAMÍ

Early in the morning I had the pleasure of meeting the young parish priest, Father Luis Hernán Miramar, who is the first and only parish priest in El Tigre. He is highly loved and respected, and I was very impressed by his commitment and dedication to the people. He told me that the place is called El Tigre because in older times jaguars (which are the Americas' version of tigers) used to come to drink water at the Guamúez River at this spot. Not

---

2. *Yage* is a Cofán word for a plant with hallucinogenic properties when mixed with another plant, chacruna, by traditional Cofán medicine men.

anymore, since jaguars have almost totally been exterminated. He explained to me how the indigenous communities have suffered terrible hunger because of the fumigations. The day before our visit, two little girls were sent to the parish to collect food supplies because they had no food at all.

We left early for a long, long walk to two reservations of the Emberá-Chamí: Argelia and Las Palmas, where there were also representatives of a third resguardo (reservation), La Italia, which is located very far away. However, all three are one community. We were very graciously received with lots of songs, dances and music in their own language (see photo on page 165). I walked most of the time along the wet, muddy rainforest path, and only at the end did I ride the horse we had with us (see next page). We were warmly welcomed by about 200 members of the Emberá-Chamí, including the Governor and the Jaibanas (religious leaders). The agenda was read by the Secretary of the Cabildo:

1. Welcoming greeting by the Governor and the Jaibanas plus the visiting organizations
2. Cultural Dance
3. A song in our language
4. Dances
5. Proposal of the joint work to do by the organizations, and discussion
6. Musical offering
7. Ending ceremony

The Governor and the Alcalde Mayor (Head of the Cabildo) welcomed us to their *chidria*, which means land in the Emberá language. He said that they represent the three Cabildos (Councils) of the Emberá-Chamí and their goal is to fight to defend Mother Earth. They want to achieve unity of territory and to keep their autonomy and culture. They want support and follow-up because they do not have defenders. They want to preserve their unique culture, clothing, practices and customs. There are provisions in the Constitution for them, but these rules are violated by the State itself. They cannot talk to the government because the government officials pay no attention to them.

As an indigenous organization, they follow the ideals of CRIC (Consejo Regional Indigena del Cauca, Regional Indigenous Council of Cauca), always in the struggle doing resistance because they have not disappeared. They struggle with their peasant brothers and Afro-Colombians, all of whom suffer discrimination by the State. The Army abuses all of them. The CIA (Central Intelligence Agency of the U.S.) is more dangerous than the FARC they say. The State is afraid of their traditional authorities. The Emberá-Chamí say, "We have leaders who are preparing themselves to defend our wealth and our land. Life is not a business, money does not give us identity but our identity gives us protection. The armed actors must be punished, and impunity has to be stopped." They are grateful that we came to see the needs of their people. They emphasized that their leaders are threatened and that they are all of them ready to give their lives for their land, and it is for this that they are struggling. They also talked about defending what they call their Law of Origin, which is the set of rules to administer their own justice so they are judged by their own Council of Elders and their Plan de Vida (Life Plan) which each Cabildo is working on. The Elders are the leaders because they have the experience.

Father Campo and Cecilia, on horseback, on the way to the Argelia and Las Palmas reservations

WEDNESDAY AFTERNOON

After lunch we started a long, long walk to the Cabildo Las Palmas, also of the Emberá-Chamí Nation. There was no horse, so off we walked.

The whole community welcomed us to their reservation. They started talking about ethno-education focused on their customs and on taking care of the environment so they can pass on their vision to the children. They consider the good handling of their own culture crucial. They are organized in a very spiritual form, which gives them strength and unity. Their culture is based on the wisdom of the elderly to be transmitted to the children who will defend their territory. For them, selling the land is like selling their mother. They should be united in resistance, taking care of their ancestors, their cultivation practices and their sacred places. According to their cosmology, unity is what gives them strength, and this ideology is what guides the principles of their Plan de Vida.

Song, dance, and music with the Emberá-Chamí of Argelia, Las Palmas and La Italia

Their main issues are:

Territory
Their territory is to be worked on. It is like a second mother that gives them life and wealth to live with harmony and freedom. It is never to be destroyed. The colonizers say that the Indians do not work because they do not cut trees, but what they do not realize is that wood is sacred to the indigenous communities. They said they also have to protect water because the Third World War would be for water, and they intend to resist to defend the waters.

Education
Based on interculturalism, the instruction in indigenous schools will impart not only general knowledge as in the Colombian educational system but will also focus on the Putumayo and particularly on the Valle del Guamúez.

The indigenous apply their own education with respect to water, following Quichua, Cofán, Pasto, Nasa and Emberá principles. They do not close their doors. They share their cultures to promote union, customs, spirituality and sacred places, so the little ones do not forget their mother's culture. All of this enriches their minds and creates a sense of belonging. Julio said they like saying, "I know who I am, where I come from, where I am, what it is that I want, what is my dress, my customs, my food, my dances. I love my land because it is my mother."

Each cultural ethnic group handles its way of thinking with respect to ethno-education. Each Plan de Vida has relation to Mother Earth. The authorities keep their philosophical traditions and they learn from them how to love nature, natural medicine and traditions which open their minds. The elders discover new things when they do their traditional ceremonies, upon which they reflect and cry, being the great philosophers that they are. Ethno-education also makes them reflect on the importance of intercultural issues and on how they have learned from many people who showed solidarity with Colombia, people from other countries who have shown interest in their culture and identity and have given support to their political process.

Autonomy

This point refers to the form of how they use arms. Others use arms to kill people. The Emberá-Chamí use their wood canes, which give them spiritual power according to the norms of the Emberá culture. This is a way to show how their culture has worked doing resistance in an organized way for so many years, accompanied by the spiritual strength drawn from those who died leaving a memory of carrying out resistance with the profound value of loving their land.

They invited Father Campo Elías to say a few words, and he reflected on their spiritual strength and the respectful accompaniment that the church is giving to them. They are the actors and the builders of the future because they pass on their way of thinking to their children. According to the indigenous theology and its respect for land, the environment and spirituality, today they are an ethical voice for the whole world. Father Hernán talked about the University for Ethno-Education, which costs $150 per semester per student. Each student prepares a thesis that should correspond to their ethnic identity and their territory.

Then Luis, another leader, spoke and said that the Emberá culture has been alive in their hands since before Christ. And he said they are descendants of the Mayas. He reminded all of us of the traumatic list of their sufferings when the Spaniards stole, massacred, enslaved and killed their philosophers. He also reminded us of how Simón Bolívar left laws respecting indigenous and Afro-Colombians. He talked about the fumigations and how they have no food, how the children suffer malnutrition and how the effects of glyphosate affect the environment. They do not want more war. They want people to think about the future for the children. He talked about how the government violates their norms and contaminates their environment. They want to grow rice as an alternative crop, but need a rice mill in order to process it and sell it.

Someone from the community requested donations of guitars, drums, quenas, flutes and charrascas for their musical group.

THURSDAY AFTERNOON AT BREAKFAST

Before going to Puerto Asís to catch my noon flight to Bogotá, I had a working breakfast meeting with Father Campo Elías, Father Hernán and Gildardo to strategize for the CSN delegation. We discussed:

1. Political Part:
   a) Vision of the region, location, geography
   b) Current political situation
   c) Indigenous communities
   d) Situation and needs in the U.S. and Kansas City in particular
2. Logistics
   a) Dates
   b) Places to stay, food and transportation
   c) Appointments with local authorities
   d) What to tell them about the Military and Police
3. Sister parish in Kansas City for El Tigre parish
4. Needs: to bring sheets, towels, lanterns, knee-high rubber boots, malaria and yellow fever vaccines, mosquito nets, wet paper towels (wet-wipes), toilet paper and other things to think about.
5. In Bogotá it was suggested the Colombia Support Network delegation visit the Minister of Interior, Section of Indigenous Affairs; the U.S. Embassy; Vice President Santos; the Defensoría; and the Embassy of Ecuador, besides the usual other NGOs.

The Sibundoy Valley
The Old Path and the Ambitions of a Coming Power

From the times of the Conquest to the current times, whoever travels to Putumayo becomes awed by the beauty of the Sibundoy Valley. Its magic comes not only from the landscape with rivers, volcanic peaks, flowers, trees, birds and other living creatures but from its horizon surrounded by the majesty of the Andes and the wilderness of the nearby Amazon jungle. The valley is the connection between these two well-defined geographic entities, and for thousands of years has played the role of a bridge to unite and not separate all the elements that live and survive in its midst.

In harmony with this place, the Kamentsá and Ingá communities inhabit Sibundoy. Theoretically, the homeland of these indigenous communities encompasses an immense extension of land in southern Colombia and even a part of Ecuador. It is a territory given to them by an officially registered will of Taita Carlos Tamiobioy as a grant from the Spanish Crown in the year 1700. The Kamentsá and Ingá cultures are refined and serene, full of artistic feelings reflected in the beautiful masks and crafts they make, which show the serenity of their souls. The Kamentsá cosmography does not indicate they came to Sibundoy from some other land nor how they ended up there. Their language is a mystery, and no one has been able to demonstrate links to any other language in the region. Contrary to all in the region, their religion is based upon the moon and little children are washed in their rivers at midnight, during special holidays, when there is a full moon.

A long time ago, there was a war between the Ingá and the Kamentsá, but after senseless fighting, they made peace among themselves. This was the beginning of an annual holiday called "Fiesta del Perdón" (Celebration of Forgiveness), a holiday for dancing and being merry and enjoying each other's company. As part of this holiday, anyone who has offended another asks for forgiveness and all of them grant pardons. This is a great lesson for the rest of Colombia to learn!

In the Andean part of the Sibundoy Valley there are mountains with forests that receive the winds from the Amazon and become factories of water. Many rivers are born there which later feed the mighty Amazon. For thousands of years, Andean and Amazon tribes have met along a primitive path called the Old Road (Camino Viejo or Ruku Nambi) to engage in barter transactions. (Even if you do not speak Spanish or Kamentsá or Ingá you can enjoy the beauty and the clear waters here: http://www.youtube.com/watcg?v=7C1wnkxHEqI.)

This path, the Old Road, is the selected route chosen by the Colombian government to construct a new highway between the town of San Francisco and Mocoa, the capital city of Putumayo Department, which will pass directly through these sacred historic lands where the indigenous have their burial grounds. The new road, with financing committed by the Inter-American Development Bank (IADB), is to replace the present road which is in poor shape. The road is planned as a part of a highway and waterway development extending from Belém on the Atlantic Coast of Brazil to Tumaco on the Pacific Coast of Colombia. It will respond to the ambition of Brazil to have an outlet to the Pacific in order to trade with China and other Asian countries. And it is one of the many roads planned by the governments of South America through the Initiative for the Integration of the Regional Infrastructure of South America (IIRSA)[1] to open up the Amazon and the rest of South America to facilitate business, especially mining and oil-drilling.

The path has an immense significance to the two indigenous nations because it is the site of their sacred places and of their cemeteries. The plan calls for cutting 97 hectares of virgin forests, which the Kamentsá and Ingá fear will destroy the water sources of the Sibundoy Valley, making it impossible for

1. Editor's note: The Initiative for the Integration of the Regional Infrastructure of South America (IIRSA) is a development plan to link the economies of the twelve sovereign nations of South America through new transportation, energy and telecommunications projects.

them to grow the crops which sustain them. Already Colombia's Constitutional Court has declared the Ingá and Kamentsá on the verge of extinction.[2]

At the request of these two communities, Colombia Support Network (CSN) has undertaken intense work to help them survive culturally and physically.

Editor's note: One of the Elders of the Kamentsá community, José Narciso Jamioy Muchavisoy, a former professor in Bogotá, discussed the challenge that the Kamentsá and Ingá communities believed the road project presented to them. "The elders say that they have walked...the path to go by foot to Mocoa and that if the San Francisco-Mocoa highway is built, this will destroy the trees of the wind that protect the Sibundoy Valley. According to the technical studies presented by INVIAS (the Colombian Government's road-building institution), approximately 15,000 hectares of natural forest will be destroyed...This destruction will make way for the spirits of the wind to become enraged and rapidly dry the lands of the Sibundoy Valley. This will have devastating consequences for the ecosystem in the valley and will affect the lives of all of its inhabitants, its flora and its fauna." (Translation from Spanish to English by Anne Schoeneborn published in Colombia Support Network's Action on Colombia Newsletter, October 2011, pg. 2.)

Responding to a decision by the InterAmerican Development Bank (IADB) to fund construction of the road as a part of IIRSA, the Initiative for the Integration of the Regional Infrastructure of South America, Aureliano Garreta Chindoy, a leader of the Ingá community in the Sibundoy Valley, directed a message to Dr. Isabel Lavandez of the Independent Consultation and Investigation Mechanism (MICI) of the IADB in which he said "This road is going to affect the ethnic, socio-cultural, environmental and economic integrity of the Ingá and Kamentsá peoples of the Putumayo and the

2. Editor's note: Three papers that discuss this project are: first, "Proyecto Vial de Integración Regional Variante San Francisco-Mocoa: Aspectos Sociales y Ambientales Reivindicados" by Mayra Tenjo in UNASUR: Opciones de Participación de la Sociedad Civil, coordinated by Héctor-León Moncayo Salcedo, pp. 95-116, located here: https://rightsandresources.org/wp-content/exported-pdf/libroparticipacionunasur5.pdf; second, "Variante San Francisco-Mocoa: la riesgosa e interminable carretera en la selva de Colombia" by Mongabay Latam, located here: https://es.mongabay.com/2020/06/colombia-variante-san-francisco-mocoa-putumayo-adelanto-video/; and third, "La Amazonía colombiana: Análisis de las inversiones que amenazan los derechos de los pueblos y sus bosques," by Mayra Tenjo Hurtado and Paula Álvarez Roa, published by Derechos, Diversidad y Selvas (Dedise), Bogotá, December, 2015, pp. 10-11. From the first article by Mayra Tenjo in UNASUR: "The indigenous people of the Putumayo possess a rich and diverse culture and ... they have demanded recognition of their culture as people who have occupied the ancestral territory of Carlos Tamoabioy for thousands of years. This is their principal tool against the developmental concept of the dominant classes...," pp. 110-111.

Colombian Amazon...we will continue to defend the preservation and the defense of the Amazon region as the World's Natural Reserve of Humanity, the largest and most important environmental reserve, in accord with our views as indigenous peoples, and for the rest of the inhabitants of the world." He noted that the Colombian government had not conducted constitutionally required prior consultations with the indigenous communities concerning "development of mining and energy mega-projects and roadways through indigenous lands..." Through the leadership of Carmenza Tez of the Kamentsá Community in Sibundoy and later with her husband Steve Bray, and the Colombia Support Network, with the assistance of Mayra Johanna Tenjo of the Instituto de Servicios Legales Alternativas (ILSA) of Bogotá, the MICI recognized the negative aspects of the road construction project and the IADB, which had invested millions of dollars in the road project, finally pulled the plug on further financing. They determined that the project could not be built as planned, as water running down from the mountains destroyed the structures on the mountain slopes that they had put in place to protect the road. The stunning photo, below, of a large concrete bridge span ending in a sheer mountain wall is the ultimate statement of failure of this project, a failure applauded by the Kamentsá and Ingá leaders.

2014

Marmato: The Mountain of Gold

One of the highlights for anyone who visits Bogotá is a tour of its Gold Museum because it contains the largest collection of pre-Hispanic gold work in the world. One of its most famous pieces is the Quimbaya poporo, or vase, a product of the most exquisite pre-Columbian gold work.[25),32)] Its function was to keep the lime needed to chew the ritual coca leaves used in religious ceremonies. It was kept with the same respect Catholics give the Chalice where wine is preserved for Mass. This was a different way, but a legitimate one, to live spiritually.

The region of the Cauca River, today's Departments of Caldas, Quindío, Risaralda and southern Antioquia, was populated by the Quimbaya indigenous people who disappeared near the Tenth Century A.D.[9),22)] This region could be called the golden belt of Colombia because it is located in the heart of the historic production of this metal in the country. In spite of there having been numerous gold-producing centers in the Viceroyalty of New Granada, we will focus only on Marmato.

In 1535 Spanish soldiers under the command of Sebastián de Belalcázar arrived in the region where today's Marmato is located. It was populated by an indigenous group called Cártama. Soon the Spaniards, when crossing their territory, realized that their main occupation was to extract gold from the mountain while living in a village surrounded by cornfields and a rainforest. On November 17, 1537, Conquistador Juan Badillo founded Marmato. Its name comes from the mining word marmaja, which is a yellow rock rich in iron, also known as fool's gold. [9),22)]

Gold has left its mark in the history of Colombia since the Conquest. Its main cities and towns were founded near or close to a gold mine. Only this can explain the foundation of Santafé de Bogotá in a high plateau on the top of the Andes far from the sea. Its founding was the result of the greed of the Spaniards seeking El Dorado, the religious ceremony which took place in a nearby lake.

Spain always saw its overseas territories in America as its principal source of precious metals such as gold and silver. This was their purpose.[24)] With that gold, the Spanish crown paid its debts to the Flemish and German bankers, initiated war actions such as those of the Invincible Armada, and kept its hegemony throughout the planet. Spain never invested the gold taken from the country in its Viceroyalty of New Granada, which corresponds to today's territory of Colombia, Venezuela, Ecuador and Panamá. The Spanish did not build roads as the Romans did, nor stimulate any local industry or the colonial economy. What was left in the country were precious jewelry, altars for the colonial churches, crowns for the Virgin Mary and many religious items.

Marmato then became a type of provisional town called Real de Minas that was assigned to a Spaniard who was responsible for a group of indigenous who were forced to work in the mine. This system was called encomienda, and the only duties for the Spaniard were to collect taxes, care for the spiritual life of his recommended indigenous peoples—which for practical purposes was to make them good Catholics—and pay the royal fifth for the King. In 1625, the Cártamas had already been wiped out, and the only thing left from them is their name and the hieroglyphs they painted on rocks nearby. Due to the scarcity of the indigenous population because of mistreatment, the Spaniards decided to bring African slaves to work in the mines to allow them to exploit the mineral resources of their American colonies. In 1627 it was registered that a group of 70 black slaves worked in Marmato and another group was assigned to agriculture to produce food for the workers of the mine.[1]

During the seventeenth and eighteenth centuries, the mine was controlled

1. Editor's note: See *Profits, Security, and Human Rights in Developing Countries: Global Lessons from Canada's Extractive Sector in Colombia*, Chapter 3: "Ethnicity, Episteme, and Gold, The Struggle for Human Security in Marmato," by James Rochlin, pp. 74–78.

by the Arboleda, Castro and Moreno families and the encomienda was under the jurisdiction of the city of Popayán. The Spanish miners used to say that the mountain of Marmato was a whole mountain of gold from its base to the top of the mountain, which they called El Burro. Marmato's gold was sent to Cali, Popayán and Spain, but the conditions of the slaves never changed. At the beginning, the miners used to live in the lowland, called San Juan, but because they had to climb every day to get to the top of the mountain, they decided to build their homes on the side of the mountain, on top of the tunnels, challenging the laws of gravity. This is why Marmato is unique, because it did not follow the traditional Spanish urban design for its colonial possessions: a square in the center with the church on one side and the city hall on another. Marmato was declared a Historic Patrimony of the country on March 2, 1982.[26, pg. 57)]

For more than 250 years Marmato produced gold for the Spanish Crown and the encomenderos. Colombia was the colony that produced the most gold in the Spanish Empire, becoming the producer of 40 percent of the total world production of gold in the Seventeenth Century. But in 1810, the time to become independent from Spain arrived, and Simón Bolívar and others sought out England, the eternal enemy of Spain, searching for political and economic solidarity. The English wanted a mortgage to back the loans they made, and Bolívar pledged to them the gold of the mines of Marmato. The inexperience of the negotiators who contracted for the loans resulted in their agreeing to usurious terms. The payments to England had to be made in gold. The amount of gold the English took out of Marmato for a century more than paid the original debt. Thus by an ironic turn of history, the English no longer had to send their pirates to assault Spanish cities in the Caribbean in order to get the gold from Spain.

During the time from Colombia's independence from Spain until 1925, a succession of English companies mined in Marmato. According to Vicente Restrepo in his classic book about mining in Colombia, the English kept a special watch over this mine in Marmato and introduced the more modern techniques of the time in order to make the mine more efficient.[28)] From 1925 on, the mines were possessed by the Colombian government, which gave concessions to private Colombian contractors. In 1955 the mine was again administered by different government enterprises with different names such as ECOMINAS, MINERALCO and MINERCOL. In 2004 the concession was given to Mineros de Caldas, a subsidiary of the Canadian company Colombia Goldfields which later became Medoro Resources. On June 13, 2011, Medoro announced from Toronto that it had merged with another company, Gran Colombia Gold (GCG).[7]

Before undertaking to analyze Marmato, it is worth considering that until very recently artisan, or small-scale, mining prevailed in Colombia. It first was regulated by colonial legislation, which was the Spanish legislation on mining that was designed in the Middle Ages. The right to royalty was reserved for the King of Spain who conceded the mines to be operated by commoners. A tax was charged that changed from between 10 percent and 20 percent, according to the needs of the Crown. Some mines were reserved exclusively for the Crown as a monopoly.[5],[6]

In modern times, from 1886 to 2001, although the legislation that ruled mining was not perfect, at least it recognized the rights and the work of the small miners. But with the globalization of the economy, the situation changed due to many factors, both internal and external. One important internal factor is the almost genetic impossibility on the part of the Colombian elite to make structural reforms that would make Colombia a more just society. The elite would prefer to do anything before regulating the financial system that gives them so much profit or before carrying out a land reform which would really use land appropriately. Nor would they change the labor laws or reverse the privatization of big sectors of the economy, such as health, energy and oil. They will make no changes that would touch their interests.

Colombia's great tragedy is to be a society that excludes the majority of its citizens from their economic, political, social and cultural rights. In September, 2010, the Office of the United Nations for Development published a report called "Rural Colombia: Reasons for Hope."[7] The statistics in this report speak for themselves: 52 percent of Colombia's substantial rural property is in the hands of 1.15 percent of the population and the Gini number referring to the concentration of landowners is 0.8. In a February 2011 report, according to CODHES, an NGO that follows displacement in the country, between 1985 and 2010 in Colombia 5.2 million people were displaced from rural areas.[6, pg. 9] Colombia's population is 47 million.

Current economic theories popular among Colombia's elite focus on economic growth and assume that if production increases wealth increases, and more wealth means more work, more income and more demand. Therefore, the theory is Colombia will be a very prosperous country based on an economy that grows and attracts foreign investment to sectors such as mining, especially focused on coal, gold and oil.

According to a Wikileaks cable published in the Madrid daily El País on November 5, 2010, the powers that be in this world decided that Latin America should go back to its destiny of 520 years ago: to be a provider of raw materials. Nobody expressed this more eloquently than the Energy Secretary of President Clinton, Bill Richardson, in a March 1998 meeting in Cartagena, Colombia. Before a group of investors from Canada and the United States he said that his country would back, with military aid, the investments in strategic sectors such as mining and energy.[26, pp. 32-33)] Is this the role of the Colombian Army as set forth in the Constitution?

Colombia rules itself by international consensus, such as the Washington Consensus, which promotes budgetary discipline, favors public spending where it presents opportunities for private profit, reduces taxes for those with large incomes, frees international trade as in the Colombia-United States Free Trade Agreement, and privatizes public enterprises (even those which make a profit).

Another angle to consider is biodiversity because mining affects Colombia's biodiversity directly. According to the Convention on Biological Diversity, Colombia possesses nearly 14 percent of all the biodiversity in the world.

In 2001 President Andrés Pastrana's government published its Mining Code, which changed the old legislation through Law 685. The Government of President Álvaro Uribe (2002-2010) diligently took upon itself the task of enticing foreign investors by giving them tax exemptions, fiscal benefits and low royalty rates. And for Uribe and his government the excuse for such investment was that it facilitated the retaking of regions that were under the control of the guerrillas. President Juan Manuel Santos himself is a firm believer that the "mining locomotive" will bring growth and prosperity. [18)]

It is worthwhile to consider some aspects of Law 685. It eliminates the difference between small-scale, medium- and large-scale mining, so the artisan miner competes under the same conditions as the multinational companies. It also penalizes and inhibits the miner who does not "legalize" himself. The Law gives advantages to mining companies using techniques which destroy the ecological environment in a country which has immense biological wealth.

The Constitutional Court clarified that before doing any mining development in an indigenous territory, the Colombian state must conduct a prior consultation with indigenous communities. Yet there are numerous examples of the Colombian government approving multinational companies' mining plans without conducting such a proper prior consultation.[2]

Meanwhile, Article 227 of the Mining Code concedes royalties which in practice amount to very small percentages. On the issue of royalties and taxes, Senator Jorge Enrique Robledo of the opposition Polo Democrático party observed in a debate in the Colombian Congress on November 22, 2011: "In 2010, for each 68 dollars in direct foreign investment ... 100 dollars left via dividends and profits." In the same speech, Senator Robledo criticized the criminalization of artisan miners. He notes that while the government itself calls them guerrillas and drug dealers, as a matter of fact, the artisan miners have been working the mines for 500 years. Today's artisan miners inherited that work from their parents, grandparents and great-grandparents. Why is this a problem after 500 years? Continues Senator Robledo: "... because the price of gold is high, and the multinationals are behind the effort to mine gold in Colombia."[30)]

In no other place is the conflict between big mining and small mining clearer than in the old mining town of Marmato. Its concession is subject to special legislation which is unique because it was given in horizontal levels as established by Decree No. 2223 of 1954. The decree established that the High Zone would be dedicated to small-scale artisan mining, and the Low Zone to large-scale mining. Regulations also cover the mine in the nearby settlement of Echandía. Almost all of the Low Zone has been provided for by concession to Gran Colombia Gold, whose concession borders Echandía. The Echandía zone is also part of special legislation which recognizes it as private property that excludes the state from owning the subsoil. In general, in Colombia, the state owns the subsoil.[3]

Upon study of the historical background of mining in Marmato, it is useful to discuss in detail the current situation in Marmato by the following sectors: the mining companies, geology, the National Government, culture and the small-scale artisan miners.

---

2. Editor's note: EcoOro was approved for mining in Santander without prior consultation with indigenous and local communities; concessions were granted to or extended to ExxonMobil and other mining companies during the 1990s without prior consultation for the large (270 square miles), open-pit mine Cerrejón in La Guajira.
3. A special status was given to the Echandía mine by special legislation, Law 20 of 1969 by means of RPP 357, which provided it to Señor Fernando Gutiérrez, who had purchased it from a Mr. Gale, of English nationality, who had worked the Echandía mine for many years. That exception is rumored to have come from the Spanish Crown. This information was provided by Yamil Amar of the Comité Cívico Pro-Defensa de Marmato (Civic Committee for the Defense of Marmato).

THE MINING COMPANIES

Direct Canadian mining investment in Colombia has expanded since the 1990s. The company Colombia Goldfields came to Marmato and specialized in exploration and buying properties rich in gold. It was founded in 2005 and on October 30, 2009, became a subsidiary of Medoro Resources, which also focused on acquiring properties with mining potential and then seeking companies which would develop the gold mines directly.

And acquire properties was what Colombia Goldfields (Medoro) did! In its exploratory activities, the company found out that the mountain of Marmato stores in its interior from 6 to 10 million ounces of gold. It also concluded that the most efficient way to mine the gold would be by excavating an open-pit mine cutting through the mountain. In other words, the historic town of Marmato would have to be transferred to another place. There are more than 400 small-scale artisan mines in the High Zone of the town. Clearly the idea is to close all of those mines and to start development of an open-pit mine because the latter would produce more gold much faster. Besides, Medoro contracted an NGO, CETEC (Corporación para Estudios Interdisciplinarios y Asesoría Técnica), in order to "facilitate the relations between the company and the community," emphasizing that it will propose agricultural and cattle-raising projects, thinking about the future when Marmato no longer has gold. Medoro donated millions of pesos for the construction of a modern hospital and schools located in El Llano, a new town in the Low Zone to which Marmato's residents are supposed to move.

On November 1, 2011, Gran Colombia Gold (GCG) published a press release in response to a series of negative articles published in the Colombian press and in the press release it reiterated that GCG intended to build an open-pit mine in Marmato that would require moving the town to a nearby community.[4]

GEOLOGY

The mountain where Marmato is located has steep slopes. The miners do not typically clean off the tailings of their mining activity, and these tailings accumulate on the mountainside. Winter rains may then cause rock slides. On May 4, 2006, strong rains produced a rock slide which damaged a part of the historic area of the town.

Nobody died, but a few buildings were damaged. The geological institute of

4. Editor's note: Medoro merged with Gran Colombia Gold in 2011, which thereafter sought the rights to construct an open-pit mine on the upper part of the mountain.

the government declared the area to be of "high risk," but the same analysis declared that projects could be designed to mitigate the landslides. The Police station, the hospital and the school have been relocated to the new town below, although a Colombia Support Network (CSN) delegation in January 2012 observed the old city hall, a hospital and school to be largely intact. Mineros de Caldas, a subsidiary of Medoro, expressed its opinion in the following excerpt from a report prepared by Scott Wilson in 2010[33)] which states on page 128: "More than ever the Company believes that the urban center of Marmato is in great danger as future landslides could end in a great human catastrophe of great significance. Lately, the position of the Company is that the urban center of Marmato be moved for humanitarian reasons, which fortunately coincides with the needs of the Company."

In a letter of February 25, 2008, Senator Robledo asked the national government if the idea of destroying Marmato and displacing its inhabitants is because of the risk of a landslide or because its subsoil contains immense gold deposits which a multinational company wants to develop. Robledo suggests that in a country where there have been floods, earthquakes, volcanic eruptions and landslides for which the government has not undertaken serious solutions for its people, the government's supposed concern about relocating the people of Marmato, who live on top of a massive gold treasure, does not ring true.

THE NATIONAL GOVERNMENT

The Colombian government acts more as if it were a lobbyist for the mining companies instead of the legal representative of a sovereign people. It looks more like an absolute monarchy showing itself to the world as a republic. We have already seen how the revision of the Mining Code was accommodated to the needs of the multinationals. The government entities of control and supervision of mining do not operate properly. In the specific case of Marmato, the government itself granted permission to Medoro to explore the High Zone of Marmato, according to the Manizales newspaper *La Patria*, February 11, 2010, which means it does not respect its own laws. (Recall, as earlier stated, the High Zone was to be reserved for the use of artisan miners.)

The government has never made an effort to seek out other options, such as to promote the development and training of artisan miners in how to use clean technologies, since the technology of the artisan miners also damages the ecosystem, although not as much as large-scale mining.

Notably, some persons who had been in high positions in the previous government of President Álvaro Uribe have easily gone to work in mining in the private sector. The former Minister of Mining of President Uribe, Hernán Martinez Torres, sits on the Board of Directors of GCG, and the President of the Company, María Consuelo Araújo Castro, is a former Minister of Foreign Relations.

The government's decision to make Colombia into a mining country never involved consultation with the people through a referendum. The political and environmental consequences are too serious not to ask the approval of the Colombian people. In fact, this decision will extend the internal war because it will produce unemployment and displacement in great proportions. People who are unemployed or displaced will likely try to solve their problems by having recourse to illicit economic activities or to violence.

CULTURE

Can economic development be justified when it destroys the cultural patrimony of a country? Was it just to give the mining concession which financed Colombia's independence to foreigners without consulting with its Afro-Colombian and indigenous groups who have lived for centuries from their mining in Marmato? What is the price for open-pit mining that will destroy water sources and soils? Social wellbeing, profit and the environment should be balanced when we talk about development. If gold were found under Cartagena, the celebrated historical city, would the government grant it to the multinationals? Of course not. Why, then, Marmato if it is as old as Cartagena?

SMALL-SCALE ARTISAN MINERS

When Colombia Goldfields arrived in Marmato in 2007 it started to offer money to the miners for their small- or medium-size mines. Some of the artisan miners sold their mines because they assumed they could keep their jobs. Others decided to move to other towns and invest the money in new businesses. Goldfields bought 84 mines and nine mills. It also bought some titles in the nearby region of Echandía. The miners had no real concept of the value of the mines. Then what happened was unthinkable. Goldfields closed the mines and destroyed most of the mills, which was an insult to the miners. As a result, 833 persons were left without jobs.[5]

Many of the artisan miners who had sold their mines returned to Marmato seeking jobs. The mines were still closed and hunger besieged their families. The Mining Code states that if you buy a mine and do not work it in the next

5. Confirmed by Yamil Amar, June 10, 2020, in an email to the editors.

six months, you lose the right to the title of that mine. When the six-month period had run without Goldfields working the mine, one unemployed miner said to another one, "Let's break the locks." They did, reopening the mine. Then they started to work. Many more did the same. These are the miners called "guacheros." At the end of 2010, the NGO hired by the company, CETEC (Corporación para Estudios Interdisciplinarios y Asesoría Técnica), arrived with a contract to be signed by the guacheros. They sought out legal advice, and their lawyers recommended that they not sign because if they did so, they would be recognizing the multinational company's ownership of the mines. On January 21, 2011, the Army arrived with representatives from the national and state governments to carry out an order to evict the miners. Within minutes more than 200 miners got together and the government started to realize the issue was not a simple one. The artisan miners concluded that what was planned was to force them to become economically displaced people who would join the 5.6 million who are already displaced. Therefore they decided to organize the Asociación de Mineros Unidos (Association of United Miners), which had the effect of unifying them for a common cause.

The Marmato leaders are tired of having only the leaders of the mining company appear in the national media and not having the media ask them anything. They dislike the fact that Marmato is presented in the national news as a poor town on the verge of disappearing. They say that the abandonment is the responsibility of the government and that when the landslide of 2006 came, it was they, the community itself, who picked up the rubble. Then, in May 2006, they founded the Comité Cívico Pro-Defensa de Marmato (CDM).

The pressure on the artisan miners continues, now with some new twists. It is forbidden to buy dynamite or wood posts to construct the shafts that sustain the artisan mines. The CDM argues that there has not been previous consultation on the issue of moving Marmato. They say that, given the fact that the town is an historic patrimony of the country, it cannot be relocated. The miners believe that it is the duty of the state to build schools and hospitals, not something to leave to a multinational mining company. In May 2011, the people declared a nonviolent general strike against the projects of the mining company and its ally, the Colombian government. Their parish priest, José Reynel Restrepo, spoke publicly against the plans of the Canadian mining company to destroy the source of life of Marmato, its culture and its inhabitants. On August 28, 2011, a video including Father Restrepo's strong statement against moving Marmato was placed on YouTube. Four days later, on September 1, 2011, Father Restrepo was murdered.[6]

On December 21, 2011, the Municipal Council of Marmato voted to keep the municipality in the historic zone and to return to it all the institutions which characterize a town, such as the Mayor's office, Police station and others. It also decided to say "no" to the open-pit mine and to support traditional artisan mining.

A new municipal government was voted into office beginning January 1, 2012. The new Council and Mayor will again have to address the open-pit mine issue. Opponents of the mine will now have the additional support of the new Governor of the province of Caldas. Undoubtedly, the mining company with the support of the national government will keep pressuring the community to accept the open-pit mine.

History has many ironies, and in the case of Marmato, they flourish. Another proposal of the mining companies is to train the people from Marmato in goldsmithing, which is to say, going back to the production of elements such as the Poporo Quimbaya. With a big difference this time: The gold of the Quimbayas belonged to them, and the designs had spiritual value. Modern goldsmithing will make designs defined by market forces, and the artisans will have to buy the gold from the multinational corporations.

In Marmato, there are a great number of cases of violations of human rights, characterized by the criminalization of social protest, jail, threats, persecution and killings. The miners believe that this combined strategy by the multinationals and the government is for war, and not for peace.

---

6. Editor's note: As of February 2024, we the Editors have not been advised of any outcome in the investigation of the murder of Father Restrepo and we believe that his murder is unsolved to this day.

CITATIONS AND REFERENCES

1. Amar, Yamil. "Gobernador de Caldas respalda al pueblo de Marmato". Message to Cecilia Zárate. January 26, 2012. Email.
2. Arenas, Darío. "Marmato, Despojo a cielo abierto". moir.org.co., MOIR, julio 23, 2010. Web. enero 7, 2012. <*http://www.moir.org.co/Marmato-despojo-a-cielo-abierto.html*>.
3. Bedoya, Ana María. "Los Guacheros: unidos y firmes en defensa de su trabajo". *Escuela Nacional Sindical, Trabajo Decente Vida Digna*. Segundo Informe (2011): 1-5. Print.
4. Bedoya, Ana María. "De acá no nos vamos". *Escuela Nacional Sindical, Trabajo Decente Vida Digna*. Tercer Informe (2011): 1-6. Print.
5. Casilda Bejar, Ramón. "América Latina y el Consenso de Washington". *Boletín Económico del ICE #2803*, pp 19-38, abril 26 a mayo 2, 2004. (ICE: Información Comercial Española.)
6. CODHES. " Consolidación de qué?" *Boletín de la Consultoría para los Derechos Humanos y el Desplazamiento*. Número 77, Bogotá, febrero 15, 2011, pp 1-30.
7. "Colombia Rural: Razones para la esperanza". Programa de las Naciones Unidas para el Desarrollo, septiembre, 2011. Web diciembre 28, 2011. <*http://www/pnud.org.co*>.
8. "Country Profile Colombia". Convention on Biological Diversity/United Nations Environmental Program, Montreal, Canada, <*http://www.cbd.int/countries/profile.shtml?country=co*>.
9. Diaz López Lyda del Carmen, Urbina Rangel Fernando, First. *Marmato: un pueblo de oro anclado en la montaña*. Bogotá Departamento Editorial, 1989. eBook. <*http://www.banrepcultural.org/blaavirtual/antropología/marmato/indice.htm*.
10. Duque-Escobar, Gonzalo. "Marmato; desaparecerán más de 500 años de cultura por reorientación minera". *Marmato Blogspot*. N.p., diciembre 6, 2008. Web. agosto 1, 2012. <*http://www.marmato.blogspot.com/*>, <*http://www.banrepcultural.org/.../antropología/marmato/mar1.htm*>.
11. Escuela Nacional Sindical. "La Disputa por el oro de Marmato". *Trabajo Decente Vida Digna*. Primer Informe (2011): 1-7. Print. septiembre 30, 2011.
12. FUNDESUMA. "Concejo Municipal de Marmato respalda al pueblo de Marmato". Message to Colombia Support Network, 28 December, 2011. Email.

13. García Hernández, Andrés Fernando. "El traslado de Marmato es posible". El Mundo [Medellín], julio 15, 2011, web Noticias. Web. febrero 5, 2012. <*http://www/elmundo.com/portal/noticias/antioquia/_el_traslado_de_marmato_es_posible.php*>.

14. Gran Colombia Gold. "Investor Presentation". *Grancolombia gold*. Gran Colombia Gold Corp, enero, 2011. Web. febrero 7, 2011. *http://www.grancolombiagold.com*

15. Hurtado Sabogal, Rodrigo. *La Contienda Política Alrededor de la Licencia Ambiental para el Projecto Minero Angostura en el Páramo de Santurbán*. Bogotá: Pontificia Universidad Javeriana, Facultad de Ciencias Políticas y Relaciones Internacionales, Maestría en Política Social, 2011. Print.

16. Inter Pares, Mining Watch/CENSAT Agua Viva. *Land and Conflict*. Ottawa: Inter Pares, 2009. 75. <*http://www.interpares.ca/en/publications/pdf/Land_and_Conflict.pdf*>.

17. "Marmato: entre el crudo presente y el borroso futuro". *La Patria* [Manizales], mayo 2, 2010, Caldas. Web. diciembre 27, 2012. <*http://www.lapatria.com/story/marmato-entre-el-crudo-presente-y-el-borroso-futuro*>.

18. Martínez-Alier, Joan. Environmental Justice (ejolt), "The Colombian Mining Locomotive has Halted," February 14, 2013.

19. "Medoro quedaría con minas altas y bajas en Marmato". *La Patria* [Manizales], noviembre 2, 2010, Caldas. Print. <*http://www.lapatria.com/story/medoro-quedari-con-minas-altas-y-bajas-de-marmato*>.

20. "Marmato: Reubicación o ambición minera?" *Terra.com*. abril 7, 2011: Noticias. Web. febrero 5, 2012. <*http://noticias.terra.com.co/minería/marmato-reubicación-o-ambición-minera,109a3eae6413f210VgnVCM10000098f154d0RCRD.html*>.

21. Molano Bravo, Alfredo. "El Espejismo de Marmato". *El Espectador* [Bogotá], octubre 1, 2011, Nacional. Web. octubre 1, 2011. <*http://www.elespectador.com/impreso/nacional/articulo-302997-el-espejismo-de-marmato*>.

22. "Nuestro municipio/Historia". *Alcaldía de Marmato*. Gobierno en línea Ministerio de Comunicaciones Colombia, n.d. Web. febrero 2, 2012. <*http://marmato-caldas.gov.co/nuestromunicipio.shtml?apc=Mpxx-1-&m=f&s=m*>.

23. O'Tuathail, Micheal. "Marmato's Gold Bonanza". *Dominion*. 51, March 18, 2008: n. page. Web. March 20, 2008. <*http://www.dominionpaper.ca/articles/1777*>.

24. Pérez Sáenz de Urturi, Juan Eusebio. "La minería colonial americana bajo la dominación española". *Boletín Millares Carlo*. 7-8 (1985): 53-120 Web. <*http://dialnet.unirioja.es/servlet/listaarticulos?tipo_busqueda=EJEMPLAR&revista_busqueda=7277&clave_busqueda=129584*>.

25. "Quimbaya en la Exposición del Museo del Oro". *Museo del Oro*. Banco de la República, 2008. Web. diciembre 8, 2011. <*http://www.banrep.gov.co/museo/esp/s_quimbaya01.htm*>.

26. Ramírez Cuéllar, Francisco. *The Profits of Extermination*. First edition. Monroe, ME: Common Courage Press, 2005. Print. Pp. 32-33, 57.

27. "Response from Gran Colombia Gold to concerns of negative human rights impacts of its mining operations in Colombia". *Business and Human Rights Resource Center*, 1 noviembre 2011. Web. November 1, 2011. <*www.business-humanrights.org/Search/SearchResults?SearchableText=GranColombiaGold&x=0&y=0*>.

28. Restrepo, Vicente. *Estudio sobre las minas de oro y plata de Colombia*. Segunda. Bogotá: Imprenta de Silvestre, 1888. 334. Print.

29. Robledo, Jorge Enrique. "Por qué están desplazando a Marmato". *Moir.org.co*. Moir, enero 11, 2008. Web. agosto 1, 2012. <*www.jorgerobledo.com/por-que-están-desplazando-a-marmato/*>.

30. Robledo, Jorge Enrique. "Para Colombia, muy poco de la riqueza minera". MOIR, noviembre 22, 2011. Web. noviembre 30, 2011. <*www.moir.org.co/web/category/jorge-enrique-robledo/page/181/*>.

31. SRK Consulting. "A N143-10 Mineral Resource Estimate on the Marmato Project, Colombia." *Grancolombia Gold*. Gran Colombia Gold Corp, April 9, 2011. Web. November 21, 2011. <*http://grancolombiagold.mediaroom.com/index.php?s=11316&item=53988*>.

32. Sánchez Cabra, Efraín. "El Museo del Oro". *Boletín Cultural y Bibliográfico*. 40.64 (2003): 3-48. Web. diciembre 8, 2011. <*http://www.banrepcultural.org/blaavirtual/publicacionesbanrep/boletín/boleti6/bol64/64-1.pdf*>.

33. Wilson, Scott. "Technical Report Medoro Resources". *Medoro Resources Webarchive*. Medoro Resources LTD, January 20, 2010. Web. January 8, 2012. <*file:///Volumes/Clip/Reporte-de-Medoro/2010.webarchive*>.

JANUARY 20, 2011

Santurbán: Gold v. Water

Greystar's Threat to Colombia

Last August 7 in his inaugural speech as President of Colombia, Juan Manuel Santos said: "We are a nation with one of the largest biological diversities in the world, and with a great supply of water. Therefore we are called upon to care for them for our own benefit and that of mankind...We will create the National Agency for Water Resources in order to guarantee greater protection of our natural resources." In another segment of his speech, President Santos emphasized the need to create jobs in order to reduce the highest unemployment rate in Latin America and he specifically pointed out focus areas which are indispensable if Colombia is to move forward, naming agricultural development, infrastructure construction, building of additional housing, mining development and technological innovation.

Based upon President Santos' speech, the challenges he must meet include protecting biodiversity, guaranteeing sources of potable water and creating employment for Colombia's millions of unemployed, while overseeing an increase in mining operations such as those planned for the Santurbán area.

Deep in the eastern mountain range of the Colombian Andes there is a collection of mountains known as Santurbán. This is a territory of "páramos," a Spanish term that in pre-Roman times meant "desolation." And the lands of the páramos are desolate, because they are found at an altitude of 3,000 to

5,000 meters. Their vegetation and grasses are appropriate for such heights. They are in permanent action, retaining water vapor from the ever-present fog and transforming it into liquid water. The secret of this process is in the nature of their soils, which are of volcanic origin and contain organic material and aluminum. The organic material accumulates, due to the low temperature in the páramos, which slows the activity of microbes. Upon combining with the aluminum, particles are formed which are resistant to decomposition. It is in this way that the soil retains water for long periods of time. Water is freed slowly and continuously. The páramos do not produce water. It comes from rain, fog and snow from higher altitudes, from snow-covered mountains above 5,000 meters. They collect water and regulate it.

For this reason the Andean páramos are considered natural "factories" of potable water. In addition, because of the very nature of their soil, the Andean páramos store carbon from the atmosphere and thus help to control global warming. These mountains may be able to offer a response to global warming and to the shortage of water.

In the specific case of Santurbán, its ecosystem shelters a high biodiversity in addition to providing water to rivers and ponds. Santurbán has 85 ponds which give origin to a number of rivers and streams that sustain agricultural production and cattle-raising in the low zones, as well as supplying water for the 2.2 million inhabitants of the cities of Bucaramanga and Cúcuta and 20 nearby municipalities.

The páramo of Santurbán holds 457 species of plants, among which stand out the frailejón subshrub, Espeletia conglomerate, ferns, orchids, mosses, lichens and the oak tree called Quercus Humboldtii. Colombia is the country with the largest number of species of birds in the world, and of these 201 are endemic to Santurbán. Many amphibians, such as frogs and lizards, and mammals, such as the Andean bear "Tremarcus Ornatus," a threatened species, live there. Santurbán also has a large expanse of swamps, called "turberas," which act as sponges with a greater or lesser amount of water, depending upon the time of year.

As the Madrid daily newspaper *El País* reported on December 5, 2010, in an analysis of the U.S. diplomatic cables released by WikiLeaks, "The priorities of Washington with respect to the South American subcontinent are clear: mines." That seems also to be true for Canada, given that the Canada-based multinational Greystar Resources Ltd. sought permission to mine for gold in the area of Santurbán, specifically near the stream of Angostura, from which the mining project takes its name.

In the municipalities of Vetas and California, the Spanish Crown took out gold beginning in 1513, in tunneled mines using artisan methods, to produce small amounts. Since that time, this is how mining has been done in Santurbán. But the technology of that time is different from the type of technology which Greystar wishes to use. Greystar, using an open-pit model, plans to excavate more than 2,700 acres and construct two piles of tailings and a dump at an altitude of 8,500 to 13,450 feet. The process uses heavy machinery to destroy the covering of vegetation for the purpose of exposing the soil, which will be removed with explosives. The hole which will be opened will be 656 feet deep and 1.075 billion tons of rock will be removed, of which 775 million tons will go to the dump, and 300 million tons will go to the leaching water basins. A total of .25 kilograms of explosives will be used per ton of rock removed per hour.

There will be two leaching water basins, one near the Angostura River and the other near a stream called Páez.[1] The cycle would be 60 days long, and the time of leaching would be 10 years. The amount of water used by the mine is calculated to be 250,000 liters per hour. Greystar plans to extract 11.5 million ounces of gold and 61 million ounces of silver over 15 years. When it leaves, it will leave behind the hole and the desert to remember it by.

This mine project generates many, many questions. What is going to happen to the 85 ponds? What is going to happen to the river basins of the Zulia and Lebrija Rivers, which are located in the mining zone? What is going to become of the Suratá, Toná and Frío Rivers, which supply drinking water to Bucaramanga? Near the city a dam is being built to supply drinking water to the one million inhabitants of Bucaramanga. Given that the Angostura project will affect the generation of water in the páramo, what is the dam for? The cyanide accumulated in the debris pile will degrade and go into the air, and therefore there is a risk of long-term contamination because it will originate acid rain. Imagine this in a region which is a peerless producer of water!

What will happen to the biodiversity and to species on the way to extinction which live in the páramo of Santurbán? What will happen to the millions of tons of earth impregnated with cyanide that the multinational is going to leave

1. Editor's note: The original article contained information for the amount of sodium cyanide used per liter of water and the amount of sodium cyanide for each water basin. The figures given could not be confirmed. For an explanation of the process referred to in this article, see Mark J. Logsdon, Karen Hagelstein and Terry L. Mudder, "The Management of Cyanide in Gold Extraction," published by the International Council on Metals and the Environment, April 1999.

behind? What will happen to the soils left sterile by the mining operation?

Some more questions come to mind. How is the groundwater going to be affected? By using so much water in the mine, the ground water currents will be weakened and the subsurface water will lose its potential at the same time as the soils that capture water are being removed. The ponds of water containing cyanide could break because of an excess of rain or an earthquake or tremor—so frequent in these mountains—and this could lead to the presence of cyanide in the rivers that come from the high areas of the páramo and that supply water to the populations and cities below. The transportation of cyanide, especially in the higher reaches of the mountains, is risky given the very nature of the mountain land, the insecure climatic conditions and the primitive construction of the roads.

Before he left office as President, Álvaro Uribe signed mining concessions in most of the Colombian páramos. The political web page *La Silla Vacía* on October 14, 2010, reported that during the eight years of his [Uribe's] presidency, the number of hectares with mining concessions increased from 1.13 million to 8.53 million, 6.3 percent of which were in the páramos. Remarkably, all of this happened after the Colombian Congress had passed a reform in the Mining Code forbidding mining on páramos. Uribe delayed signing the legislation for eight months; meanwhile, his administration granted numerous mining permits to multinational mining companies.

The 1991 Colombian Constitution orders the protection of areas of ecological importance and of natural resources. In fact, Law 1382 of 2010 expressly amended Article 34 of the Mining Code to forbid mining in páramos.

Colombian leaders will do anything except solve the structural problems of injustice. If developing the economy brings with it the destruction of the great biodiversity of the country, so be it. There is no hurry to find other forms of development that do not include mining. To give the páramos to the rapacious multinational corporations, which are only interested in extracting the mineral wealth, knowing that mining always brings environmental consequences in a country like Colombia, is as suicidal as if Saudi Arabia would decide to burn its oil fields.

And, as far as creating employment is concerned, experience in other Colombian mining operations shows that the permanent positions created are quite few in number. According to George Pierce, a truck mechanic from the U.S. who worked for several years at a Drummond coal mine in Colombia, after the infrastructure of the mine has been set up, much of the permanent employment goes to experienced workers from abroad.

There is a new element in this case in relation to Greystar. The Colombian Constitution provides that the local population must be consulted before mining may start and only with local permission can work start. Greystar has assured the local people that its presence will bring benefits, such as giving scholarships for the children and taking them on field trips, building greenhouses to grow endemic plants for reforestation and, of course, creating jobs. It is true there will be new jobs while the mine site is being prepared, but after that most jobs will be for technical personnel coming from outside. The locals are really enthusiastic and support the coming of the mining company.[2] This is different from what mining companies have done in southern Bolívar state, where they have used paramilitaries to displace the local population. Worthy of note is the participation of the World Bank, which has investments in Greystar through its International Finance Corporation.[3] This seems inconsistent with the Bank's presenting itself as defending the environment. See www.ifc.org/.

The Colombian government ought to suspend the concession of mining rights in the zones which are producers of water. Its responsibility is not only to Colombia, but also to the planet itself. Santurbán should be declared a national park, and the small-scale local and informal mining in the lower areas should be regulated. Ecological tourism could offer an excellent alternative. It is time for the government of Colombia to put aside the insanity of exploiting the natural resources of the country at the service of the highest bidder. It

2. Editor's note: When Greystar announced its plan to develop an open-pit mine in Santurbán, a crowd estimated at 100,000 people took to the streets of Bucaramanga carrying signs reading "Agua Si, Oro No" ("Water Yes, Gold No") and chanting these words. Given the strong popular reaction against the mining plan, a public hearing was scheduled to determine if a license should be granted to Greystar for the mine. An estimated 2,000 persons attended the meeting, which was held in a large auditorium in the city of Girón, a suburb of Bucaramanga, on March 4, 2011. Most speakers at the meeting, including Santander Governor Horacio Serpa and a representative of Bucaramanga's Mayor, spoke out against the mining plan, and Senator Jorge Enrique Robledo, who was in attendance, indicated his objection to the proposed mine. The meeting was adjourned when a fist fight broke out between an opponent of the Greystar plan and a supporter of the plan. No permit was granted to Greystar Resources Ltd. The description of the proceedings at the March 4 meeting is based upon the observations of Jack Laun, who attended the meeting. Reference "REPORT ON SANTURBÁN MINING PROJECT OF GREYSTAR RESOURCES" by Jack Laun, March 14, 2011.

3. Editor's note: Greystar Resources Ltd. changed its name to Eco Oro Minerals Corp effective August 16, 2011. Eco Oro has pursued a multi-million dollar claim against the Colombian Government for lost potential revenue due to restrictions on its proposed mining activities at its Santurbán site. See "Eco Oro Minerals Corp. v. Republic of Colombia, ICSID Case No. ARB/16/41." A request for arbitration was filed on December 8, 2016.

should begin to think about the benefit to the people of Colombia, who deserve a future of respect and wellbeing for all, and not place itself at the service of the greed of foreign investors.

President Santos must take seriously his promise of defending Colombia's immense biodiversity and its water resources by making creative proposals that respect the environment. If he has the courage to do so, he will have an important place in Colombia's history.

2005

Background on San José de Apartadó

San José de Apartadó is a little village, and also a corregimiento, or district, in the old Spanish system, located in the Abibe Mountain Range, which is a natural corridor connecting the provinces, called "Departments" in Colombia, of Córdoba, Antioquia and Chocó in the northwestern part of Colombia. Administratively, it is attached to the municipality of Apartadó, Department of Antioquia, in the Urabá region.

The zone of Urabá, originally a jungle frontier region, began to be cleared by peasants who in the 1950s fled from the partisan violence in the rest of Colombia. Soon it was obvious that the region was ideal for the growing of bananas as an agrarian industry, besides having the advantage of being close to the sea.

The urban center of San José and the settlements of La Unión and Arenas Altas make up the Peace Community, which has a population of 1,200 persons. The municipality of Apartadó has a population of 125,000 inhabitants. Both the highlands and the low areas are fertile and bananas, cacao, avocados, fine wood trees and vegetable gardens grow well there. The headwaters of the Apartadó, Río Grande, Carepa, Currulao and Mulatos rivers form in San José.

At the end of the 1980s and in the 1990s, committees of social scientists were brought together by the Colombian government to analyze the terrible violence in the region. They concluded that it originated in the labor-management relations in the banana industry. A 1987 report described the banana business leaders as rapacious and absentee owners. Others indicated that the violence in the region came from the militarization of the social conflicts and that its roots were in the terrible inequalities brought about by the enclave economy, inasmuch as the great profits generated by the exportation of bananas were not invested in the region, and the concentration of wealth left the workers without decent minimum wages for subsistence. [20)]

It is worth remembering a little history. Colombia traditionally has had two political parties, the Conservatives and the Liberals. These parties have excluded other organized political movements, relying upon the assassination of political opponents if necessary. This exclusionary characteristic is one of the reasons for the appearance of guerrilla movements, together with the social and economic exclusion of the majority of the population on the part of the Colombian elite. In the 1980s in an attempt at a negotiated solution, a third party, the Unión Patriótica (Patriotic Union), was created as a result of an agreement between the Colombian government and the FARC (Fuerzas Armadas Revolucionarias de Colombia) guerrillas. Many persons not only from the FARC but also from civil society who were not satisfied with the two traditional parties joined the new party.

The region of Urabá was a stronghold of the Liberal Party until the Patriotic Union arrived. The majority of the population of the banana belt began to elect mayors from the Patriotic Union (Unión Patriótica, UP). These UP mayors improved the road to San José, the health center and the school serving the community. Before the road was built, the peasants had to carry their products on their backs or on mules.

The Liberal Party decided to retake these mayorships through something they called "Operation Return." They did not find it inconvenient to ally themselves with paramilitaries, drug traffickers and the region's economic powers. Almost all the UP mayors of the region were assassinated or put in prison after they were set up on the basis of false information, as was the case for Nelson Campo, who is still in prison, or is the case of José Antonio López-Bula, who upon leaving prison was forced to live in exile. Much of what we saw in San José has to do with its history.

In one visit by a Colombia Support Network delegation to Apartadó, the then Mayor from the Patriotic Union Party, José Antonio López-Bula, told us that the municipal government had attempted to collect municipal taxes from the banana business owners. They simply refused to pay. The municipality appealed the decision but their refusal was upheld by the national government, leaving the municipality without the valuable resources that would have come from taxing the banana-growing sector.

This situation of outright exploitation gave rise to a very active civic and labor organization movement. Cattlemen and drug traffickers, with the tacit approval of the Army, established private forces which not only resorted to killing leaders of the people, but also used the atrocious strategy of mass murders to eliminate the popular movements. Their purpose was to spread terror. Between 1988 and 1990, figures show that in Apartadó more than 400 people were murdered for political reasons, especially workers, political activists and labor leaders.[20] These "paramilitary" forces aided by the Army were trying to "clean up" the region, as General Rito Alejo del Río, Commander of the 17th Brigade and a graduate of the School of the Americas, plainly told a Colombia Support Network delegation, "We invite you to invest in the region. There are no union problems. The region is clean."

On June 9, 2005, the Office of the Comptroller General of Colombia published a document entitled "The Effort at Agrarian Reform and the Process of Attachment and Extinguishing of Rural Properties," in which it concludes that what has happened in Colombia is a counter-agrarian reform due to drug trafficking. Land ownership has been concentrated, and 48 percent of the best lands of the country belong to the drug traffickers, while 68 percent of the other landowners—peasants—possess only 5.2 percent of such lands. The report states as a certainty that the food security of the country is threatened. (*El Tiempo*, Thursday, June 9, 2005)

These lands are located in frontier zones and are linked to the production of illegal crops and cocaine laboratories. In this way, by buying land, the drug traffickers become linked to legal activities and appear to be businessmen. Behind this lies the forced violence by which the lands are acquired, using private armies as paramilitaries. This is the origin of the 3.5 million displaced persons in Colombia. The enviable location of San José and its admirable political organization are the principal reasons for its martyrdom.

DON BARTOLO FOUNDS A LITTLE TOWN

Don Bartolomé Cataño, a 75-year-old peasant, founded the small settlement of San José de Apartadó in 1970. With a sweet smile and a quick speech, he welcomed the CSN delegation and told us that he represented the peasantry of the region at the city council on the ticket of the Unión Patriótica. He came to Apartadó in 1966, seeking an opportunity after working for others since he was seven years old. He bought a small plot in the beautiful lands he found in the Serranía de Abibe, got married at 36 and started to raise pigs and chickens. He built a small house and took leadership training courses offered by the Peasant Association. He liked the courses because they not only trained him but spoke of the need for agrarian reform.

Soon 17 other peasant families came to live in the area where he was located. They worked the land from 5 a.m. to 6 p.m. planting food crops such as bananas, manioc, plantains, corn, beans, avocados and cocoa beans to sell. They built a school and a health center and constructed the road. They called it San José because he is the patron saint of the peasants who till the land.[25)]

The Community of San José got along well with the labor movement, and a number of its young people even joined the guerrillas. The political movement Patriotic Union was especially popular in the region. The Patriotic Union originated in a negotiation between the Colombian Government and the guerrillas of the FARC. The purpose was to reach a negotiated solution to the conflict. The people of San José were especially attracted to one of the methods of emancipating the peasant farmers, namely the establishment of agricultural cooperatives. This seemed to lead to healing because what the powerful owners had been trying to do was to annihilate the social and political dissent militarily. Don Bartolo and the Community organized the Balsamar Cooperative to process and market their cocoa beans rather than sell them to middlemen.

On August 17, 1996, at 11:30 a.m., unidentified armed men burst into the City Council chambers in Apartadó and shot Don Bartolo twice. He started calmly to pick up his papers when a third shot, directed to his face, killed the founder of San José de Apartadó.

Its support for the Patriotic Union contributed to make the San José Community a target in the war. In addition, the location of the settlement, together with the existence of a coal deposit in the region where it is located, made it particularly attractive to those who wished to take possession of the land away from the peasant farmers. Thus began the abuses, and many San José residents were exiled to the city of Apartadó, protesting the repression. A committee sent by the national government negotiated with the leaders of the exiles in order to get them to return to their land.

On September 6, 1996, a group of armed men dragged the leaders of the protest out of their houses and killed them. In February 1997, a group of 40 paramilitaries which had opposed the Patriotic Union's electoral successes, most of the paramilitaries "reinsertados"[1] from the EPL (Ejército Popular de Liberación/Popular Liberation Army) guerrilla movement, entered the town at 6 in the morning, pulled the four leaders of the Balsamar Cooperative from their beds and beheaded them, leaving their bodies in the road. When the brave Mayor of Apartadó, Gloria Cuartas, called the government prosecutor's office so that the bodies could be removed by the Police following judicial inspection, she was able to observe how the paramilitaries gathered around the improvised grave where the bodies had been placed and how the paramilitaries greeted the soldiers who were guarding the prosecutors as their "cousins." 25)

Beginning in March 1997, the paramilitaries took absolute control of the road from San José to Apartadó. They controlled the transport of food and medicine; they inspected every passenger with lists in their hands. Whoever appeared on the lists or whoever looked suspicious was murdered. The paramilitaries' checkpoint was located about five minutes from a military post in the Policarpa neighborhood of Apartadó. A delegation from CSN had the opportunity to observe these paramilitaries, armed and wearing numerous gold chains in order to demonstrate their authority. Multiple disappearances, murders and pillage took place at this checkpoint, where they behaved as if they were agents of the government.

THE SIXTH OPTION

The bloodshed in the Community of San José, because its location in a corridor of confrontation between the FARC guerrillas and a bloc made up of the Army and the AUC paramilitaries made it so vulnerable, was profoundly worrying to various entities of the church. Because of that, beginning at the end of 1996, the Diocese of Apartadó began to discuss with members of the Community a proposal to establish themselves as a "Peace Community," which would adopt some very precise and verifiable rules calling for no collaboration with any of the armed actors. The idea was to get the war out of their Community by declaring themselves neutral. They carried out numerous educational programs with leaders of the Community to achieve a collective reflection agreement of what this proposal meant.

Given the political environment, the peasants of San José courageously decided to declare themselves to be neutral, which means not allied with any of the armed actors: Army, guerrillas or paramilitaries. This single act was

1. Editor's note: A *reinsertado* is an armed actor who gives up his arms and re-enters civilian society. In this case, however, the EPL guerrilla became a paramilitary member.

one of the first public demonstrations of non-violent resistance in a country where traditionally only violent means are used to solve conflicts. The option of nonviolence was compared to their other alternatives which were:

1. They may join the paramilitaries or become supporters of their agenda, which is to maintain the socio-economic status quo.
2. They may leave for the cities, where they will live in slums and become beggars, prostitutes or street children.
3. They may join the guerrillas and engage in conflict with the Army-supported paramilitaries.
4. They may journey to the rainforest in southern Colombia, cut trees and plant coca to make cocaine paste, the only crop which can bring them profits, given the lack of roads, agricultural credit and extension services or price supports for growing and marketing traditional crops.
5. One armed actor or another may kill them if they do not accept one of the four alternatives preceding this one.

After carefully thinking about these options, the peasants from San José, with the help of the late Monsignor Isaías Duarte Cancino, Bishop of Apartadó at the time, Gloria Cuartas, Mayor of Apartadó at the time, and Colombian NGOs such as Justicia y Paz and CINEP, decided to create an alternative, or a sixth option: to remain together tilling their lands and caring for their orchards and animals. They concluded this was the only thing they knew how to do.

After a period of preparation, on March 23, 1997, Palm Sunday on the Catholic calendar, the declaration was signed in a solemn ceremony. A number of members of the Parliament of the Netherlands were present. The peasant farmers committed themselves to comply with the public declaration which established that they would:

- Participate in Community work projects
- Fight for justice and against impunity
- Not participate in the war, directly or indirectly
- Not use weapons
- Not manipulate or deliver information to any of the parties
- Look for a peaceful and negotiated solution to the country's conflict [20),22)]

In that month of March, the process of nonviolent resistance of the Community of San José de Apartadó began, joined by peasant farmers from 16 small settlements in the region, including La Unión, Arenas Altas y Bajas, La Cristalina, Mulatos Medio y Alto, La Resbalosa, Las Nieves, El Guineo, La Linda, Alto Bonito, Las Playas, Porvenir, Buenos Aires, La Esperanza and Bellavista.

WHAT DOES IT MEAN TO BE A PEACE COMMUNITY?

The Peace Community is three things: a territory, a political decision and a peasant farmer association for raising and selling food products.

The Peace Community is a territory clearly designated and demarcated as a neutral zone, with flags and fences that identify the territory as a neutral territory. It is made up of the town limits of San José, the settlement of La Unión, the fields and workplaces of Community residents and the sources of water and energy. In this way geographical limits were established against the war. As small settlements join the process, they are also being demarcated. The members of the Community carry an identity card stating that they are accredited members of the Community.[2]

The Peace Community is a political decision or option because it was created as an organized response to a situation of war whose principal victims are members of the civilian population. In joining together, they seek power not just against the armed actors but against their ways, which are vertical, exclusionary and discriminatory. By opposing these ways, the Community generates participation that is pluralist and that reinforces the autonomy of these communities in constructing an alternative that is different from that of weapons and economic power.

In order to belong to the Community, every person takes part in workshops where the essence of the process and the commitments that are made are explained. The decision is free and voluntary. The workshops are produced together, and they set forth ways of relating to one another so that the Community struggles as one unit to protect the lives of all. The relationship among them is circular because all take part and all have the right to make decisions.

Ethically, the Community shares the conviction that you cannot think in terms of "you and I," but you have to think of "we," so that every time they take an action, they do it with the knowledge of how it affects others. That is why it is so important for them to strengthen Community ties, especially through work and through the celebration of the system every three months. The purpose of that is to reinforce their group consciousness. Their unity is their strength.

2. Editor's note: As discussed later in this article, the Peace Community responded to the vicious murder of its designated representative, Luis Eduardo Guerra, and seven other persons on February 21, 2005 by moving to a new settlement they built on land they owned about one kilometer away from the town of San José. They called the new town "San Josecito."

The respect for pluralism and individual liberty is another source of strength because every Community and every member makes decisions autonomously, without pressure and without feeling excluded when they are not part of the majority. Another admirable quality is their transparency. Before, in order to survive in a war zone, they had to tell lies to the armed actors. This Community bases its possibility of survival upon speaking openly to the armed actors, telling them that they cannot collaborate with them because that would involve them in a war in which they have declared their neutrality.

By seeking the common good, they are seeking to humanize their living together; creating relationships takes into account the situation of everyone because they are talking about defending their very lives. When a situation arises that puts one person's life at risk, the others have to insist on respect. That is what they experienced when the paramilitaries installed their checkpoints for nine months. They stopped cars and killed whomever they wanted to. The Community demanded that their process of neutrality be respected.

Pretty soon in the workshops people started asking: Why are we resisting? We are resisting because this is an unjust situation. We resist because they are attacking us. Out of that discussion came one of their most important principles, which is to fight against injustice and impunity as an integral part of their strategy.

The philosophy of the Community creates a kind of relationship and attitudes based upon new values, such as liberty, equality, respect, solidarity and dialogue, as an answer to the old ways of thinking based above all on power over everyone and everything. Another new idea is the manner of conflict resolution, departing from violence and based on dialog and working for the good of all. Good places for settling differences are the workshops in the different towns, or work groups or committees, where town residents discuss their accomplishments and the difficulties they are experiencing, and they can all meet face-to-face.

The initiatives for confronting problems are taken together. For example, one of the decisions the Community made is that they prohibit the sale and consumption of liquor. The decision was taken because it is a method for avoiding any violent situation or disturbance which might serve as an excuse for the intervention of any of the armed actors.

HOW ARE THEY ORGANIZED?

Part of their training is that the Community exercises leadership and every person has the capacity to raise her/his voice to suggest plans, to discuss and to make demands. As they told our CSN delegation, "Before when we would go alone to work up in the mountains, we were afraid to go because, as a peasant farmer, a person feels afraid; but now when we go in a group, you feel more strength and you can see how fear had kept us apart..." As was said before, all of the members commit themselves to work together. This allows them to practice the principle of solidarity and of unity, so that a person isn't thinking so much of his/her own interests but rather of the well-being of the whole Community.

Internal Council

This is the highest authority in the Community. Its fundamental mission is to guide the survival and development of the Peace Community (respecting and requiring respect for its rules and principles), and to represent the Community in its relations with the Government and national and international institutions. The Council is responsible for strengthening the experience of neutrality and resistance from the political and solidarity point of view and for seeing to it that the rules and declarations of the Peace Community are carried out.

The Internal Council is chosen democratically by the people aged 12 years or older, because it is from this age that all the men and women can decide freely if they want to take part in the Peace Community. (Only persons 18 years or older may serve on the Council.) The Council gathers those who represent the agreement to carry out this experience of civil resistance.

The Internal Council coordinates activities and resolves conflicts through dialogue, tracks the work groups and coordinates visits of delegations to the Community. Every six months the Community chooses the members of the Council and the Coordinators by means of a free and voluntary vote.

The Community gets together in the small towns and reflects on the characteristics that a member of the Internal Council ought to have, and based on that, the people in the towns propose candidates. Later they make a list of the candidates and a day is chosen for elections. The eight people who receive the most votes are the new members of the Council.

There are several work groups, and each one has a coordinator who sees how the work is going and reports on the needs and accomplishments of each group. There are a number of work groups made up just of men, some made up just of women and some that are mixed. These work groups are not only in charge of accomplishing private production (cacao and banana primarily) but also of cultivating products for the self-support that guarantees a certain security of food supply for the Community. For example, the coordinators organize the assistance that comes into the Community.

There are also committees that interact with the Internal Council. The committees propose and carry out, according to their specific areas of work, the tasks necessary for the sustenance and progress of the Peace Community.

Formation

This committee is made up of four women who work with Community members to carry out workshops and meetings on subjects that reinforce the internalization of the process of nonviolent resistance. Given the high percentage of illiteracy, they prefer to use teaching techniques that favor unwritten expression: drawing, singing and poetry.

Communication

This committee has been responsible for the establishment of a radio station that is available to the Community, and they have trained personnel to arrange for programs that they want to put on. Unfortunately, up to now it has not been possible for them to obtain a license from the Ministry of Communications to put this Community radio proposal into operation. In the same way, the communication committee has coordinated the carrying out of several written publications about the Community and has furnished the photos and graphics that appear in those publications.

Sports

This committee coordinates the carrying out of games (especially soccer). The members of the Peace Community and neighboring villages take part.

Economics

This is possibly the most active committee. It coordinates the purchase and later marketing of cacao, baby bananas and avocados as the principal products for the economic support of the Community.[3] This committee has led an interesting process of formation and training in order to obtain products of export quality in the case of baby bananas. 22)

THE REACTION

Of course the Army and the paramilitaries did not accept this type of "neutrality." Cutting relations with the guerrillas would amount to neutrality for them, but that a community would decide not to participate in the war, also

3. Editor's note: The Peace Community of San José de Apartadó has since obtained certification for export of cacao to England to be made into skin cream. This is now a major source of income for the community.

denying to *them* information and sale of food, and would require that *they* not enter the territory with weapons, that was too much. Because of that, they determined to destroy the Community.

For their part, the FARC targeted the Community because it would not sell them food and would not offer them any kind of collaboration. On October 6, 1997, the FARC killed Ramiro Correa, who was a member of the Internal Council. Since then the FARC have killed 19 members of the Community.

The moving ceremony of March 23, 1997, was an incentive to repression by those who opposed the Community. The Community had to become accustomed to living with terror because the murders, the disappearances and many other strategies of extermination, such as the blockade of food supplies, just motivated them. By now some six drivers who transported necessary food supplies between Apartadó and San José have been killed. The Community had to organize planting of Community crops for the emergency. Often when they have had to go out to work in fields not very far from the town, there would be 40 or 50 persons, hand-in-hand for mutual protection, and they would return in the evening surrounded by armed squads who would point their machine guns at the group. [20)]

By the end of 1997, the Peace Community of San José counted 47 victims killed, the majority murdered or disappeared, with great barbarity. It was a high price to pay while other communities had been forced into total disintegration and hiding out. But the existence of the Peace Community of San José continued in heroic resistance in the midst of the terror.

In December 1997, the Inter-American Commission for Human Rights visited the Community because of the difficult situation they were experiencing, because of the numbers of murders that were taking place and because the number of widows and orphans was increasing. By December of 1997, the little hamlet's residents had left because of the terror that was spread by the joint actions of the military forces and the paramilitaries. The inhabitants of San José have never been able to discover any differences between the Army and the paramilitaries, especially when a paramilitary checkpoint was installed about five minutes from the military checkpoint on the road between San José and Apartadó. It was not even necessary to complain to the Inter-American Commission about this situation because they themselves were able to see it directly. But they were not the only ones observing. The United Nations Office of Human Rights and many other international organizations had seen it. [20)]

The Inter-American Commission adopted *precautionary protective measures*

Cecilia with Father John Dear, Director of the Fellowship of Reconciliation, as he presented the Pfeffer Peace Prize to the Peace Community of San Jose de Apartado Leader Tuberquia in Madison in 1998.

in favor of the Community and demanded that the Government take the measures necessary for the respect and preservation of the lives and the rights of the Community. In spite of that, impunity and terror continued. The Commission was witness to the increasing number of actions taken by the paramilitaries against the Community and to the fact that they acted together with the Armed Forces. At that time, the Attorney General, the Public Prosecutor and the Ombudsman made visits to the Community, heard testimony and summoned people to Apartadó where the people got together. In spite of that, the facts have demonstrated that impunity reigned and reigns to this day. [20)]

On February 19, 2000, the Army was all over and located on every part of the road. More than 15 soldiers, wearing uniforms that they wore regularly and insignias of the 17th Brigade, entered the town. Among them soldiers who had taken part in murders were recognized. They had acted as informants at the checkpoints on the road located at three and six kilometers from the Community. During that incursion they killed five people without any hesitation or shame.

After that came the threats from the Army: They said that they were going to finish off both the leaders and the Community. As a matter of fact, there was no need to wait. In July of the same year, after explicit threats from members of the Armed Forces against the Community of La Unión, unknown men entered La Unión wearing hoods and supported by a helicopter from the 17th Brigade that was flying over at a very low altitude. They assembled the members of the Community and sought out the leaders, those who had proclaimed the principles and the decisions of the Community, according to which no armed actor was to enter the territory, since the decision was that the Community would rather die than renounce those principles. And, in fact, that is what happened. The paramilitaries ordered them to lie down, but the leaders refused to do so, and they were killed standing on their feet, defending their Community. There, on July 8, 2000, lay, in the very center of the town, the bodies of six Community leaders, while the hooded men returned to the Army's location. 1)

One week earlier, a CSN delegation had visited La Unión, and the leaders who were murdered on July 8 had proudly showed delegation members how they were stocking fish in a lake to add to the Community's food supply and how they were rebuilding the cacao plantings that had been damaged after the last displacement.

SEEKING JUSTICE

As the years passed, the atrocities multiplied.

The situation reached incredible levels. In February 2000, after the Community had talked directly with the military commanders in order to explain to them their system and after the commanders had promised to respect it, expressing their admiration for the decision, there came actions so brutal and so painful that the Community reached the unavoidable decision not to have further discussions with the Armed Forces, a decision that they maintain today.

Because of this situation, the same Inter-American Commission requested that the Inter-American Court adopt provisional remedies in favor of the Community. When that request was made of the government of then-President Andrés Pastrana, the Community met with Vice President Gustavo Bell and proposed the creation of a Special Investigation Commission. After a number of discussions, the Commission was created, made up of the Ombudsman's office, the Public Prosecutor's office, the Attorney General's office and the office of the Vice President, with the observation of the United Nations Office for Human Rights.

In September of 2000, members of that Commission made their first visit to the places where the crimes had taken place. Right there they began to find evidence of the participation of the Armed Forces and they expressed their astonishment at such circumstances. They combined the visits that they would be carrying out in order to comply with the two objectives that had been proposed at the creation of the Commission: to understand, in spite of impunity, and to halt these actions of death against the Community.

The years went by, and the atrocities multiplied, evidencing the circle of impunity and the perpetuation of terror against the Community. More than 80 declarations were made to the Investigating Commission by members of the Community. There were meetings held to receive reports, as had been agreed to, but no progress could ever be perceived.

The Government never took any measures that would show compassion, in any degree, for the terror that was being inflicted on the Community. The killing and threats continued to increase; the burning of houses was frequent, and above all, every military operation was accompanied by paramilitary operatives supported by the Armed Forces. Almost every day there was displacement and the murder of members of the Community increased without let-up. They were robbed of their produce and of the money they obtained by selling it. Many women were raped. They also killed many members of the Community or inhabitants of the area at the checkpoints. Frequently they would carry out target practice very early in the morning in locations near to the Community.

The Community has collected many testimonies, offering declarations before prosecutors and attorney general's staff and before the members of the useless Investigation Commission. Instead of seeing resulting justice, they have seen death and threats to the people who made the declarations, without any unit of the justice system showing any interest in protecting them nor offering any measure of protection. Obviously, the testimony of the Community is limited because they don't have the means to demand that their victimizers identify themselves or give them their name, rank and serial number, nor are they able to photograph or videotape them or write down their license plates or insignia, which they don't ordinarily wear. That is what the investigating agencies have demanded in order for the testimony to be valid. Many of the files that are being stored only contain the testimony that the Community has given, and that turns into a high risk for those who have made statements, but you can see that they are not looking for proof in the camps of the victimizers. They only look in the area of the victims. And those proofs, given the little credibility that the functionaries of the justice system give to the testimony of the victims, and given the disdain, and not infrequently, the aggression and suspicion with which they treat those who are victims of those same agents of the Government, these files are turned into proceedings that are useless as well as dangerous. They only serve to "demonstrate" that the justice system is not permanently inactive. But the overwhelming truth is that there is no result that can be shown. [18)]

Because of all that and because of the number of inquiries that prestigious international organizations have made to the Prosecutor's office, with some very worrisome indications that the Prosecutor's office has been infiltrated by the paramilitaries, the Peace Community has begged that members of their Community not be asked to make any more declarations. They ask that formulas be sought so that the information that they have and that they could furnish to the investigation of these crimes be provided in another manner to the judicial process, preserving the safety of the witnesses because they don't want to have any more murders.

And it is thus that in November of 2002, the Community proposed to Vice President Francisco Santos that there be an evaluation of the Investigation and that a Truth Commission be created, to be made up of delegates from national and international organizations of high credibility, that there be an inventory of all the crimes of which the Community has been the victim, evaluation of responsibility for such crimes and delivery to the government of recommendations to avoid such crimes being repeated.

On that same date, they asked that the office of Vice President Francisco Santos assume the coordination of preventive actions, with the goal of stopping the bloodshed and the acts of terror against the Community. At the same time, they asked that preventive measures be taken, such as: repair of the road; the prompt return of displaced persons; projects for education, especially in the little towns; projects that permit the assimilation of the culture of peace; furnishing regular health services, since the terrible stress in which they have had to live aggravates all illnesses; as well as normal transportation of food, which is related to the elemental right to life.

On April 15, 2004, the Constitutional Court of Colombia issued its decision T-558/03 in which it emphasized the obligation of the Colombian government to carry out the interim equitable relief and provisional remedies ordered by the Inter-American Commission and the Inter-American Court for Human Rights.

THE POLICY OF DEMOCRATIC SECURITY[4]

Attempting to appear as if they were complying with the order to protect the Community issued by the Commission and the Inter-American Court, the government of Álvaro Uribe Vélez made a proposal for Security and Protection to the Peace Community. This proposal was made within the parameters of

4. Editor's note: For a critique and additional understanding of the concept of "democratic security," see Cecilia's article "The Insecurity of Democratic Security" in this volume.

Democratic Security, which plans a military presence in every corner of the country. In this case, it means proposing the presence of the Police. It should be clarified that in Colombia the Police are national and part of the Army.

After analyzing this proposal, the Internal Council expressed profound discomfort with the proposal that the National Police would carry out the project of security and protection, given that the Peace Community has suffered so many attacks by the Police and given the close relationship between the Police and the paramilitaries in this area.

Elements of the Police have facilitated and protected the movements of the paramilitaries when they come to commit their crimes against the Peace Community; they work in coordination with them and they have demonstrated their complicity with them. In areas where there is strict control by the Police, such as the Transportation Terminal in Apartadó, the paramilitaries are at large; they threaten members of the Community; they announce and carry out blockades; they rob and kidnap members of the Community, many times before killing them or “disappearing” them. [18)]

The Internal Council asks what could be expected in the way of protection and security from two government institutions like the Army and the Police, made up of officers and soldiers and police who torture, who carry out massacres, murders, disappearances, sexual abuses, and burn down houses, force displacement, threaten, plunder, perform acts of terrorism, deceive, arbitrarily and illegally detain, etc. They act without even the slightest reparations for the victims, whose losses make it hard for them to continue surviving in the difficult conditions of their social situation. Reparations such as, for example, returning the stolen food and money, returning the mules that are their fundamental means of transportation, returning their domestic animals and their work tools, and rebuilding the houses they have destroyed. There have never been explanations, punishment, correction or reparations for the crimes done and no convincing or credible explanations.

The other concern is that the presence of armed persons in the village could attract insurgent groups planning to attack them. This puts the civilian population in the midst of the conflict. For the last several years, the Community has been demanding respect for its neutral position. They will not collaborate with any armed actor, and they require that no arms exist in their Community space where they live and work. The Army, just like the Police, when they have penetrated into the Community space, trampling its internal regulations, have been very explicit in saying that they do it so that the guerrillas can attack them all together so that all can "die together under the weapons of the guerrillas."

It is worth remembering that in 1998 the then Commander of the Armed Forces of Colombia, General José Manuel Bonnet, told a delegation from CSN that he did not believe in neutrality, and that whoever is not for the Army is against it.

PECULIAR CHARACTERS FOR THE APPLICATION OF DEMOCRATIC SECURITY IN APARTADÓ

In this history of pain and anguish, of love and hate, of loyalty and treason, of sincerity and cynicism, of heroes and villains, of justice and injustice, there are some characters that stand out. One is Wilmar Durango. Another is Colonel Néstor Iván Duque, commander of the Bejarano-Muñoz battalion attached to the 17th Brigade with its headquarters in Carepa. The things that these two have done are inexorably linked to all the development of events in San José, just as cloudy skies are linked to storms.

On December 9, 2003, at 2:40 p.m., a jeep of Peace Brigades International (PBI), an organization that accompanies the Peace Community, was detained by paramilitaries as it left Apartadó on the road to San José. Two persons of the Peace Brigades and a leader of the Peace Community were in the jeep. When the car braked, three men with small arms and one with a bag over his head, which covered his face, surrounded the vehicle. The three armed men pointed their guns at the passengers. They identified themselves as paramilitaries, and after insulting the people in the car and threatening them, one of the paramilitaries opened the window and took away the money which the Community leader was carrying, which had come from the sale of cacao and totaled 24.5 million pesos. This money was the fruit of the Community's work in planting, harvesting and selling the cocoa beans, which was one of the Community's sources of income. In addition, the paramilitaries took away the cellular phones of the PBI accompaniers. They then ran away through the nearest banana fields. Five minutes later the jeep came upon a military checkpoint. There the two PBI persons and the Peace Community leader told the soldiers at the checkpoint what had just happened to them. [15)]

Clearly, by taking away the money of the Peace Community the paramilitaries attacked the subsistence of the Community, which has an economy of a communitarian nature. This was the fifth time that the resources, which the Community had obtained with so much suffering and work, were lost. The objective of those effectively in power in the region is to combine a political attack with an economic one to exterminate this process of nonviolent resistance.

On December 14, 2003, at 4:30 p.m., a leader of the Peace Community received a telephone call in San José de Apartadó. On the line was Wilmar Durango, who began to insult the Peace Community leader, telling him that he was a son-of-a-bitch and the Community was a son-of-a-bitch, and telling the Community leader that he (Durango) was working with the paramilitaries. Durango went on to ask how the Community felt about the robbery of its money, which he said they had done, saying it was a beautiful job done by the paramilitaries. Then he said the next step would follow, which would be that they will begin to kill the Community's leaders one-by-one. Even if they are especially careful, he said, these sons-of-bitches Community leaders would wind up in a tomb, that the son-of-a-bitch leaders of the Community did not have any way of escape, and that he who is not killed now would be killed in prison. [4),5),12)]

On February 3, 2004, Wilmar Durango was seen patrolling with the Army in the settlement of Guineo Alto. Besides this, he was with Army troops on February 23 when they stole cattle from one of the Community members. Durango entered San José with a mask on and he walked around the houses of several Community leaders.

On March 3, 2004, in the bus terminal of Apartadó, Durango stopped a member of the Peace Community and told him that he, Durango, was working with the Army and one of the essential objectives which they had was to assassinate Wilson David (Coordinator General of the Community). In addition, he said they had to kill several other persons from San José. In January 2004, Durango had announced that he had orders from paramilitary commander Salvatore Mancuso to do away with the Community. He also said that even though the Community had international accompaniment, they were going to destroy it, especially the president of the Internal Council, Wilson David. [6),13)]

Since he was working with the Army and the paramilitaries, he felt very secure. He asked for silence with respect to the theft of money and repeated that the sentence against Wilson David would be carried out. "If you continue to denounce what happens to you," he said, "it will be even worse for you."

On June 3, 2004, Wilmar Durango again approached members of the Community to tell them that there were three witnesses who would be disposed to make declarations against Wilson David and others, and if this did not work out right, the decision had already been made to murder them. [16)]

On October 2, 2004, at 12:30 p.m., four paramilitaries intercepted a public vehicle which was traveling between San José and Apartadó. They ordered all passengers to get out of the vehicle, except Yorbelis Amparo Restrepo, a 27-year-old woman who lived in the Community. While the passengers were getting out of the vehicle, the paramilitaries insulted them, telling them they were going to exterminate the Community because it was a guerrilla community. The paramilitaries then drove off with the vehicle. At 6 o'clock that afternoon the lifeless body of Yorbelis was found. Wilmar Durango had threatened her with death. Yorbelis, a single mother, left three children.

Colonel Néstor Iván Duque, Commander of the Bejarano-Muñoz Army Battalion, which is assigned to San José, has distinguished himself as being the very incarnation of the application of the policy of Democratic Security of President Uribe for the Peace Community. The objective of this policy is to resolve the Colombian conflict by military means.

In practical terms this signifies that Colonel Duque engages in activities which are not within his competence, such as carrying out investigations, issuing judicial verdicts, impeding the right to free marketing of products and impeding the right to transportation and movement of persons of civil society. It would seem that for Colonel Duque the concept of Democratic Security signifies food insecurity. The Colonel ignores the existence of civilian noncombatants, and instead of contributing to the strengthening of the institutions of the state, his actions produce more insecurity and less protection.

Some of the actions which explain the activities of the Colonel can be summarized as follows: constantly appearing in the testimony of the Community members' illegal detentions, use of paid informants, threatening with beheading, carrying out tortures and doing warrantless searches. He defends the use of paramilitaries to achieve his goals, and what is important to him is to achieve these goals, insulting and mistreating women and children and making belittling comments about human rights organizations.

On July 23, 2004, at about 10 a.m., Durango was again in the bus terminal where he told several persons from the Community who were waiting for transport to San José that he and his associates were looking for the right moment to assassinate the leaders and that he personally was taking part in all of these threatened actions. He said that Community residents could make all of the denunciations they wished to, that they all will reach him and they will just cause him to laugh, since he was working with the Army. For this reason they could not do anything to him because the Public Prosecutor's office had cleared him of all charges. After saying this, he named the Community leaders and accompaniers with whom they were going to begin the killings. [15),16),17)]

THE VISIT OF CSN IN JUNE OF 2004

As is traditional, CSN takes delegations to its sister Community every year. Six persons visited the Community on a CSN delegation in June 2004. For one week we shared our lives with Community residents and not only came to admire their incredible organization and tremendous moral strength, but we also enjoyed the beauty of the place and daily life in this small hamlet.

The crowing of the roosters, the sound of the burros, the songs of the birds, the smoke from the chimneys of the houses, the children going to school and the simple but delicious meals delighted us. We observed the packaging of the baby bananas and the drying of the seeds of cacao in the tropical sun. One of our favorite sports was observing the meal of the pigs, which were fattened on fresh coconuts. We became aware of everything. It is a transparent Community which has nothing to hide and which does everything it can to keep its residents from being converted into part of the 3.5 million displaced people in Colombia. In the words of the Peace Community, "... what we know how to do is farm the land; if we were to be displaced we would become beggars, and we do not wish to live that way. Farming the land is our dignity."

On this occasion we also heard freely without pressure and without being forced, spontaneously, the testimony of several survivors of experiences which were the product of "democratic security." Let us listen to them.

Among the people we spoke to were Conrado David, his wife and seven-year-old daughter. They told us that on March 18, 2003, there was a military operation in La Cristalina, the rural zone where they lived. Conrado was returning to his home when he was met by soldiers who ordered him to lie down on the ground and threatened to kill him. He pleaded with them not to shoot because his elderly mother was coming behind him with his two young daughters. While lying on the ground, Conrado heard shots, and his three-year-old daughter, Mildred, was injured by one of the shots. She suffered a wound from which her intestines came out. The soldiers called for a helicopter, but after waiting for an hour and a half, they were informed that the helicopter would not come and that Mildred would have to be taken to the hospital by the unpaved road from San José de Apartadó. While she was being taken to the hospital in Apartadó on the road from San José, the little girl died. The soldiers said to Conrado's mother that she had to say that the little girl died in an attack by the guerrillas, even though there were no guerrillas in that area.

We were impressed by the unity of this family and its tremendous sense of dignity. Mildred's older sister told us that she was never going to see her little sister again.

Another person we spoke to was Elkin Darío Tuberquia. Elkin spoke to us in a sincere manner, spontaneously, without pressure and full of incredible dignity. He came to give us testimony about his personal experience with the 17th Brigade. He said he was in the house of his mother and father-in-law because they had come from the settlement of Las Nieves after paramilitary incursions which produced an exodus beginning at the end of February. While he was crossing the river that runs through San José, he came upon a group of Army soldiers who detained him on the night of March 12, 2004. Elkin had collaborated with the guerrillas some 12 years previously in Mulatos. However, he had retired and cut-off all ties with the guerrillas because he organized his home, which was a requirement that his fiancée made of him if he were to marry her. In fact, Elkin had been detained in 1997 as a result of other inquiries into his past, and he was in prison for three years. But even prior to this detention, he had broken off all links to the insurgency, as has been confirmed by testimony of his relatives and those who had known him for the last eight years in Las Nieves.

Elkin was taken to the 17th Brigade and subjected by Colonel Duque to recognition by hooded persons. He was deprived of his liberty illegally for nine days during which he suffered multiple forms of violence upon his body and upon his conscience. Elkin told us that Colonel Duque personally tortured him, struck him, kicked him and broke open his mouth until he required him to say that he was a FARC militiaman. Elkin said that if he had not confirmed that he was a FARC militiaman they would have taken him outside where the paramilitaries were waiting to kill him. When he said that he had been a FARC militiaman in order to gain his freedom and avoid assassination by the paramilitaries, Colonel Duque called persons to come and film his confession.

Another person who was detained illegally the same night and taken to the 17th Brigade together with Elkin was Apolinar Guerra, who was 18 years old. However, Apolinar did not wish to give testimony to us because he was still very traumatized by the experience at the 17th Brigade.

The experience of these two persons told to us by Elkin gives us a good idea how the strategy of Democratic Security functions in the rural regions of Colombia. It deprives persons of their liberty in an illegal fashion, since Elkin and Apolinar were not committing any illegal act, nor was there any warrant for their arrest. They were detained without being given the reason why and they were taken to a place which is not designated by the law as a place where prisoners are to be kept, for the purpose of creating ex post facto an appearance of legality for their being deprived of their liberty. Methods of torture, which are prohibited by international law and by the law of Colombia, were used. And "witnesses" were paid money to accuse them. Through torture and threats of death, they got "confessions" out of Elkin and Apolinar which were false and had absolutely no legal value. They called a prosecutor to take their testimony, and our question is: How independent is the judicial system, given that in regions of conflict, the prosecutors generally live in the Army installations for reasons of security?

The mother of Gloria Helena Tuberquia, an 18-year-old girl who was detained in the 17th Brigade with her baby and accused of being a guerrilla, also came to talk to us. But she was so terrorized by the Army's actions that in the end she did not give us any testimony, because she was afraid that something might happen to her daughter, whom she has not seen since the moment of her detention.

THE SEVENTEENTH BRIGADE

Throughout the more than 18 years during which CSN has worked in this region, we can give testimony of multiple violations of human rights and international humanitarian law by the 17th Brigade.

Torture, sexual assault, plunder, pillage, displacements, illegal detentions, false testimonies, robbery, patrolling openly and cynically with the paramilitaries whom they call "cousins" are the mark of this Brigade. Threats of the military officers against the Community are constant, and they frequently tell them they are going to use "heavy machinery," which means using the paramilitaries. That is what Colonel Duque did on the evening of March 12, 2004, when he illegally detained two women who were members of the Community and referred to them in a demeaning way as "big bellies" because one of them was pregnant. [7)]

A very serious crime by this Brigade is its custom of "legalizing the death," which is to say dressing the cadavers of members of the civilian population in guerrilla uniforms so that they will appear to have been killed in combat.[5] This was the case reported for the Zapata and Valle families who four days

5. Editor's note: Innocent civilians killed then dressed as guerrillas and presented as guerrillas killed in combat came to be known as "false positives." These cases were perpetrated by the Army and paramilitaries as documented by Javier Giraldo.[20]

after they declared themselves part of the Peace Community lost five of their members. These five had gone out on that Holy Thursday to get coconuts from some nearby palm trees to prepare the typical meal for those days. They ran into a patrol of Army soldiers and paramilitaries combined. Their clothes were burned and military uniforms were put on their bodies in order to present them as "guerrillas killed in combat." That afternoon the mother of one of those killed recognized pieces of his clothes in the remains of a fire pit. [20)]

The merciless treatment and lack of respect by the members of this Brigade toward the civilian population whom they are supposed to protect is almost natural. But in none of the cases is it crueler than in the treatment of children and women. Besides, the 17th Brigade is responsible for violations committed as much by the guerrillas as by the paramilitaries, by omission, since their function is the protection of the non-combatant civilian population.

What will become of the children of Miriam Tuberquia, who on June 16, 2003, saw their mother detained in Las Nieves hamlet by members of the 17th Brigade and ordered to lie down on the soil which had been wet from rain until June 18 because she was considered "suspicious?" Miriam had some syringes in her backpack because she needed to inject herself every day for an illness she had, and she also had money with her from the sale of cacao by which she lived. What will become of her little two- and three-year-old children, whom the "courageous" soldiers threatened with their guns? And what will become of the children of Yorbelis Amparo Restrepo, the single mother who was murdered by order of Wilmar Durango?

At the checkpoints, it is common for soldiers to pull children away and take them to members of the Army where they are asked about the leaders of the Peace Community and later given candy. The signatures of the Colombian government for treaties for the protection of children are a dead letter in practice, since the treaties are signed only so that the international community celebrates the oldest democracy in Latin America and so that the Colombian government does not lose money coming from the international community.

REMEMBRANCES OF GREAT INTEREST

As Program Director of CSN, I recall that on February 12, 2003, I visited the Peace Community in one of the routine visits of CSN. After spending several days in the Community, I was preparing to return because I had a family gathering later that day in Bogotá. That morning two of the most outstanding leaders of the Community, Gildardo Tuberquia and Wilson David, traveled down from San José to Apartadó with me and accompanied me during the morning, since my plane was to leave at noon that day. Calmly, I accompanied them while they carried out some errands, and then we went to a restaurant where we drank some fruit juice. Then they said good-bye to me fondly when I took a taxi for the airport. How was I to imagine that the same day after they had left me they would be illegally detained?

Wilson and Gildardo took a public vehicle to return to San José. That vehicle was inspected by some soldiers who came out from behind some trees where there was no checkpoint. The soldiers made all of the passengers get out with their belongings and show an identification document. A small cardboard box remained in the vehicle which nobody recognized as theirs. The soldiers returned the documents to all of the persons except a woman named Amanda. They said they had found explosives in the box and they detained everyone. They also invaded the Community where they took several persons into custody.

The Peace Community has brought together reliable information that leads to the interpretation that the stopping of the vehicle was part of a set-up planned by the 17th Brigade, and the "finding of the box with explosives" was designed to damage the good name of the Peace Community and to create judicial processes against some Community members and leaders. The Office of the High Commissioner for Human Rights of the United Nations documented all of the information about this case.

Another occurrence that is worth mentioning is the case of the hand grenade which exploded in San José. In one of the visits to San José, while we were walking casually through the town, some persons told us that a hand grenade had been left by the Army in a field. They said that they had called the local Ombudsman's office in Apartadó and the Ombudsman had come and taken photos of the grenade and had consulted about it with the Army. The Army said the grenade was a smoke grenade, and the inhabitants of the Community then kept it in a house which happened to be Luis Eduardo Guerra's house. CSN suggested to them that they throw the grenade into the river so that it would lose its explosive power, but they did not do so. This is the grenade which exploded and killed the wife of Luis Eduardo Guerra and seriously injured his son Deiner.

On Friday, February 18, 2005, a person from the CSN office called the Peace Community to discuss the marketing of small bananas with one of the Community's leaders. While they were talking the incessant sound of helicopters was heard in the background. When the CSN person asked the Community leader if the sound was that of helicopters he replied that it was. He said that all day long they had been flying over the Community and that the Army was carrying out an operation in the zone.

CSN has worked with the Peace Community since its beginning. Through the years we have not only visited the Community frequently, but we have also lived with them for long and short periods. CSN had one person living there for six months and another for one year. Never did they observe relations with the guerrillas, which would have been easy to detect. This is a transparent Community that follows the norms of International Humanitarian Law accepted internationally. It has not made the formal arrangements for the declaration of neutrality because these require the signature of the agreements by all of the parties involved, so that the said zones would be respected. They have not carried out these formal steps because of the irregular nature of the Colombian conflict which does not permit it, and particularly when the very government of President Uribe Vélez does not recognize that there is an armed conflict in Colombia.

Editor's note: On February 21, 2005, the legal representative of the Peace Community, Luis Eduardo Guerra, was murdered with his son Deiner and companion Bellanira and five other persons in the rural area of Mulatos, part of the Peace Community's lands. The Colombia Support Network sent a delegation, of which Cecilia was a part, to Colombia to investigate what had happened and who was responsible for the murderous attack. The delegation found paramilitary forces collaborating with the 17th Brigade of the Colombian Army were responsible for the murders.

Cecilia was very moved by the murder of Luis Eduardo Guerra and wrote a remembrance of him, as follows:

WHO WAS LUIS EDUARDO GUERRA GUERRA?

Any person who would have known the social, human and ethical qualities of Luis Eduardo Guerra and of his profound commitment to nonviolence and to construction of peace and a negotiated solution to the Colombian conflict would have been tremendously impressed by the testimony and the beauty of spirit of Luis Eduardo. Although he was a peasant, he possessed an intelligence and political clarity which many postgraduate students in famous universities would have desired to have. His personal warmth, his moral courage and his great sensibility won for him the most profound respect of the persons who knew him.

He came to Urabá as a very young boy when his father brought him fleeing the political violence in the center of the country and riding on his shoulders he saw the first cadavers of persons killed for political reasons, as is all too natural for Colombian children. Luis Eduardo had been nominated by the Community as its representative to the Inter-Institutional group, which included representatives of the government and of the Inter-American Commission of Human Rights, in order to follow up on the provisional measures ordered by that commission for the Peace Community. The last meetings in which Luis Eduardo participated took place in the office of the Colombian Vice President Francisco Santos on December 13, 2004, and in the offices of the Minister of Foreign Relations on January 28, 2005, 24 days before he was assassinated.

Luis Eduardo traveled to Europe where he visited several countries, Italy and Germany among others, where he reported on the situation of the Peace Community. At the invitation of Colombia Support Network he visited the United States. In Wisconsin, he promoted the sister community relationship with Dane County. He was received by Dane County Executive Kathleen Falk, by Wisconsin Secretary of State Douglas La Follette and by State Representative Mark Pocan, who were all very favorably impressed by his presentation and who later lamented profoundly his horrible murder.

From Left: Dane County Executive Kathleen Falk, an assistant of Kathleen Falk, Cecilia, and Luis Eduardo Guerra Guerra, leader of the Peace Community of San Jose de Apartado.

During his visit to the United States, Luis Eduardo traveled to Columbus, Georgia, where he spoke at a rally of thousands of persons who had come to attend the annual vigil to close the School of the Americas organized by the School of Americas Watch. We kidded him there because all of the girls recognized him since he was one of the most outstanding speakers, and they did not stop greeting him with a kiss on the cheek upon recognizing him. In 2004 he participated in a Social Forum in Ecuador as a delegate of the Community of San José and of other communities engaged in nonviolent resistance. He was interviewed by many of the members of the diplomatic corps accredited in Colombia and by the office of the High Commissioner of Human Rights of the United Nations in Bogotá. These persons all appreciated him very much. Luis Eduardo leaves three young children who are orphans of both father and mother.

In an insulting manner and one injurious to his memory, officials of the Colombian government have said that Luis Eduardo was ready to leave the Peace Community and disassociate himself from it. Anyone who had known Luis Eduardo and recognized his profound commitment to his beloved Peace Community would never believe the absurd suggestion that he wished to leave it.

I, Cecilia, remember that the last time that I, as Program Director of CSN, met Luis Eduardo as a friend, was in Bogotá at the home of my aunt in June of 2004. There he predicted his death. He explained to me that the Colombian Army in Córdoba has a border with the 17th Brigade in Antioquia, precisely on the border area of the two provinces. He told me that given the peace conversations which the government is carrying on with the paramilitaries, which are taking place in Ralito, both the paramilitaries and the Army think it is necessary to clear out this corridor in order to leave the area and zone "free" to control as a measure of protection for the paramilitaries. He said that they were going to begin to carry out operations for this purpose and that the Peace Community would be their first objective. How could one imagine that eight months later this prediction would be carried out and he himself murdered?

Editor's note: This article by Cecilia Zárate-Laun was completed after the February 21, 2005 murder of Luis Eduardo Guerra and seven other Community members from the Peace Community of San José de Apartadó.

> From April 16-19, 2005, five members of Colombia Support Network (CSN) visited San José de Apartadó to investigate the massacre that took the lives of Luis Eduardo Guerra, three children and four other adults. The five members of CSN who visited San José de Apartadó

were: Cecilia Zárate-Laun, Eunice Gibson, John Gibson, Conrad Weiffenbach and Norman Stockwell. On June 26, 2005 they issued a report on the massacre entitled "The Massacre at Mulatos in Colombia: An Investigative Report." This report was submitted to U.S. Senators Feingold and Kohl of Wisconsin and U. S. Representative Baldwin of Wisconsin as well as others. The full report is appended to the end of this article.

A very brief summary of some of the conclusions of the Report and some more recent facts are as follows: 1) The Colombian Army and paramilitaries planned and carried out the massacre. Subsequent to the Report members of the military and paramilitaries were indicted, tried, convicted and sentenced for the planning and complicity in carrying out the massacre. 2) The Peace Community of San José de Apartadó is an experiment in direct, democratic, nonviolent community which has chosen to remain neutral and nonviolent in the face of internal violent upheaval. The Community has existed since 1997 until the present, 2024. They do not allow any weapons within their Community. 3) In violation of the Inter-American Court's recommendations to negotiate all decisions pertaining to San José de Apartadó with the Community and to locate any Police facilities on the outskirts of San José in order to respect their adherence to nonviolence, the Colombian Government acted unilaterally in disregard of the Community in locating, without prior consultation, the Police within the town of San José. This violated the San José Peace Community's desires for an area of no weapons and also put the members of the Community at risk, since the Police facilities were liable to attack by the FARC as had happened in the past. 4) The Colombian Government has made no efforts to protect the Peace Community of San José as recommended by the Inter-American Court and Colombia's Constitutional Court. 5) When the Government located a Police station and an Army installation in San José de Apartadó after the murder of Luis Eduardo Guerra, the Peace Community made the decision to move out of San José and build a new settlement on land about one kilometer away which the Community owned in farmland called La Holandesa. The Peace Community had obtained this land from human rights support out of Holland. The new settlement was called San Josecito and remains their home to this day in 2024.

The role of the Colombia Support Network with respect to the Peace Community of San José de Apartadó since the February 21, 2005 massacre has consisted of maintaining a close relationship with the Community through annual visits by delegations from Madison, Wisconsin. These visits, together with members of the Peace Community coming to Madison for special visits, carry out the sister community relationship between Dane County, Wisconsin, in which the capital city of Madison is located, and Apartadó, which is represented by the Peace Community. In 1993, two members of the Dane County Board, Tammy Baldwin and Mark Pocan, who led the effort in the Dane County Board which resulted in the official sister community relationship, joined a Colombia Support Network delegation to Apartadó, met with civic leaders in Apartadó, including Mayor José Antonio López Bula and municipal council President Albeiro Bustamante and members of the Partido Union Patriotica (Patriotic Union Party) and went to San José de Apartadó. There they met with several leaders of the Balsamar Cooperative who later became leaders of the Peace Community. Sadly, several of the leaders of the Patriotic Union Party with whom they met, including Albeiro Bustamante, shown with them in the attached flyer, were murdered in the violent partisan conflict which broke out shortly after their visit. Tammy Baldwin, now a United States Senator, and Mark Pocan, now a Congressman, have continued their interest in CSN's support of the Peace Community. As a part of the current relationship with the Colombia Support Network, each month reports from the Peace Community in Spanish are translated to English and posted on the Colombia Support Network webpage.

REFERENCES

The references listed below, numbers 2-11, are to emails from the Peace Community of San José de Apartadó between August 8, 2002 and March 1, 2005. These emails could not be located by the Editors. The references listed at numbers 12-17 refer to Petitions made to Colombian President Álvaro Uribe by Father Javier Giraldo on behalf of the Peace Community. Some information on these submissions is available on the webpage "Desde los márgenes" of Javier Giraldo Moreno, S.J.

1. Historical Evidence directed to President Andrés Pastrana on August 6, 2002 by the Commission of Justice and Peace.
2. "New Military Aggression against the Peace Community," email from the Peace Community of San José de Apartadó on February 22, 2003.
3. "Again We are Struck by Terrorist Actions," email from the Peace Community of San José de Apartadó on December 10, 2003.
4. "The Actions of Death Continue," email from the Peace Community of San José de Apartadó on December 19, 2003.
5. "New Aggressions," email from the Peace Community of San José de Apartadó on February 24, 2004.
6. "The Threats of Displacements Continue," email from the Peace Community of San José de Apartadó on March 3, 2004.
7. "New Abuses Against the Community," email from the Peace Community of San José de Apartadó on March 13, 2004.
8. "An Urgent Call for Solidarity," email from the Peace Community of San José de Apartadó on May 28, 2004.
9. "The Actions of Death Continue," email from the Peace Community of San José de Apartadó on August 5, 2004.
10. "Indiscriminate Bombardment and New Aggressions," email from the Peace Community of San José de Apartadó on February 23, 2005.
11. "The Road of Terror," email from the Peace Community of San José de Apartadó on March 1, 2005.
12. Right of Petition to President Uribe, filed January 5, 2004, number 741719.
13. Right of Petition to President Uribe, filed February 26, 2004, number 260021.
14. Right of Petition to President Uribe, filed April 5, 2004, number 279992.
15. Right of Petition to President Uribe, filed May 20, 2004, number 300313.

16. Right of Petition to President Uribe, filed July 6, 2004, number 320803.

17. Right of Petition to President Uribe, filed September 20, 2004, number 369840.

18. Reply of the Peace Community of San José de Apartadó to the Proposal of Security and Protection, sent to the National Government, Community of San José de Apartadó, December 13, 2004.

19. Right of Petition to President Uribe, presented on January 5, 2005.

20. Giraldo S.J., Javier. "San José de Apartadó: Perfil de una Comunidad de Paz," Unpublished document, Bogotá, June 2000.

21. Giraldo S.J., Javier. "San José de Apartadó en el nudo de la 'Seguridad Democratica'," http://www.archivodelosddhh.gov.co/saia_release1/colecciones/Noche%20y%20Niebla/30/No.%2030%20San%20José%20de%20Apartadó%20en%20el%20nudo%20de%20la%20seguridad%20democratica.pdf, Bogotá, 2005.

22. San José de Apartadó, Paths of Resistance, Alternatives of the Civilian Population in the Midst of the Conflict, Collective Production of the Peace Community, with the cooperation of OXFAM and DFID (Department of International Development of Great Britain), published by ARFO, Bogotá, without a date.

23. Ministry of National Defense, Peace Communities, April 2005, www.minddefensa.gov.co

24. Mayor's Office of Apartadó, "For Apartadó and Its People, 'Póngale Corazón!'". www.apartadó.gov.co, 2005.

25. Zárate-Laun, Cecilia. "A Ray of Hope in Colombia's Nightmare," written in 1995 but first published in the current volume.

Addenda to Background on San José de Apartadó

INTRODUCTION

The entire report with the exception of the Interview with Massacre Witness #1 (this interview is missing) is available online at "The Massacre at Mulatos in Colombia" if you put that title into a search engine. Several entries appear. Choose the one from CSN. Or you can go directly online to https://colombiasupport.net/2005/6_26_rpt/san_jose_investigation.htm. There are several hyperlinks within the online version of the report to photos, interviews and other reports hidden on the CSN website, some of which are contained in the Addenda here.

There is also an English translation available at that site of a statement by the Peace Community about the massacre and notes in English about the investigatory delegation's meeting with Carlos Franco, the Director of the Colombian President's Human Rights Program.

The addenda that follow are:

Addendum #1: The Massacre at Mulatos in Colombia, An Investigative Report

Addendum #2: Summary Notes on the Massacre and Related Issues by the CSN Delegation Investigation, June 2005

Addendum #3: Interview with Massacre Witness #2

Addendum #4: Interview with Massacre Witness #3

Addendum #5: Interview with Massacre Witness #4

Addendum #6: Interview with Massacre Witness #5

Addendum #7: Interview with Sr. José Phidalgo Banguero-Zapata, Mayor of Apartadó, along with the Asesora Jurídica

Addendum #8: Interview with General of the XVII Brigade, Héctor Fandiño-Rincón at Brigade Headquarters, Carepa, Antioquia, Wednesday, April 20, 2005

Addendum 1
The Massacre at Mulatos in Colombia, An Investigative Report

Colombia Support Network
PO Box 1505, Madison, WI 53701
June 26, 2005

DEDICATION

This report is dedicated to the memory of Luis Eduardo Guerra, Deiner Guerra (age 11), Bellanira Areiza, Alfonso Bolívar Tuberquia, Sandra Milena Muñoz, Natalia Tuberquia (age 5), Santiago Tuberquia (18 months) and Alejandro Pérez, who died in Mulatos, Apartadó, Colombia, February 2005.

Lullaby for Dead Colombian Children

Parents sing their children to sleep,
Death came the other night.
Raw murder made a deeper sleep.
Now they sleep a deep, deep sleep.

Soldiers with guns and long knives put parents to sleep.
Knives were sharp, brought swift pain.
Now the children sleep.
Now they sleep a deep, deep sleep.

Some children ran and ran and hid.
They need someone to lullaby so they can sleep.
But fear makes sleep hard, less deep.
Now they sleep a deep, deep sleep.

Their eyes shone. Their ears could hear songs.
Visits from pain and hurt were wrong.
No lullaby will ease their fear, help them sleep.
Now they sleep a deep, deep sleep.

The children of San José are now asleep.
Eyes can't see. Ears can't hear.
Now their sleep is deep.
Now they sleep a deep, deep sleep.

Please, God, help all Colombian children
So for all,
So for all,
Now they sleep a deep, deep sleep.

John Gibson, Madison, June 2005

PURPOSE

By act of Congress, renewal of United States aid to Colombia ($700 million per year to the Colombian government, mostly in military aid) depends on their meeting conditions on human rights. This report presents the information we have gathered and the basis for our recommendations, which appear at the end of this report.

Apartadó, in northeastern Colombia, is the sister community of Dane County, Wisconsin, our home. Our delegation from the Colombia Support Network (John Gibson, Eunice Gibson, Norman Stockwell, Conrad Weiffenbach, and Cecilia Zárate Laun) visited Colombia from April 16 to 26, 2005. The visit was supported with letters from Wisconsin Senators Russ Feingold and Herb Kohl, Dane County Executive Kathleen Falk, and Wisconsin Secretary of State Douglas LaFollette, sent in advance to people in the agencies with which we wished to meet. We met with people in Apartadó, in the Peace Community of San José de Apartadó, and in the offices of a large number of government and non-government organizations in Medellín and Bogotá.

We offer this information to the United States Congress, Department of State, and other concerned groups and individuals wishing for information to guide their discussions on human rights in Colombia.

To recap events briefly, on February 21, 2005, Luis Eduardo Guerra Guerra, one of the founders and leaders of the Peace Community of San José de Apartadó, was murdered in an area near the Mulatos River. Three children and four other adults were also murdered in this massacre. Paramilitary checkpoints present in prior years on the road between San José and Apartadó have been removed, but there are now checkpoints of the Colombian Police and Army. A Police station was put within the village of San José, against the wishes of the Peace Community, which observes a non-violent resistance to the armed conflict. In response to the placing of the Police station in the village of San José, the Peace Community has abandoned their village, moving to a new site a few km away, where they are living in a new settlement, for which construction has begun.

The background of events in this region of Colombia is comprehensively summarized in a background section of this report. A list of 500 violations of human rights, including other massacres that the people of San José de Apartadó have suffered, is also presented. San José's website (in Spanish) offers more recent information. San José represents the experience of many rural communities in Colombia: The aggression toward them is systematic. (Editor's note: As indicated in the Introduction to these Addenda, further information can be found on the CSN website.)

The culpability of the armed forces in the most serious of human rights violations has been acknowledged by the Colombian Procuraduría, which in May 2005 issued a decision (document in Spanish) that disciplinary action will be taken against units of the Army and Police that were in command of the region in which San José de Apartadó is located in the years 2000 to 2002, for their responsibility in the same types of violations of human rights then in San José, including massacres. Please see the Background document and list of violations from the community for details on those violations (Editor's note: Online at CSN website as per Introduction to Addenda).

U.S. aid must not support the Colombian Police and Army in such behavior.

We expect that similar action from the Procuraduria will result in due time following the massacre of February 2005, which they are now investigating.

But whether the sanctions against those responsible in the military will be effective remains to be seen. Often in the past such sanctions have not been so.

INFORMATION WE GATHERED DURING OUR VISIT:

- We met April 18th and 19th with the people of San José, who told us among other important things that when they travel through the checkpoints along the road to Apartadó they still suffer personal harassment and confiscation of purchases and other belongings. A group of leaders summarized their concerns (notes of interviews with community leaders) about the Police station placed in the village after the massacre, inability to get justice from the government, their stigmatization in the media by government officials, and the history of recent abuses. In private meetings, witnesses shared information on the massacre of February 21 and related events with us. Some were able to identify forces in that area during the massacre as Army, and one said soldiers there told them the Army did it. Please see our summary notes on this point, and our notes from interviewing Witnesses 2, 3, 4, and 5. (Editor's note: notes for Witness 1 are missing; others are in later addenda.) For their protection, information that could lead to the identification of these witnesses has been expunged. Witnesses were assassinated after giving testimony following a massacre in San José a few years ago.
- We had supper on the evening of April 19 with five members of the Apartadó Municipal Council, and met with the Mayor (Alcalde of Apartadó) in his office on April 20. Please see our notes (Editor's note: Addenda 2, 7 and 8 below) regarding their hostile attitudes toward San José.
- We met with General Héctor Jaime Fandiño-Rincón, Commander of the 17th Brigade of the Colombian Army, stationed in Carepa, near Apartadó, in his office at the Brigade Headquarters for an hour on April 20. Our notes on the discussion there outline how he argued that his troops were not involved in the massacre of February 21, and his ideas implying it was due to an internal dispute within the Peace Community or an action of the FARC guerrillas.
- The historical context regarding some persons mentioned in these notes is in the section, *Peculiar Characters for Application of Democratic Security in Apartadó*, beginning on page 208 in the Background document. (Editor's note: CSN website)
- We met with Colonel Yamik Armando Moreno of the National Police, in charge of the region in which San José and Apartadó are located, in his headquarters for two and a half hours on April 20. As indicated in our notes from that meeting, he presented a version of events surrounding the massacre, and a theory of who did it, that was nearly identical to that of General Fandiño. He expressed a very hostile attitude toward the Peace Community, while maintaining a friendly one toward us.
- We met with the Procurador of the Nation, Edgardo José Maya-Villazón, who told us that the investigation by his office of the February 2005 massacre in San José and related events there was in an advanced state. He arranged for us to meet with his staff to discuss our findings. He said the Police station should be in the place where the Peace Community wants it, which would be consistent with the ruling of the Inter-American Court of Human Rights, a ruling which he said the Colombian government should follow.
- We met with Carlos Franco, Director of the President of Colombia's Human Rights Program, on Monday April 25, 2005. He strongly defended the principle of a Police station in San José, and listed a large number of events (such as hand grenades exploding in the village) that he felt discredited the Community. Please see our notes of the meeting.
- The representative at the office of the UN High Commissioner for Human Rights (UNHCHR),

Luis Carlos Monge, with whom we met, as well as Procurador Maya and his staff, told us that the location of the Police station within San José does not meet conditions imposed by the Inter-American Court for Human Rights, nor with Colombian law.

- The members of the Procurador's staff who met with us told us that:
  - "Unfortunately, the public forces also violate human rights and the law."
  - "High Army powers have recently trained people who historically do not respect Human Rights."
  - "Current negotiations re demobilization could intensify paramilitary presence, making the situation like the massacre more common." Stated with regard to a perception that the Peace Community is "taken ideologically by the guerrillas," and similar statements from the Police, some Apartadó council members and the Mayor, and some other Colombians with whom our delegation met.
- We would not expect members of the Peace Community of San José de Apartadó not to know guerrillas personally. Members of the Peace Community have grown up with and been friends with a wide variety of local people, some of whom wound up with the guerrillas.
- San José presents non-violent resistance in a country that only knows violent resistance. That is why they are important and why FARC guerrillas have killed nineteen residents since the community declared itself a Peace Community.
- We would expect some residents of San José, as neutrals, to be in touch with friends in the guerrillas, just as they would be in touch with friends in Apartadó who may have been, for example, trained by the Army to act as paramilitaries. Their lives are in Apartadó.
- So when, as Colonel Moreno of the National Police reported, a cell-phone call from a woman in San José to a friend in the guerrillas was intercepted, with the essence of the conversation being. "Did you do that?" (referring to some guerrilla action), this does not mean that San José is violating neutrality. When members of the community encounter guerrillas out in the countryside and talk with them (as Col. Moreno reports the Police have observed), this does not mean that San José is violating neutrality. We would expect friends to keep in touch for a variety of social reasons (including births, deaths, personal support), and that conversation would flow at those encounters. Officers and others who grew up in privileged circumstances may not personally know any guerrillas or campesinos, and may not appreciate the above points.
- Colonel Moreno told our delegation that another reason he believes the leaders of the community are overtly against the government is that their website billboards contain the word "RESIST". One's perceptions are often influenced by one's peer group. The authors of the website more likely intend an exhortation to resist the kind of population displacement that has already been forced on several million Colombian campesinos.
- San José is caught in a Civil War. The most principled stance is to be neutral, not contributing to the killing of friends, in-laws, brothers and sisters who may be guerrillas, paramilitaries and Armed Forces of the nation. The position of the Peace Community is one that we recognize and respect, and you may very well respect it too.

SAN JOSÉ DE APARTADÓ IS A GOOD COMMUNITY THAT CAN DEVELOP THE COUNTRY

Contrary to views expressed by members of the Apartadó Council, Police, Army, and some government officials, we found in visiting and talking with people in San José that the members of the Community are properly and exceptionally well-motivated. San José de

Apartadó provides an alternative model for peaceful rural development of the traditional agricultural sector in Colombia.

We visited with work teams taking care of children, constructing sidewalks and housing; cutting trees into lumber across the river and up a hill from the camp, carrying the cut lumber from where the trees had been felled, and carrying rocks and gravel from the river for the walkways, all without gasoline-powered vehicles. We saw no gasoline-powered vehicles on site, only a gasoline chainsaw, human labor and a very few draft animals. No bulldozers, shovels or trucks. The road from Apartadó goes by outside the barbed wire fence behind which the new camp is located, and no road goes into the new site.

The fact that their community works as a collective could be seen as an asset to the nation, not a threat. We believe that San José de Apartadó is a highly respectable, indeed admirable, community, especially because they have maintained their ideology and resisted displacement while 150 members have been murdered and massacred over the past fifteen years.

OUR CONCLUSIONS

We believe the following conclusions are well based on the information we have gathered:

The Army was responsible for the massacre of members of the Peace Community on February 21, 2005.

The Peace Community has developed a highly respectable and principled stance toward the war in Colombia: an active peaceful resistance. We found no credible evidence of willing participation of the Community in the armed conflict or of Community support for the FARC guerrillas or any other armed actor.

The Peace Community of San José de Apartadó is an experiment of non-violence which is unique in the world. One of its most remarkable features is the truly democratic form in which decisions are made with the whole Community deciding on every important measure.

The Colombian Government made a mockery of the Inter-American Court when it chose not to follow the Court's recommendation which specifically says to negotiate decisions with the Community. The location of the Police station was agreed to tentatively in the discussion between Luis Eduardo Guerra representing the desires of the Community and Vice President Francisco Santos. The Community's request was to locate the Police on the outskirts of the town, not inside. The Colombian government used the massacre as an excuse to impose the authoritarian decision of locating the Police station inside the town.

We believe the Community's decision to oppose the placement of a Police station within the Community to be eminently reasonable for the following reasons:

a) it is consistent with the Community's principled opposition to having arms in their midst; and b) the Community would leave itself open to becoming engaged in the armed conflict, as the guerrillas might carry out an armed attack against the Police station which might injure or kill Peace Community residents and damage their homes, as happened to the indigenous community of Toribio in Cauca Province while our CSN delegation was in Colombia.

We found credible evidence of extensive cooperation and coordination between the Army and the paramilitaries in the massacre of February 21, 2005 and other events involving the Peace Community of San José. It is clear to us that the Colombian Government has failed to curtail these paramilitaries, whose activities are illegal under Colombian law. Under these circumstances the Peace Community's rejection of Army presence in the Community appears sensible and reasonable.

We believe on the basis of the evidence we received during our visit to San José, Apartadó, Medellín and Bogotá that the Colombian Government has failed to take measures to protect the Peace Community as ordered by the Inter-American Court and by Colombia's Constitutional Court.

In one sense the Peace Community of San José is a representative of rural communities throughout Colombia which have organized as civil society and in constituent assemblies to oppose the armed conflict, but have experienced aggression by the Colombian state, rather than protection, with their institutions and lands subjected to attack by paramilitary forces acting in concert with the Colombian Armed Forces.

We ask that you incorporate the above information regarding human rights in Colombia, including information in linked documents, in your reports and deliberations, in so far as you recognize it to be useful.

OUR RECOMMENDATIONS:

We recommend, based on our information in this report:

- That United States aid to Colombia's Armed Forces be cut off until Colombian Armed Forces' collaboration with paramilitaries ends and until changes are made by the Colombian government in its policies toward rural agrarian communities like San José de Apartadó.
- That the United States require investigation by the respective Colombian authorities of all military and Police commanders of the region encompassing Apartadó since 1997, when San José declared itself a Peace Community
- That the United States deny visas for Colonel Duque, General Fandiño and other Army and Police officers responsible for the soldiers and policemen who have abused the residents of the Peace Community of San José de Apartadó since 1997.
- That the United States withhold aid from Colombia unless the Colombian authorities:
    - Respect the desire of the Peace Community to have no armed actors within their borders and demonstrate that Army and Police collaboration with paramilitaries has ended, and also develop a just alternative to the proposed government plan for demobilizing and "reinserting" paramilitaries into civilian society.
    - Respond effectively to conditions required for Colombia by the Inter-American Court of Human Rights and by Colombia's own Constitution.
    - Cease using military (including National Police) professionals in civilian functions, such as teachers and doctors that the government is obliged to provide in rural communities.
    - Remove the local offices of the Judiciary (Fiscalía) from military bases, to enable their impartiality.

The United States can help to end the continuing, severe violations of rights of peasants like those of San José de Apartadó, who hold and embody the highest moral position consistent with the conditions forced upon them.

Millions of Colombians have already become internally displaced. The toleration and (yes) support by US aid of ongoing massacres and harassment of the populations of San José and many other rural communities can be halted.

We hope that the information gathered by our delegation will help lead to a foreign policy towards Colombia based upon the principles upon which our nation was founded.

Addendum 2
Summary Notes on the Massacre and Related Issues

by the CSN Delegation Investigation
June 2005

I. It is almost beyond a reasonable doubt that some element of the Army carried out the massacre. Here is why we believe that is true:

1. There are quite a few people who saw readily identifiable Army personnel in the area of the murders at the time they took place.
2. While the Minister of Defense and the Vice President both told the press that the Army had been two days' march from the atrocity, and those statements have never been formally retracted, General Fandiño told us that the statements were not correct and that the Army was in the area.
3. Apartadó hospital records show treatment of a soldier who had been in the area at the time of the now-admitted Army operation.
4. The people who saw and identified soldiers connected with the killings are believable. We talked to a number of them. Their accounts match the account that was carried in *El Tiempo* on Easter Sunday.
5. The people who talked to reporters and who also talked to us relayed verbal admissions made to them contemporaneously by various members of the Armed Forces.
6. The people we talked to know what the FARC look like. None mentioned seeing any at any time between Feb. 19 and 21, except for the one who was shot by the Army while he was visiting his daughter.
7. The version offered by the Army is not credible. Here is why:
   a. They lost credibility by first giving out a story that was patently incredible (the two-days' march story).
   b. They have presented two "guerrillas" who they claim will testify that Luis Eduardo Guerra was about to quit the Peace Community and thus was killed by the FARC. But Luis Eduardo had only weeks before his murder spoken to Vice President Santos on behalf of the Community on two occasions.
   c. At least one of these "guerrillas" (Elkin Tuberquia) talked to our delegation last June and told us of being beaten and tortured by Colonel Duque at 17th Brigade headquarters.
   d. A Spanish NGO has a recent tape made by Luis Eduardo Guerra only a few weeks before his death in which he sets forth his plans for the Peace Community.
   e. General Fandiño claimed that the Peace Community emailed details about the atrocities before the Fiscalía dug up the bodies, which he insists were buried very deep. He thinks that that proves that the Peace Community knew in advance that the victims would be killed, mutilated and buried.
   f. That isn't true. Several witnesses arrived in San José on the evening of Wednesday, February 23. They had found the bodies of the Bolívar family covered with cacao brush and a little dirt. The emails weren't sent until Thursday, February 24. The email says Luis Eduardo and his family were captured by soldiers from the 11th Brigade at about 11

a.m. on Monday, February 21. A witness saw that. We talked to him.

g. Contrary to General Fandiño's claim, the Thursday, 8:21a.m. email does not say that Luis Eduardo's body has been found. Because a witness saw him and his family taken away by the Army, and heard him yell, the witness and the sender of the e-mail reached the reasonable conclusion that the soldiers had killed them.

What is the best way to make sure that the Colombian government responds adequately?
What should be the position of the US government?
What will happen to their property?
Will they be treated as displaced persons under applicable Colombian law?
If not, how can they retain their property?
If yes, will the law be applied fairly and promptly?

II. From meetings with the agencies listed below, we confirm that there is a campaign of stigma against the Peace Community, by

The Mayor and Council of Apartadó
The Antioquia Governor's office
The Army
The Police

III. Accounts of the massacre

1. Published accounts
   a. *CAMBIO* No. 610, March 7-14, 2005
   b. *EL TIEMPO*, Jesús Abad Colorado, Easter Sunday, March 27
2. Formal reports (not yet available to the public)
   a. Report, interviews with a group of embassy representatives in Bogotá by the international observers who accompanied the group of 100 from the Community to the site of the massacre. CSN believes a lot of statements were taken in this visit. CSN has followed up with Jerome Hohman, US Embassy Human Rights Officer, by email, requesting information as to whether a report exists.
   b. Report from the OHCHR. This could only be released to the Colombian Government at its request. The Procurador told us that he had requested it and that request is within his authority. So by now it should have been released.

Addendum 3

Notes: Interview with Massacre Witness #2

Old San José de Apartadó
Morning of April 18, 2005

Luis Eduardo visited the witness on Saturday, February 19 in the afternoon.

On Sunday (February 20), they heard shooting in Las Nieves. Luis Eduardo wanted to go to Cantarana, his farm, to harvest cocoa beans. The witness had heard helicopters and shooting, so the witness told him not to leave the house. He had his son and his girlfriend with him. The witness said, "The Army is going to go to Cantarana." So he didn't go on Sunday, but waited until Monday morning.

On Monday morning the witness said to Luis Eduardo, "What are you going to do?"

He said, "We're going to get the cacao. I have to. If you can harvest cacao, I should be able to do so." The cacao farm was Luis Eduardo's father's, but he had planted the cacao. Luis Eduardo said, "I just need a little money for the doctor for the child. I'm making you a gift of the rest of the cacao." He gave the witness a gift of some colts also.

It is about 5 hours from the house where the witness was to San José and about an hour from the house to the cacao farm. Luis Eduardo was going to return on Tuesday so that he and the witness could talk about the colts. They made a lunch for him to take along, then waited.

The witness was worried about Luis Eduardo and his family, and wanted Deiner to stay, but he wanted to go along and they left. At 2 p.m. the Army came. One soldier asked the witness if the witness knew Luis Eduardo Guerra. When the witness said yes, that Luis Eduardo was like a son to the witness, the soldier said, "We killed him down there".

Then the soldier asked the witness, "Do you know who Alfonso Bolívar-Tuberquia was?"

The witness replied, "We are related." The soldier said, "Unfortunately, he and his family have been killed." The witness was very upset and did not say anything.

Then one soldier sat down and told the witness that someone had told him that the witness is a guerrilla. The witness said, "Bring that person to me. It is complete nonsense."

Eleven people in all were held captive from Monday to Sunday. The witness told us: "We couldn't eat. They ate our food. They were digging holes." They said they were looking for weapons. The witness said, "You can tear down the house. We don't have weapons." They said others there, including a baby, were guerrillas.

When the committee from the Peace Community arrived, the soldiers said, "You are lucky the group from the guerrillas have come to rescue you." He said they were going to kill all of that guerrilla committee that came to get the bodies.

A soldier told the witness, "We are the Army. The paramilitaries are up there in the hills and they will get you. They will sweep clean. They will burn all your houses and cut off everyone's head."

One soldier said they were from the 17th Brigade and some others said they were from the 11th Brigade. The soldiers said there were 2,000 of them in all.

During the time they were kept in the house, the witness and others woke up in the morning and made themselves a little breakfast. The witness said the soldiers were there all day. They wrote a lot on the wall.

A little girl was sent out to get some water for cooking. A soldier looked at her and said to another soldier, "Could you cut this little girl's head off?" The other soldier said, "Sure, if they tell me to, I will."

The little girl was with us and the witness in the interview. A delegation member held her hand and asked her, "What did the soldier say to you?" The little girl just burst into tears. She could not speak, but she cried softly.

When the 11 family members left with the Peace Community committee, the soldiers remained in the house. The witness said when they left the soldiers stole 2 mules and some gold chains from a neighbor.

Addendum 4
Notes: CSN Delegation Interview with Massacre Witness #3

April 19, 2005

The witness said he has escaped death 4 times. He is very young.

On Thursday, February 17, he went down to San José from the hamlet called La Linda. That takes about 40 minutes. He talked to people in San José. He said he was going to Mulatos to pick up cacao. The witness said he spoke to Luis Eduardo, who said: "I'm going on Saturday." On Saturday afternoon, Luis Eduardo arrived, while the witness was working.

On Sunday they wanted to go to Luis Eduardo's farm, so they went to look for the horses. The dogs were barking, and they heard shooting from Las Nieves, so they stayed in the house all day with Luis Eduardo and others. The witness and Luis Eduardo decided not to go out to the cacao farm but they did go to the river to fish and to cut some plantains. They left the river about 7 in the evening.

They ran into a neighbor and asked, "How's everything?". The neighbor said the whole area is full of the Army, in Cristalina, La Unión, and Las Nieves. That day they had heard shots in Las Nieves and at noon had heard a helicopter land. Luis Eduardo said, "That is the Army. Who knows what they have done there!"

Monday in the morning they heard on the radio that the Army had killed a guerrilla named Machorucio. They ate breakfast. They took a packed lunch with them and were ready to return to San José, when Luis Eduardo suggested they go to Cantarrana instead to harvest cacao.

About 8 a.m. Luis Eduardo and the others left for Cantarrana. Our witness said, "If we see the Army here I am not going to Cantarrana. If they surprise us, I will be quiet." If they asked about the guerrillas, he said they would tell them they had not seen anything of them. They went along the Mulatos riverbank talking and laughing.

From a distance our witness said he saw a uniformed man straight ahead, going up a hill. "It is the Army," he said to Luis Eduardo, who said, "We are going there". Then our witness said he saw another Army soldier closer. Our witness said the soldier held up his rifle and said, "Stop, don't run!" When he said this, several other soldiers came out of the brush.

Then our witness said he saw Luis Eduardo raise his hand. He said he told Luis Eduardo he would not run and Bellanira asked the witness what he was going to do and he said nothing. But as the soldiers came closer, he decided to run. He said as the soldiers drew near he saw they wore green berets, which the Army uses. The soldiers hollered, "Grab him! Grab him!" Then he heard one of those who had been with him say, "Ay, Ay," and he said he thought to himself that the Army soldiers were beating that person. He kept fleeing through the hills (monte).

At 2:30 p.m. he arrived at Alfonso Bolívar's house. He told Alfonso Bolívar that the Army was coming. He told them, "They got Luis Eduardo and his wife and his child". Bolívar said things are bad and our witness said yes. Alfonso Bolívar was eating lunch with some workers. One of them, Alejandro, was going to tell his wife that the Army was coming so that she would know that. Bolívar told him "OK, but finish eating first and then go." A short while later, Alejandro left going downhill. He reached a point like a corner when the witness said they heard some shots. Then our witness told us he said, "Boys, let's run. It is the Army". And they began to run and from above the house the Army soldiers shouted at them to stop running. They heard sounds and were frightened, but kept running until they all met again. Our witness said he thought, "Thank God nothing has happened to us".

Then Alfonso Bolívar told them that soldiers had killed or injured his wife because he saw her when she fell, her head covered with blood, on some straw on the floor. He said he saw her fall. Our witness said he told Bolívar that maybe it was just his imagination, but Bolívar said he was going to go back to see what had happened.

The witness said he told Bolívar to go back the next day, but Bolívar turned back right away. Our witness then ran on with the other workers and said he told them that he was afraid, and they would sleep up in the hills (monte).

The next day, having heard that Bolívar might not have gone back to his home, our witness returned with the other workers very carefully to Bolívar's house. They found blood where Bolívar had said he saw his wife fall, and blood elsewhere in the house.

Our witness said that the soldiers who had come to Alfonso's house were the same ones who took Luis Eduardo. The others asked "How do you know?" He said, "Because those are Luis Eduardo's horses over there."

After looking for Alfonso Bolívar and his family for quite a while they were about to leave when our witness saw a high stack of cacao branches which appeared suspicious.

When our witness went to see what this was, he said he and the others saw freshly moved soil and they knew that people were buried there.

They wondered, "What should we do? We know they are buried here." They went up in the hills (monte). They slept in a house that they found.

The next day our witness thought about going with one of the others to San José to tell the Peace Community what had happened. But he decided instead to go back to see what had become of the people in the house he had left that morning. As he did so, the next day, he began to see helicopters and so returned to where his companions were. There were 4 families. The next day they saw helicopters in La Resbalosa. They spent the next 15 days in the hills, fishing in the river for food, and going up into the hills during the day.

Finally the witness said, "I can't stand it anymore." On a Tuesday he walked to a place where he could buy a little food: a kilo of cheese and some brown sugar. He slept in the hills. Then at 6 a.m. he started walking and he got to San José on March 9. Some of the people that had just been threatened in the hills were there. He thought the "lost families" would be OK.

Addendum 5

Notes: Interview with Massacre Witness #4

San Josecito

Monday afternoon, April 18, 2005

The witness is a relative of a massacre victim. He is very young. He is kind of afraid and does not want his face shown. He said that he, Alfonso Bolívar and two others had been working in the cocoa bean fields in the morning and had come into Bolívar's home for lunch. They were just finishing lunch and preparing to go back in the fields, when a relative of Luis Eduardo's arrived at the house and told them that the paramilitaries were coming and the Army soldiers were with them. He said they were scared but they thought they would go on working. He said they were just ready to go back to the fields when they heard shooting nearby. He said they walked out of the house and the soldiers saw them and started shooting. He said, "They were trying to kill us. We took off running."

The witness told us he heard Bolívar's wife screaming, "The children." He said he could hear the children crying. He told us, "That's all I heard. I ran for it. That night we slept out in the hills."

The witness said the next day he and the others went back to Alfonso's farm to see if they could find Bolívar and his family. Nobody was in the house. There was blood all over. There was blood in the living room. Our witness said he figured they killed them with machetes, because there were small pieces of the flesh of the children. There were children's clothes and Bolívar's wife's bloody clothes.

Our witness said he believed they must be dead. He and the others looked around but could not find anyone. He told us he thinks Bolívar's wife was raped, because they found her blouse and footprints and it appeared she had been tied. There was also blood on the mattresses.

The witness said they found a pole with Alfonso's shirt on it. He said he told his friends that he thought Alfonso had been killed. They said no, but he said "I am sure they are dead."

They found a shallow grave. The bodies were covered with a little earth and a lot of cacao brush that Alfonso had cut from the cacao trees. He saw Alfonso's body first. It was cut into pieces. He said it was very painful for him to see his relative cut up like that.

The witness said the grave was about 70 meters from the house. It was in the cacao field. The bodies were also covered with blankets. They found a place full of blood where the killers probably had cut them up.

Our witness said the Army and the paramilitaries were the same. He, himself, did not see them. The people who came to warn Alfonso did see them. They are very afraid and they have all gone to other towns to work.

He said the FARC guerrillas are present in the area, but he did not see any of them in the place where the shooting took place that day.

He said he used to ask Alfonso, "What are you going to do?" He said, "I won't run. I don't owe anyone anything."

Our witness said that the witness who fled at Luis Eduardo's capture was the one who came and warned them. They all heard the shots and said, "Run, Run, Run." They saw the dirt fly from the bullets.

Alfonso ran too. They told Alfonso not to go back but he heard his wife calling so he went back. He said to them, "Come with me," but they didn't. They were too scared.

Addendum 6

Notes: Interview with Massacre Witness #5, a person who was part of the search team

San Josecito
April 19, 2005

The witness said that those who were in San José learned of the killings on Wednesday evening, February 23. The witness had walked with a group of about 100 members of the Peace Community as a search committee up to the massacre site, where they found the corpses.

Alfonso Bolívar had a fairly big cacao farm. This is cacao country and there is lots and lots of cacao. Our witness said, "When the bodies were found, there were signs of cuts on Bolívar's wife (Sandra) and on the laborer, but they were not totally dismembered."

In the witness' opinion, the Army is trying to create mass displacement of the people.

The witness told us that "the Fiscalía who worked on the exhumation of the bodies said that the torture cuts were the same type as those seen on the bodies of the victims in the massacre at Mapiripán."

The witness also said "Everyone knows that the contra-guerrilla battalions are the craziest of all the soldiers. They are recruited for craziness." When the witness met them in the hills as part of the search committee, the witness was afraid that they would ignore their officers and just fire at the gathering of people.

The search committee left at 5 a.m. on Thursday morning, February 24. There were about 100 in all when they all joined. They were walking single file at one point and this witness counted them. They went as 3 groups. The groups were to meet at Buenos Aires. There were men, women, children, old people, and pregnant women.

One of the women fell behind and got lost, and she is the one who found Deiner's head. She retraced her steps then and found the group but it took a lot of time. They sent a group down right away to watch the bodies, because they had already been so damaged by birds and animals.

The first group got to the farm by about 4 p.m. Some children had run ahead and the soldiers almost killed them. Our witness observed a lot of tension between the 2 groups of soldiers at the farm. A big group of soldiers surrounded the first batch of civilians to arrive and pointed machine guns at them. Someone yelled that they were civilians with babies and old people. Those soldiers did not back down until Captain Gordillo from the other unit yelled at them repeatedly. Finally they obeyed.

There were lots of helicopters. Representatives of the Fiscalía, who arrived while the search committee was there, looked at Alfonso Bolívar's house. It had been ransacked. There was a big pool of blood and a bloody axe. There were machete cuts in the mattresses, furniture, everything.

The Fiscalía did not finish the investigation because it became late in the day. They left for Carepa at 5 p.m. on Friday. They carried a great deal of evidence with them in bags. The soldiers took a great number of photos, including posing with each other next to the body bags and next to the ransacked and bloody house.

The witness understands that regular Army soldiers are not allowed to carry machetes, but they are frequently seen carrying them.

Addendum 7
Notes: Interview with Sr. José Phidalgo Banguero-Zapata, Mayor of Apartadó, along with the Asesora Jurídica

Wednesday, April 20, 2005

We learned from the Council members at our dinner Monday evening that there are 15 council members. They receive enough pay so that they do not have to have jobs or businesses on the side, but some of them do. They are elected at large from the whole municipality (municipio) and at present all of them live in Apartadó and none live outside it.

We were told that the Mayor was returning on the flight from Medellín, just to be able to meet with us. He was in Medellín to attend a debate by the provincial Congress on what to do about the Peace Community.

We saw an office labeled Asesor Jurídico, so we introduced ourselves and asked if we could talk to the City Attorney. She was very polite. She showed us her job description and said that she had competed for the position. We were concerned that the houses in San José might be expropriated as abandoned, so CSN asked her to explain the condemnation (expropriation) law. Her explanation described a system not very different from the one in Wisconsin.

When we went in to see the Mayor, she came along.

We introduced ourselves and gave our usual listing of the concerns of the Peace Community. The Mayor insisted that the Police are community Police, a separate division, and that they respect human rights. He said he has demanded that the authorities investigate (esclarecer) the murder of the eight persons. He said it was important to him that the murders took place up in the monte and not in the city or the towns.

He described the gathering where they took truckloads of good things out to San José, after the massacre to inaugurate the new Police station in San José. He says there were 2,500 people. He explained that the Police have a civil branch. He said they answer to the Mayor, but he also said they are a branch of the National Police.

The Mayor said that the Abibe mountain range is dominated by the FARC.

He said that on April 3, the general promised that the houses in San José would be taken care of. The lawyer (asesora jurídica) said that there is a national law protecting the property of displaced persons. But she backed away from saying that the former residents of San José are displaced persons entitled to the protection of that law.

You can go to the Personero (municipal clerk) and demand return of your land. That has happened in other towns, but not here.

The Mayor indicated he is offended that the Peace Community goes to international groups for help.

Addendum 8

Interview with General of the XVII Brigade, Héctor Jaime Fandiño-Rincón

Brigade Headquarters, Carepa, Antioquia
Wednesday, April 20, 2005

At 11:30 a.m. we met with the general for an hour in his office.

Detailed notes of meeting:

- We opened the interview by introducing ourselves and expressing our interest in the progress of the investigation of the massacre. General Fandiño was very courteous, but also very self-assured.
- He said that Apolinar Guerra and Elkin Tuberquia had been captured and accused of being guerrillas, but that the Defensoría had gotten them freed, arguing that they were not guerrillas and that they had been tortured.
- The General said that they came in in January and denied what the Defensor and Father Giraldo had said. They insisted they were not tortured.
- He said they gave this testimony to the Fiscalia and to the Procuraduría, so the FARC took revenge against their family.
- General Fandiño said that Luis Eduardo Guerra called Elkin Tuberquia and told him that he wanted to quit the Peace Community. He said the FARC found out about that and killed him.
- General Fandiño said that [Apolinar] Guerra and Tuberquia are safe in Bogotá and he would arrange for us to interview them if we would like to do that.
- General Fandiño showed us a list of 500 complaints. He said, "All of them except a few are lies." (We really did not see the list close up. It appeared to just be a list of names. It was only a few sheets of paper.)
- On Dec. 6 the FARC decapitated 3 Indians in Las Playas, which appears to be true.
- The General does not believe the Peace Community's version of events. He states that the bodies of the victims were discovered on February 25 and were not removed by the Fiscalia until February 26. And the bodies were buried very deep. The witness could not have found them by just removing a little bit of earth.
- He also said that already on February 24, the Peace Community sent an email accusing the Army of the killing. Also the Corporación Libertad sent out the message on February 24 with all the details. He asked how they knew what had happened.
- General Fandiño does not believe what the Peace Community has said, that a witness escaped and came back and found blood and found the grave and the bodies all cut up. General Fandiño does not believe that could have happened.
- General Fandiño said he has a complete record of the whereabouts of all his troops. Each commander has a Global Positioning Satellite (sic) (GPS). (Editor's note: GPS stands for Global Positioning System.)

- The General said that the Feb. 24 email was on the Peace Community's website. The Defensor called General Fandiño on February 24 to tell him about the massacre and he was completely surprised. So how did the Peace Community know all this on February 24?, the General asked.
- He said, "They did all this to make the Army look bad in front of the Inter-American Court."
- We asked about the status of Wilmar Durango. We said that the members of the Peace Community had made a lot of complaints about him, stating that he was living at Brigade Headquarters, that he wore the uniforms of Police on some occasions, of Army on some occasions, and also acted as a paramilitary. He had held them up and taken their money, saying that the guerrillas would get it otherwise. He had taken part in a lot of illegal blockades and used them to steal property. And he had threatened the life of Yorbelis Restrepo, who was killed just a few days after the threat.
- General Fandiño said that he thought that Wilmar was a criminal and that he had brought charges against him, but the Fiscalia had let him off. He said that if there were any more complaints against Wilmar, he would have him charged again.
- General Fandiño said he thought that Gloria Cuartas and Father Giraldo "ought to be in jail". He showed us a civil complaint (demanda) that he has filed (or will be filing) against the two of them and the Corporación Libertad. It claims calumnia (defamation).
- General Fandiño gave us each a slick folder full of information against the Peace Community.

FALL 2008

Tiquisio: A Community Beset by Violence with a Unique Response

Tiquisio is a small village located in the heart of the beautiful Serranía de San Lucas in Bolívar state in northern Colombia and literally sits on top of a gigantic gold mine coveted by multinational corporations, particularly AngloGold Ashanti from South Africa, that is known in Colombia as Kedahda.

The good people of Tiquisio, who work both as small-scale miners and peasants, have suffered under the guerrillas, the paramilitaries and the Colombian Army. From 1978 to 1997 the ELN (National Liberation Army) was present in the area. This group assassinated whoever refused to pay their "taxes." In 1997, 1998 and 2001, the area was taken over by the paramilitaries who stole cattle, raped women and committed a series of massacres and killings. They claimed to be "cleaning" the area of guerrillas because the multinationals were coming and would give jobs to everyone. The "cleaning" carried out, the Army has controlled the region since 2003. The Army occupies a small hill in the middle of the town and from the hill shoots mortar shells above the small community, supposedly directed against the guerrillas. The Army assassinates, detains and disappears people, according to testimonies given by the people to a Colombia Support Network (CSN) delegation. The soldiers sing a song saying: "We want to swim in a pool full of guerrilla blood."

They are paid money and given two weeks vacation for every guerrilla they kill. The Army carries lists of local people branded as guerrillas, without evidence.

Since the Colombian government has declared it a "red zone," it receives very little investment from the government. For the same reason there are no public services: The community lacks clean water, a proper sewer system, health services and education. The sanitary system drains into a branch of the Magdalena River where people fish, children swim and women clean clothes. Their school has a ratio of 52 students per teacher, and the health services have been dismantled. All of this on top of a gold mine. For all the above reasons, many people have left and gone to join the four million internally displaced people in Colombia (almost 10 percent of the population of 44 million in the country). It has also created distrust and the disintegration of society.

Recently, Kedahda has increased its presence in the area, and people are afraid that the multinational is going to get all the privileges. In the years 1988-98, tons of gold were taken without the profits being invested in the region. Tiquisians have always considered the mine communal property. They worry that the multinational will take all the profits, forcing local people to leave their small mining and work long hours with low salaries. Others expressed their concern for the effects big mining operations could have on the environment. And others worry that many people will leave and this would be the end of their community. Responding to an Urgent Action launched by CSN on April 22, 2008, the multinational openly declared that when they see their security threatened they seek the Colombian Army. This Army receives yearly millions of dollars from the U.S. government despite their terrible human rights record.[1]

But the people of Tiquisio decided to reconstruct their community as a civilian alternative to the armed conflict and the humanitarian crisis in a collective way to protect their self-determination, life, human rights and a space for dialogue. Therefore they created the Proceso Ciudadano por Tiquisio, PCT, (Citizens Process for Tiquisio) since they do not want to leave Tiquisio, and they remain attached to their little plots. The PCT organized mothers, youth and small-scale miners to develop a community life plan and the conditions for a better life. They develop cultural and educational activities, try to improve their economic problems through community agriculture and seek to help achieve a negotiated solution to the conflict in the area. The CSN delegation was impressed by their tremendous sense of community.

1. Research article by Colombia Support Network published February 6, 2012, reporting on incidents from 2005-2012: CSN Report: The Colombian Army: Terrorism, Thievery, Bungling and Massacres-Update, at www.colombiasupport.net.

Citizens Process for Tiquisio is a community organization that seeks to build a humanitarian space for the integral development of the people of Tiquisio. Tiquisio has 13 unincorporated towns called corregimientos and 72 veredas or rural neighborhoods. Its people's main economic activities are agriculture, cattle-raising, fishing and gold mining. The municipality has 20,000 people. Because the armed conflict has generated forced displacement, deterioration of the social fabric, distrust among former neighbors and friends, detachment from their land, the disintegration of social organizations and losing the sense of belonging to the community, the people of Tiquisio decided to build the Citizens Process for Tiquisio as a civilian alternative to the conflict in order to strengthen its social organizations, gain spaces for dialogue, guarantee people do not have to leave the region, and improve their situation by building peace in the region. Tiquisio means "land of gold." The community was very hospitable and gracious. They opened their hearts to the CSN delegation.

In 1975, armed groups started to appear, attacking the guerrillas and starting the confrontation with the guerrillas. Families abandoned the countryside, and in 1998 there was a battle between the paramilitaries and the ELN (Ejército de Liberación Nacional, National Liberation Army) guerrillas, and the town ended up between the two warring groups. People fled to the mountains seeking refuge. This happened on August 10, 1998. War keeps going on, and since then they have had no tranquility, as the Army keeps killing in the rural neighborhoods and keeps threatening the inhabitants and damaging their homes.

SMALL-SCALE MINERS

The multinational Kedahda was granted a concession from the government of 200 hectares, and in the middle of those, 36 hectares were left for the small-scale miners. This is a concession to start mining. In other words, the 36 hectares in Las Nieves are in the middle, and sooner or later the small-scale miners will have to leave. There are no roads, but the multinational has indicated it will build them along with hospitals and schools; this means that little by little, they are usurping power. Technology and money buy everything. The small-scale miners say, "We work the rivers and forests with our hands, but they come with backhoe loaders, and soon the water from the mountains is gone, rain stops and many species will disappear. The people will leave." There is not only gold here but also oil, uranium and emeralds, they say.

Tiquisio residents should be concerned about the effects of the Tratado de Libre Comercio (TLC, Free Trade Treaty), which is a form of neocolonialism.

Most of the money of the country goes to the Armed Forces. With TLC, there will be more unemployment and more conflict. Tanks protect the gasoline. The Army is the largest employer and Democratic Security[2] does not bring development but brings war to the homes of the residents of Tiquisio with the creation of the peasant soldiers.[3] President Uribe also undertook to create a civilian informant network of one million volunteers to function as additional "eyes and ears" for the Police.[4] Shells have fallen near the school and near the cemetery. The soldiers know where they are shooting. On another occasion in 2004, the ERP (Ejército Revolucionario del Pueblo, The People's Revolutionary Army) threw five gas cylinders inside the town. That tells us how vulnerable the civilian population is.

Our delegation spoke with a couple, Felix and Minerva. Felix is the President of the Miners' Association and belongs to the Citizens Process for Tiquisio and Minerva, his wife, is the head of the women's group. The following summarizes their comments: They said that mining was very good in the first years, but the state never paid attention to the mining sector: It does not engage in training, and the profits from the mining are not invested in the region. In an indirect way mining favored the guerrillas of the Ejército de Liberación Nacional (ELN) in all of Southern Bolívar Department (province). Between 1988 and 1998, 120 tons of gold were mined without a cent invested from the Colombian state. The ELN guerrillas saw the boom in the area and started to charge a "war tax." On their own, the miners organized communal workdays to build primitive roads and organize community action. Mining in Tiquisio has the potential to engage all its inhabitants in the mining industry. At the beginning, gold was on the surface, but now they have to dig deeper, using oxygen and equipment. Everybody participates in this economic activity, and the people consider the mine communal property. Even people from other countries came and mined here, they said, and the people shared with them. People keep mining, and the ELN guerrillas keep demanding their "war tax" even now that they are talking

2. President Álvaro Uribe Vélez spoke of 'three little eggs' when he became President of Colombia in 2002. The three eggs were the three requirements he saw for Colombia's long-term prosperity. They were democracy, security and foreign investment. Substantial increases in spending for the Armed Forces of Colombia addressed the second requirement of Uribe's.

3. President Uribe created a category of "peasant soldiers" as part of his military structure. He sought to recruit 15,000 peasant soldiers who would receive three months of military training, serve in their hometowns and return to their homes at night. See "'Peasant' Force Takes Shape in Colombia" by Scott Wilson, *The Washington Post*, March 13, 2003.

4. See report by the Washington Office on Latin America (WOLA) of September 24, 2002, at http://www.wola.org/analysis/colombia-governments-controversial.

to the government about demobilizing.[5]

The Nariño Battalion does not give security to the small-scale miner. It is there to protect the multinational mining company. Small-scale miners are not considered important. They themselves paid teachers and health brigades. The government has never taken into account children, the displaced or widows. Some peasant widows do not know how to defend themselves, and their children are taken to become guerrillas or recruited for the Army. The Army uses young girls, makes them become women, makes them pregnant, and destroys homes. Since this is considered a Red Zone (high-conflict zone) the government does not invest. Kedahda wants an open-pit mine for itself. People are afraid of the contamination this would bring. In Mina Seca (a corregimiento of Tiquisio), all the streams are going to disappear because the water will be contaminated, and that will be the end of the swamps. There is oil and uranium; that is why there is war, Felix and Minerva indicated, and girls 12 and 13 years old are made prostitutes and are bringing AIDS. With the money from Plan Colombia, a poly-sports center was built that nobody uses. Is that justice, when there are no schools and there is hunger and malnutrition?

The paramilitary demobilization is a lie because they are there. The forest guardian project[6] is a way to legitimize the paramilitaries. Wherever the paramilitaries go, they set conditions for the population so they control everything, like in the town of San Pablo, where all of the businesses, the bars, the clothing stores, etc., belong to them. The paramilitaries issue an identification card (carnet) that functions as a credit card in order to control businesses and the economy of the towns.[7]

Education: The diocese of Magangue has an agreement with the Department of Bolívar to hire teachers. There are 16 schools in the region and 1,600 students, but they need to cover more since there are places without teachers. There are not enough classrooms or teachers, and no library.

We members of the CSN delegation also visited the local military battalion. The Colonel greeted us with a copy of the Constitution in his hand, explaining that their function was to protect the civilian population. When questioned,

5. Editor's note: The ELN guerillas on more than one occasion have engaged the Colombian government in peace talks, but the two sides have never proceeded to a signed agreement. Several years ago, CSN was represented as an observer organization in talks held in Costa Rica. Those talks did not result in an agreement and none has been reached as of February, 2024.

6. Another part of President Álvaro Uribe's security plan.

7. Editor's note: The description of the paramilitary presence relies upon the comments of Tiquisio residents with whom the delegation members spoke, as is the case for the description of schools in the paragraph which follows.

they said the shells are for practice, and they are after guerrillas only. CSN delegate Ann George[8] had the pleasure of holding a shell in a symbolic way: She was holding her country's military aid in one hand.

A part of this Citizens Process for Tiquisio is their community radio station called "Ecos de Tiquisio: the Voice of the Feeling of Tiquisio," which has goals such as the construction and development of peace in the town and region and the stimulation and recovery of their cultural identity. They seek to create consciousness in the audience of the importance of participation, of building a public space and for becoming active citizens to help in the strengthening of democracy and to oversee that their rights as citizens are respected. And a very important goal is to integrate the community so they will be the leaders of the radio station.

Contacts were made with regional radio networks, such as the Network of Community Radio Stations of the Middle Magdalena (AREDMAG), to train the locals. The radio station started to broadcast in 2003.

On April 19, a threat was received, signed by the "Aguilas Negras" (Black Eagles), a wing of the paramilitaries. The threat said "from today forward, consider yourselves dead guerrillas, you sons of bitches of anarchists, you bunch of bandits of the FARC and ELN." One of those mentioned in the paramilitary threat was Father Rafael Gallego, who is in charge of the Ecos of Tiquisio community radio station, a great supporter of the PCT, who has repeatedly called attention to the fact that the Colombian Army keeps the military base on the hill controlling the town. Father Gallego is the parish priest and is a philosopher and theologian specializing in Human Rights and International Humanitarian Law. He is a first-class community organizer. He has led the creation of the radio station and the peasant school-farm, and above all, he is considered a threat by all the local economic, political and military powers. After leaving town for a few months because of the threats, Father Gallego is back in Tiquisio. The PCT wants to become a Constituent Assembly Process focused on defending their rights as set forth in the progressive 1991 Colombian constitution.

CSN has invited Father Rafael on a speaking tour to the United States and Canada. Plans are set for October 26 to November 22, 2008. Let's get ready to receive him with open arms![9]

8. Cecilia's companion on the trip to Tiquisio was Ann George of Winthrop, Washington, head of the Methow Valley, Washington, CSN chapter-in-formation.

9. Editor's Note: Subsequent to this article the State Department denied Fr. Gallego a visa to travel to the United States, and the speaking tour had to be canceled.

2007

Merchants of War: The Case of Colombia Shown in Three Examples

Kedahda, Drummond Coal, and Occidental Petroleum

KEDAHDA

Since 1998 the war for the control and exploitation of natural resources in the region of southern Bolívar State in the northwestern region of Colombia has been destroying social organizing in this region. The region is known for having one of the largest gold mines in the Western Hemisphere, besides oil, emeralds and a great variety of biodiversity in fauna and flora and water. The rural peasant and small mining communities which inhabit the area have been taking care of the natural resources, exploiting them only with simple tools. The Colombian state has practically abandoned the area: There is almost no infrastructure of roads, telephones, sewer systems or water treatment plants for these rural communities which have lately decided to cultivate coca plants for the production of cocaine to survive. The inhabitants cannot take their products to the markets because of a lack of roads. The area has also featured the presence of guerrillas, among them the Ejército de Liberación Nacional

(ELN, National Liberation Army) and the Fuerzas Armadas Revolucionarias de Colombia (FARC, Revolutionary Armed Forces of Colombia).

On March 3, 1997, a paramilitary group invaded the town of Río Viejo and assassinated the head of the miners' union, posting his head on a pike facing the Serranía de San Lucas, where the gold mine is located, and telling the community they should allow the entry of the multinationals into the region since they would bring economic development and jobs.

At the end of 1997, the paramilitary group known at the time as Autodefensas Campesinas de Córdoba y Urabá (ACCU, Peasant Self-Defenders of Córdoba and Urabá) announced its intention to wrest control of this territory from the hands of the guerrillas. On November 7, 1997, combat started, and the ACCU took over the mountains and blocked the entry of food and medicines into the area for the inhabitants. ACCU attacked by land, river and air, aided by helicopters and small planes. In their path they left death and destruction by massacring civilians, burning their homes, stealing their cattle and property, raping women, engaging in torture, beheading people and displacing most of the inhabitants of the region, accusing them of being guerrilla collaborators. The paramilitary group openly spoke of preparing the region for the exploitation of its natural resources through the investment of large sums of capital.

Here is a description of some of the actions of the paramilitaries when entering the region as described by the Regional Working Group of the Magdalena Medio, taken from direct testimony from the communities of southern Bolívar state:

On Friday, November 6, 1997, 180 men dressed in uniforms and carrying arms approached the community of Sudán at 1 p.m. They came in nine motorboats and had a list of names. First they killed a citizen named Michel Hernández near Sudán, then they went to Sudán and removed Nilson Polanco, who was 20 years old, from a boat and beat and decapitated him in front of the population. Then they killed another youth who was 23 years old. With a list in their hands, they asked about several families from the town. Former Mayor of Tiquisio Arcesio Pérez introduced himself as the commander of the paramilitary group. Hilario Torres, a former City Council member, was one of his main helpers.

On Saturday, November 7, 1997, at 8 o'clock in the morning, about 50 ELN guerrillas waited in trenches for the arrival of the paramilitary group. They arrived in 10 motorboats, starting the attack. After two hours of combat, the guerrillas retreated because they were being attacked by helicopters. The conflict between paramilitaries and guerrillas has continued to take place in the area of the Serranía de San Lucas (San Lucas Mountain Range) to the present time.

The inhabitants observed that when there was fighting and there were dead paramilitaries, their corpses were picked up minutes later by a gray helicopter. People believe this helicopter left from Corozál, near the military base there. Brigadier General Fernando Millán of the Colombian Army publicly admitted that two Army helicopters and two private ones were in the area under his command.

In the hamlet of La Mocha, the paramilitaries burned 40 houses and kidnapped an undetermined number of peasants to use as human shields. The whereabouts of these persons is unknown. When the paramilitaries arrived at Pueblito Mejía, the inhabitants had left the town. Some 200 houses were burned and two persons were killed there. On the outskirts of this town, the paramilitaries burned the cooperative of the Peasant Association and killed 12 people. On Friday night they burned 100 homes in Mina Azul. In the hamlet of Buena Seña the paramilitaries burned 205 homes, from a total of 211. On Sunday, November 22, in Norosí, 42 houses were burned. On November 26, the paramilitaries laid siege to the town of Monterrey, preventing the whole population of the town from leaving.

In the town of La Cooperativa, two children, aged three and five, were beheaded. They were taken from their mother's arms. The men in this family were killed by machetes, as the paramilitaries accused them of being guerrillas. In town after town the paramilitaries destroyed and killed whatever they found, according to the people who ran up into the mountains escaping from the invasion: widows, mothers and relatives who lost their loved ones. People describe bombings and the use of machine guns. The paramilitaries carried laminated lists of names. There was no food in the area. People were cut up into pieces, dismembered and decapitated. Meanwhile, the guerrillas used land mines and occupied community places. The ELN denounced acts of cannibalism by the ACCU.

There are no official reports to establish the numbers of people in the region who were killed or displaced.

Counterinsurgency Battalion #27, Rogelio Correa Campos of the Colombian Army, arrived in the community of Arenal after the paramilitaries had left. The same was true for the Los Guanes and Nariño Battalions. People saw the Army patrolling with civilians, and it did not go after the ACCU but rather stayed in the territory, setting up checkpoints and seeking out landmines. The Army units did not stop the helicopters which were helping the ACCU.

As a consequence of these actions there was a massive displacement of the population in the area which had no place to return to. To summarize, in this first incursion, 10 towns were destroyed, more than 1,000 homes were burned, 400 persons were massacred and 35,000 persons were displaced.

Since that time, the situation has not changed for the population of this region. Last September 9, 2006, the Colombia Support Network (CSN) received the following statement from the Association of Miners:

"Our communities have worked and lived in this region as miners and peasants for several generations. Beginning about 10 years ago, multinational corporations (MNCs) from the mining sector, attracted by the great mineral wealth of this region, have wanted to take over our territory, developing as years pass the same strategy that is used in other parts of the country: terror and killings with the support of the State and the paramilitaries. This strategy calls for the total militarization of the region in order to displace those who are the legitimate owners of the region so that the mineral-rich lands in our territory will be left in the hands of the MNCs (Multinational Corporations). On September 19, 2006, members of the Colombian Army's "New Granada" Battalion cowardly assassinated our leader ALEJANDRO URIBE, accusing him of being a guerrilla. The same Battalion confiscated documents of the Federation of Miners and Peasants, according to an Urgent Action message sent by communities in the region. These same communities ask the national government to reject the plans of the multinational KEDAHDA to take over their territory by legal and illegal means."[1]

A more detailed description of the killing of Alejandro Uribe and the aftermath of that killing follows:

On September 19, 2006, Alejandro Uribe, a well-respected leader of the community of Mina Gallo in the South of Bolívar Department, was murdered by Colombian Army personnel. Mr. Uribe, a peasant and small-scale miner, was president of the Mina Gallo Community Action Board. The Army misrepresented his killing to the news media as that of a guerrilla in combat. About 600 inhabitants of the region traveled to the headquarters of the Nueva Granada Battalion of the Army's Fifth Brigade in Santa Rosa demanding the return of the body of Alejandro Uribe.

1. Kedahda SA is a subsidiary of AngloGold Ashanti, the third largest gold-mining company in the world in terms of production according to their website, with headquarters at the time of the events described in this article in Johannesburg, South Africa.

On September 21, the Army responded by threatening the assembled community members, saying "... he [Uribe] will not be the only dead person you are going to have. There will be more dead leaders." The Army had previously indicated it had a list of leaders of the region and members of the miners' federation whom they hoped to find walking alone on paths in the vicinity of their homes.

General José Joaquín Cortés of the Army's Fifth Brigade suggested that Alejandro Uribe was an ELN guerrilla carrying an AK-47 rifle and was accompanied by five guerrillas, and died in an Army-guerrilla combat, all of which the community residents totally reject.

What really is going on here is that the Colombian Army is engaged in uprooting peasants and small-scale miners by attacking their leaders, such as Alejandro Uribe, so that the multinational mining corporation Kedahda can enter the region and undertake mining operations on peasants' and miners' lands which the government of President Álvaro Uribe has improperly licensed or conveyed to this company for mining development.

The Colombian Government should:

1. Investigate the atrocities committed by the Colombian military and punish those responsible.
2. Protect small-scale miners and peasants, recognizing their legitimate right to the lands they are occupying and the mines they have been working.
3. Refrain from entering into bogus contracts with multinational corporations such as Kedahda to give them valuable mining concessions in lands where small-scale miners and peasants have already established their right to possession.
4. Demand that the Army deliver the list of proposed victims to the Procurador General's office for an investigation.

The representatives of diverse organizations, many based in the southern Bolívar Region and others from elsewhere in Colombia or in the world, invited groups representing or working in solidarity with farm workers, miners, indigenous peoples, Afro-Colombians and students to convene in Santa Rosa in Bolívar Department on August 15-16, 2006, to hold hearings related to a lawsuit against the Kedahda Mining Company. The Company's natural resource extraction projects have seriously compromised miners' rights in the regions of the Kedahda Company's mining development activities, particularly through its use of ad hoc armed forces to control its workers.

Their findings, expressed in their own terms, after these two days of deliberations, include the following:

1. When miners in this region have applied to the Bolívar Region's Mining Office for permits, or to add on to their existing mining titles, they have found that the Kedahda Company had already established contractual rights to nearly all of the untitled known mines in the region. This Company has now requested similar priority rights in 336 Colombian municipalities. These same operational strategies were reported in Quinchía in the Department of Risaralda, among many other sites.
2. These strategies have succeeded because of changes made just a few years ago in Colombia's Mining Code to benefit multinational mining interests. These changes have harmed our miners who for decades have risked or lost their lives to maintain their sole source of income. The changes have also compromised the quality of life of our communities, our regions, our indigenous peoples and our Afro-Colombian population.
3. Under the current Mining Code, impoverished miners are unable to meet the requirements for obtaining legal mining titles. This leaves many miners and their families no alternative but to continue working in the mines and selling the gold on the black market. Many have thus faced extreme poverty due to the vagaries of this secondary market. It was also noted that these new provisions in the Mining Code have inured to the benefit of municipalities and regions that are not even mining gold, given that some of the resulting profit is used to finance paramilitary activities in various non-mining regions in Colombia.
4. Although it has only been proven that the Kedahda Company is now surveying mining sites under the jurisdictions of Buena Seña, San Martín de Loba and La Cruz, all indications are that over the next decade this multinational will have established the requisite infrastructure to survey the southern Bolívar region as well. The Company will by then have gained title to those mines that seem most profitable, without any regard for the presence of farm workers, many of whom have worked on the lands for decades. Our early research indicates that this Company ignores concerns related to proper decontamination. This region's great gold wealth could soon help fund further violence, displacements and plundering instead of benefiting our people.
5. Our miner and farm worker community participants have further testified that many government bureaucrats and workers from international

agencies have obtained valuable information from them, then gone on to work for the Kedahda Company. They have exploited our good will, betraying our communities' trust in their motives. We have also heard testimony which indicates that the region's Police and Armed Forces are increasingly prone to defend this multinational corporation's interests. Now, more than ever, they work to convince our fellow farm workers that this Company represents progress for the region and that they should therefore comply with the Company's demands. We also learned that many government workers have negotiated substantial kickbacks from this Company in exchange for their direct support or for their deliberate complacency.

6. Before the Kedahda Company was incorporated as a legal entity, its parent company, Anglo Gold Ashanti, tried to obtain titles through shady dealings, to an extensive 7,000 hectares (over 17,000 acres) in the southern Bolívar region, specifically to lands under the jurisdiction of San Pedro Frío, El Paraíso, Mina Gallo and Montecristo. It has been proven that when their negotiations were faltering, the region was invaded by paramilitary forces who committed many crimes against miners, creating a veritable reign of terror through forced displacements, "disappearances," closing off certain areas to food imports, routine threats and even assassinations. This proves how badly a situation can deteriorate when economically powerful entities seek to exploit natural resources in or near communities that won't simply cede their rights.
7. Recently, since we began to define and expose this Company's modus operandi in our region, there has been a growing paramilitary presence, even after these 'armed actors' were to have been disbanded. We've also noted an increased use of private security forces to defend Kedahda Company's interests. Some of our communities must now live with the intimidation of having government soldiers announce the imminent arrival of paramilitary forces. We are told, for example, that the paramilitary *Aguilas Negras* (Black Eagles) will "not look favorably upon" those who oppose the Company's presence. This makes it all the more worrisome that a special Army battalion has recently been assigned to the mining zone of San Pedro Frío.
8. Given the testimony that has been presented at this public hearing, the People's Court participants declare our commitment to defend our fundamental rights, territories and communities against these violations.

We call for a unified, widespread resistance movement among the farm workers, miners, indigenous peoples and Afro-Colombians affected by the Kedahda Company's plans and activities in our area.

THE CASE OF THE DRUMMOND COAL COMPANY

The Drummond Coal Company is being sued in a United States Court in Alabama for conspiring with paramilitaries to kill union leaders after years of abuses. The Company has used standard procedures to work with private security agencies to protect their grounds. Drummond buys armaments, munitions, uniforms, communication equipment and gasoline, and provides salaries and transportation vehicles. The Company hires former officers of the Colombian Army.

In 2001, Valmore Locarno and Victor Orcasita sought to organize a union at the coal mine in César State in northern Colombia where they worked, a mine which was developed and being run by the Drummond Coal Company of Alabama under an extremely generous concession from the Colombian government. The two men were riding in the Company bus with other employees leaving the mine after work when the bus was stopped by a group of paramilitaries who took them off the bus and murdered them. A former DAS (Departamento Administrativo de Seguridad, Colombia's FBI) official now in prison in *Bogotá*, Rafael García, has testified that he observed the head of Drummond Coal's operation in Colombia pay a paramilitary leader money to carry out the killing of the two union organizers, Locarno and Orcasita, as well as perform other death squad activities.

The violence perpetrated by Drummond has a clear political and economic logic: to clear areas for globalization and to welcome foreign investments and exports, diminishing the social responsibilities of the State and increasing poverty and inequality.

THE CASE OF OCCIDENTAL PETROLEUM

The Colombian State of Arauca is located in the eastern part of the country, bordering Venezuela. It is a new state created by the 1991 Constitution and has about 600,000 inhabitants. Arauca is one of the areas most affected by the armed conflict. The region has a large variety of social organizations, such as 57 cooperatives and peasant associations, 14 unions, 570 community action organizations, two indigenous associations and two committees for the defense of human rights, according to a report of the Spanish organization Observatorio de la Deuda en la Globalización (https://www.traficantes.net/

autorxs/observatorio-de-la-deuda-en-la-globalizaci%C3%B3n).

Political violence increased exponentially in this region after the discovery of oil there in 1980. Caño Limón, one of the most important Colombian oil fields, is administered and exploited by Occidental Petroleum, a U.S.-based multinational corporation intimately linked to Plan Colombia. Plan Colombia is a U.S.-proposed, largely U.S.-funded plan, ostensibly to fight the war against illegal drugs, but in reality created to exploit natural resources with no meaningful controls. Whoever opposes this Plan experiences genocide, forced displacement and human rights violations. In 1983, Occidental found oil in Arauca, and by 1985 had drilled wells and was pumping out oil. The Laguna de Lipa, a lake which was a spectacular biological reserve, was destroyed, and the indigenous Guahibo population was almost annihilated as Occidental's operations decimated the lake, which represented their spiritual and cosmological center. An 800-kilometer-long oil pipeline was built to take the oil from Caño Limón to the town of Coveñas on the Caribbean Sea. This pipeline also destroyed many small farms and tropical rainforests. Caño Limón has reserves of 1.1 billion barrels of oil. Oil has also been searched for in nearby areas, and one of the possible sites is in the region of Capachos. This oil field is partially located in the ancestral territory of the U'Was, the indigenous group which is the last living remnant of the Chibchas, the original native group at the time of the Spanish Conquest. In 2001 and 2002, the U'Was carried out an intense international campaign denouncing the threat that the exploitation of Capachos presented to their sacred territories.

As a consequence of this situation, detentions, disappearances and killings of social leaders and unionists have been a part of the everyday life of this region. For example, on December 13, 1988, eighteen civilians were assassinated, among them six children, and 27 were injured as a consequence of the bombing of the small town of Santo Domingo, Arauca. Reliable witnesses indicate that members of the Colombian Air Force used a U.S.-supplied cluster bomb against the town. In days prior to the attack on Santo Domingo, townspeople had heard the sounds of combat, presumably between guerrilla forces and the Colombian Army. According to reports cited by Amnesty International, the bombing was planned by the Colombian Air Force and Occidental Petroleum at the site of the company's facilities in Caño Limón and supported by the private security company Airscan.[2] A Tribunal co-sponsored by the Colombia Support Network

---

2. Airscan is a private military company formed in 1984 by former U.S. Air Commandos Walter Holloway and John Mansur. See *Wikipedia* article: https://en.wikipedia.org/wiki/AirScan.

at Northwestern University Law School on September 22-23, 2000, later determined that the Colombian Air Force was responsible for the murderous attack on civilians using the U.S.-supplied cluster bomb that was dropped on the town with technical support from Airscan.

On another occasion, more than 2,000 people were detained at the soccer stadium of Saravena, Arauca, where they were photographed, videotaped, interrogated, and branded with permanent ink on their arms. Several were detained, among them the most notable members of the human rights community in Saravena.

One of the most curious effects of the discovery of oil in Arauca is that it coincides with the entrance of the paramilitary forces into the region. As an example given by Observatorio de la Deuda en la Globalización, in the town of Saravena, a municipality of 55,000 inhabitants, in the last five years there have been 763 violent deaths caused by paramilitary forces or the military in their name [Eds. note: “in their name” signifying that the military attributed their own actions to the paramilitaries]. In 2000, the town had 43 violent deaths, in 2001, it had 74, in 2002, it had 138, in 2003, it had 210, and in 2004, there were 298. There have been 16 massacres in Saravena and more than 7,000 persons displaced. The horror and methods of these crimes are too gross to be described. On many occasions the collaboration between the paramilitary forces and the state security forces has been evident.

All of these examples taking place in Colombia teach us that as a routine process the arrival of the paramilitaries is a preamble to preparation of mineral-rich areas for the establishment of mega-projects by multinational corporations. Paramilitarism is being used to prevent civilian resistance by communities that oppose foreign capital projects.

2024

A Shock from the FARC Guerrillas in February 1999

Reported by Jack Laun from notes and observations of Cecilia Zarate-Laun

In an act of thoughtful collaboration, two indigenous women from the United States, Ingrid Washinawatoc of the Menominee community in Wisconsin and Lahe'ne Gay of a Hawaiian community traveled to Colombia in February 1999, where they worked with a young man from California, Terry Freitas, who had spent time in the U'Wa indigenous community, to promote a culturally appropriate school education. They arrived to apply their experience in developing educational programs for indigenous communities to the indigenous community of the U'Wa in the Colombian province of Arauca. They came at the invitation of the U'Wa community.

After they had completed their work with the U'Wa, the three visitors entered a car accompanied by the spiritual leader of the U'Wa community, Berito Kumer-Uwa, and, we were later told, with an indigenous guard bearing a cane, and a driver. They set off for the airport in the town of Saravena on February 25, 1999 but were stopped by armed men in a vehicle shortly after leaving the U'Wa community. The armed men, who were guerrillas of the Fuerzas Armadas Revolucionarias de Colombia (FARC, the Revolutionary

Armed Forces of Colombia) appeared along the road and stopped the U'Wa vehicle. Among them was a member of the U'Wa indigenous community whom Berito recognized and knew had joined the FARC. The three visitors were forced into the vehicle of the kidnappers, who then took off with them.

No word about the U.S. visitors was received for several days, although the U.S. Government was given notice of the kidnapping, and presumably sought to learn where they were being held and to seek their release. But in the week following the kidnapping word was received that they had been shot and killed and their bodies had been dumped in a field just over the border in the neighboring province in Venezuela. No reason for the murders was given and it remains an unanswered question for the families of the three Americans. The editors do not know how or for what reason the three visitors from the U.S. were murdered. Although Terry Freitas had spoken publicly against actions of Occidental Petroleum Company to establish oil wells in U'Wa territory, it is unclear if this was the reason the three were murdered. FARC leadership responded to questions of why the kidnapping and murder had occurred by saying it was "a mistake." Although the FARC commander in Arauca Department at the time was Noe Suarez Rojas, alias "Grannobles," the brother of one of the FARC's top leaders, Victor Julio Suarez Rojas, known as "El Mono Jojoy," no public explanation for the reason the three captives were killed was made by either of the brothers. Grannobles was reported to have been killed by the FARC a few years later, very possibly for having given the order to murder Ingrid, Lahe, and Terry.

Cecilia was the only Colombian to attend the funeral services on the Menominee Reservation in Keshena, Wisconsin, for Ingrid, who was accorded a funeral and burial of special importance as a leading environmentalist and a prestigious activist in the indigenous rights field in the United States. Cecilia later led an effort which brought together in Keshena, Ingrid's Menominee community, her husband Ali; Lahe'ena'es' husband John; an attorney and friend, Bruce Ellison of Rapid City, South Dakota, representing John and Ali; representatives of Terry's family including his girlfriend, Abigail Reyes; and Leslie Wirpsa, a journalist from Colorado and friend of Terry representing Terry. The lead attorney for the FARC in their peace negotiations with the Colombian government in Cuba, Spanish Attorney Enrique Santiago, came from Madrid to meet with the relatives and representatives of Ingrid, Lahe'ena'e, and Terry. Little additional information about the reason for the kidnapping and the murder of the three U.S. visitors to the U'Wa community was revealed in the

Keshena meeting, and a proposed trip to Havana, Cuba for relatives of the three to meet with peace negotiators, including FARC officials, which Cecilia tried to organize with the assistance of the government of Norway, was not agreed to by the relatives of the murdered persons.

The relatives of Ingrid wondered why the U'Wa guard, who was in the car when the FARC unit stopped the car and ordered the three U.S. passengers to get out, did not take action to stop the kidnapping. When the U'Wa leader, Berito Kuwaru'wa, who had won the Goldman Environmental Award in 1998 for his environmental protection leadership, returned to San Francisco later, the Colombia Support Network invited him and an U'Wa companion to CSN's office in Madison, Wisconsin to explain to relatives of Ingrid how the FARC kidnapping had occurred and why those in the car had not confronted the FARC who came to kidnap the three visitors. CSN invited Ingrid's relatives to come to the CSN office, where her mother and an aunt met in a closed-door meeting with the U'Wa leader and his companion to raise any questions they might have. The principal question they had was why the U'Wa guard in the car did not shoot to stop the kidnapping. Berito's answer: because the guard had only a wooden staff, while the FARC kidnappers were armed with guns.

The answer by Berito could not bring Ingrid, Lahe or Terry back to life, nor did it answer why the three visitors were murdered by the FARC, but at least it answered why the U'Wa were unable to prevent the kidnapping.

2014

La Mala Fortuna de Buenaventura

The Misfortune of Buenaventura

The city of Buenaventura, the principal port on Colombia's Pacific Coast, was founded by Adelantado Pascual de Andagoya on July 15, 1540. The conquistadores, who were always so creative in giving names to cities, could not have chosen a more tragic name for this city, since Buenaventura signifies good luck and complete felicity.

Located on the Pacific Coast of Colombia, it forms part of the bio-geographic region of the Chocó, which runs from the border with Panamá to the border with Ecuador, and is a region of immense biological, hydrological, forest and mineral richness, being considered one of the regions of greatest diversity on the planet. It is populated principally by an indigenous and Afro-Colombian population. One of the greatest shames committed by the Spanish was to begin from very early in the conquest to import slaves from Africa to mine minerals such as gold and platinum in the Chocó.

The Chocó has always experienced processes of extraction of its natural resources through the use of violence, force and exclusion against its population. It has a history of suffering in different periods. From the final years of the Nineteenth Century up to the present in the Twenty-first Century, the region has been 'being prepared' for implementation of the neo-liberal policies dictated by the Washington Consensus, which puts in practice a social and economic policy based on the market. The Afro-Colombian and indigenous communities have a deep-rooted culture of solidarity, mutual accompaniment and giving priority to that which is common among us all and not to 'myself,' and they are suffering from the impacts of this new invasion.

Buenaventura, two hours by car from the city of Cali, has a population of approximately 350,000 inhabitants. Eighty percent of them live in poverty and 63 percent are unemployed. They live surrounded by water on all sides but there is no potable water nor a garbage collection system. Fifty percent of Colombia's foreign trade moves through Buenaventura.

The Colombian government is developing mega-projects in Buenaventura to increase the competitiveness of Colombia in the Pacific. It plans to expand its cargo structure and build a new port in Málaga Bay[1] for larger ships since it has deep waters. Several highways have been built to facilitate the passage of merchandise, and a fresh-water port is being built by a Philippine firm associated with one from Singapore. One of the highways would connect the Pacific with the Orinoco River region on the border with Venezuela. Other projects are a marine terminal for the Dagua River, a dock for Cruz Bay and a duty-free zone. All this has generated a displacement of the population to rural areas.

One of the objectives of this modernization is that of taking the neighborhoods close to the sea, called the *bajamar* (low tidelands). The inhabitants of these neighborhoods are principally fishermen and workers in wood or other similar trades. The people say that the government wants to force them out. In the words of one of the inhabitants: "These lands we won from the sea...we worked to fill the streets with clay and sawdust...we put up with everything in order to have a house near the sea and go out to work fishing...Now they want to throw us out because they say it is a high-risk area and they are concerned about our safety. But after they force us out, here in our territory they are going to build hotels, restaurants, stores, offices...No one has asked us if we want to go..."

It is clear to see that the objective of the Colombian government is to make Buenaventura a "pole of development." That is why President Santos declared it to be the capital of the Pacific Alliance (Alianza del Pacífico). The cost is very high: The use of violence and cruelty. A development plan like this is by

1. The area around Málaga Bay is a zone of great importance for its flora and fauna, continental and marine, and it is known worldwide for being a breeding grounds for the humpback whale (*Megaptera novaeangliae*).

definition violent because in its name it drives out a part of the population. The government only emphasizes the economic part. After the demobilization of the paramilitaries in the government of Álvaro Uribe,[2] many of the old militants and new recruits from youths who grew up in poverty and without hope formed what the Army calls *bacrim* (bandas criminales, criminal bands), who are the same paramilitaries with another name, to take control of the territories.

These groups are in charge of "cleaning" Buenaventura—"cleaning" with massacres like that of Punta del Este committed on April 19, 2005, when a paramilitary invited 12 youths of the neighborhood to play football,[3] offering 200,000 pesos to the winning team. The young men never returned. Three days later, their bodies appeared floating in an estuary with their eyes torn from their sockets and with coup de grâce shots in their skulls.[4] The displacement of the population, the torture and the disappearances add to a population already in fear, despair and wretchedness. Every day is witness to the violent and systematic deaths of their relatives, neighbors and friends. Girls and women are raped. People are killed in broad daylight on the street and in the market, or they are taken to so-called "chop houses" (casas de pique) where they are quartered alive, their bodies opened and cut into pieces to be thrown into the sea.

In the first three months of 2014, according to Medicina Legal (the government's Medicine Law Office), 96 persons have died by violent causes. When the people asked for help from the military to prevent the murder of a person, the reply was that "they could not do anything because their function is to look after the wealth." The situation was described with pain and irony to an investigator by an inhabitant of Buenaventura as follows: "For the government and the powerful genocide is more profitable. The equation is simple: The monthly pay for a common paramilitary member is 500,000 pesos. His job is to kill an average of 10 persons per month, while building a decent home for a person who has to be resettled costs 40,000,000 pesos. If there are 10 persons who are provided with housing, you would be talking about 400,000,000 pesos that would need to be invested. It is cheaper for the government to allow ten people to be killed than to relocate one."[5]

---

2. Editor's note: Álvaro Uribe was President of Colombia from 2002 to 2010.
3. Editor's note: Colombia's 'football' is known as 'soccer' in the United States.
4. Gearóid Ó Loingsigh, page 104
5. Editor's note: This dramatic description of life for poor residents of Buenaventura is consistent with the desperate situation described by Gearóid Ó Loingsigh in "La Reconquista del Pacífico."

The Mayor of Buenaventura wrote an emotional note to President Santos, telling him that it was ungrateful, disconcerting and illogical that he organized the VIII Presidential Summit of the Pacific Alliance in Cartagena, a city situated on the Atlantic, on the Caribbean Coast. Buenaventura is not ready to be exhibited. Lots of blood needs to flow yet, many cries of the cut-up and disappeared, and many tears, in order to wish good fortune (buenaventura) to the international visitors.

REFERENCES

1. *Environmental Justice Atlas*. http://www.ejatlas.org/country/colombia http://www.elespectador.com/search/destierro%20bajamar

2. *Justicia y Paz*. http://www.justiciaypazcolombia.com/Herederos-de-la-esclavituwd-en-buenaventura, 22 Mar 2014

3. *Noche y Niebla*. CINEP

4. Ó Loingsigh, Gearóid. "La Reconquista del Pacífico, Invasión, Inversión, Impunidad," Proceso de Comunidades Negras, Bogotá, 2013

1998

A Ray of Hope in Colombia's Nightmare

Don Bartolomé Cataño greeted the delegation from Wisconsin warmly. We were visiting our sister city of Apartadó. With his sweet smile, he explained to us that he represented the peasantry of the region at the City Council. He ran on the ticket of the Unión Patriótica, the third alternative party that represented the hopes of many Colombians who did not feel represented by either of the two traditional parties, Liberals and Conservatives.

With a quick speech, smiling eyes and his cane, the 75-year-old founder of San José de Apartadó told us his life story. He came to Apartadó on May 4, 1966 seeking an opportunity after working for others since he was seven years old. He found beautiful lands near the Serranía de Abibe. He bought a small plot, got married at 36 and started to raise pigs and chickens. He built a small house with a zinc roof. He received leadership training offered by the Peasant Association and liked it very much because they not only trained him but spoke of the need for agrarian reform.

Soon 17 other peasant families came to live in the area where he was. Then the Army came, and a Sergeant Rodríguez, along with a notary who typed quickly, started to ask him questions. Who orients you? Nobody, myself. Why did you come? I came from the town of Andes where the rich are very rich and the poor very poor. Who sent you here? Necessity sent us here. We have been tilling this land for more than 60 days, and if nobody claims it, you can settle here. Don Miguel Flórez says you are guerrillas. We work this land from 5 a.m. to 6 p.m. We plant food—bananas, yuca, plantains, corn. Come and see for yourself.

We built a school, a health center, and we constructed the road. We are not rich people. Why did you call it San José? Because he is the patron saint of the peasants who till the land. Sometimes—he tells us—I am afraid but I keep it inside. Where do I go? God gives me peace. I study my conscience, and I do not owe anything to anybody. In 30 years here I have no enemies.

San José's peasants sold avocados, cocoa beans and other products. Don Bartolo and the community organized the Balsamar Cooperative to market and process the cocoa beans rather than selling to middlemen.

On August 17, 1996, at 11:30 a.m., unknown armed men burst into the city council and shot Don Bartolo twice. He started calmly to pick up his papers when a third shot, directed to his face, killed the founder of San José de Apartadó. In February of 1997, paramilitaries entered the town at night, pulled the four leaders of the Cooperative from their beds and beheaded them, leaving their bodies in the street. The paramilitaries shut the market and forbade the selling of foods and the tending of crops, accusing the villagers of running a supply post for the guerrillas.

The above description repeats the scene that for the majority of this century has taken place all over Colombia: a war against the poor. In the 50s and 60s it was called La Violencia. Now it is called a war on drugs. The name is not important to the people who suffer from it. The root problem of Colombia's tragedy lies in the poverty of so much of its population in a country of great wealth. Ninety percent of the wealth is owned by 2.5 percent of the population. From this situation two guerrilla movements were formed: FARC, the oldest in Latin America, and ELN in the 1960s.

A formal constitutional democracy to the outside world, Colombia with its 35 million people in reality has been a façade democracy, where the military were given "carte blanche" to control the population during most of this century. According to the Comisión Colombiana de Juristas, there are 10 people killed every day for political reasons. Since 1988, 30,000 have been killed, with an average of 3,000 a year, making each year more killings than during the 17 years of Pinochet in Chile. The targets are peasants, leaders such as Don Bartolo, labor leaders, teachers, grassroots organizers, priests, nuns, human rights activists, NGO leaders, lawyers, journalists. In fact, anybody who thinks.

The Army and its paramilitary allies carry out nearly three quarters of the killings. The other quarter is done by the guerrillas. The Army, constrained by international public opinion from doing the killings itself, has allied with landowners, drug lords and even multinationals to create paramilitaries. They do their dirty work—killings, disappearances and horrible torture—knowing that in 97 percent of the cases of killings in Colombia no one is ever convicted. Any attempt to organize a legal opposition in this "democracy," has been eliminated. Such is the case of the Unión Patriótica, Don Bartolo's political party. It was founded in 1985. Since then, almost all its members and leaders have been killed. About 4,000. Nearly one killed a day.

Drug dealers have become landowners. Big international capital wants to join the elites to "develop" areas such as San José where there is a coal deposit nearby. In Urabá, a canal is being planned to replace the Panama Canal. People have fled in terror when paramilitaries arrive, producing one million internal refugees, more than Rwanda has according to UNICEF.

Paramilitary, guerrilla and Army actions grew greatly from the last quarter of 1996, creating a context of terror and death by killing humble unarmed people—mainly peasants—in open violation of international human rights codes.

Seeking to recognize community life and to strengthen ties of citizen unity and not let members become involved in military action, espionage or support for the armed actors, and to give value to their constitutional rights, the inhabitants of 28 settlements, with San José de Apartadó in the center, declared themselves a Comunidad de Paz on March 2, 1997, on Palm Sunday, after High Mass, in the presence and with the support of Pax Christi Holland, members of the Dutch Parliament, the Diocese of Apartadó, Justicia y Paz, CINEP and the then Mayor of Apartadó, Gloria Cuartas.

This admirable peace initiative developed a program based upon absolute neutrality as to the bands confronting each other and the creation of a Special Mixed Commission of Observation for any violations of their commitment and rights on the part of the armed groups.

The people commit themselves:

- Not to bear arms, munitions or explosive materials.
- Not to provide logistical support to the bands in confrontation.
- Not to produce, provide or manipulate information for the sides of the conflict.

- Not to turn to any of the actors in the war to solve personal, family or community problems.

The Community members are clearly identified with flags, billboards or other signs with a white background and a red circle which can be seen at great distance.

The Community obeys the recommendations of an Internal Council composed of four elected citizen delegates, two representatives of national NGOs and one delegate of the Diocese of Apartadó.[1]

The Community seeks stable peace, and through active neutrality and participation, tries to recover civilian and communal space. This peace initiative springs directly from Don Bartolo's influence in the community. It seems to recover his deep desire to live free, work his fields and think about one's wishes, respecting everybody else's right to do the same. Don Bartolo's spirit is alive. Peace Community members want to give value to their rights and autonomy as citizens and Colombians.

This is an alternative allowing the civilian population to express resistance, autonomy, a dignified life and a peaceful expression of opposition to the status quo. It is a novelty in Colombia because it redefines popular power, focusing on exercising fundamental rights as citizens in a democracy, and breaks the dynamics of war and injustice, creating a space to survive.

Since it declared itself a Comunidad de Paz, San José has seen the death of 38 members, 33 executed by paramilitaries and five by FARC guerrillas. On February 11, 1998, coming from harvesting crops, four people, among them a boy of 16 and another of 14, were confronted by a heavily armed paramilitary group in military uniforms. They threatened them with decapitation holding machetes to their throats. Despite public commitment by the Colombian government to dismantle paramilitary groups, no effective action has been taken and they operate, on and off, a checkpoint on the road leading to San José de Apartadó from Apartadó.

In the middle of an atrocious reality created by both paramilitaries and guerrillas, civilian peace initiatives, even as fragile as the San José de Apartadó Comunidad de Paz, represent one of Colombia's greatest hopes.

In my last visit to San José, I went to the small cemetery where among wildflowers Don Bartolo's body rests. There I promised him that I would tell the world the story of San José. And thus this account.

1. Editor's note: In future years, the Internal Council became an eight-member body, drawing members from the central community, San Josecito, and from other rural parts of the Peace Community.

PART E

Opinion Pieces by Cecilia related to different parts of the country, its political institutions both formal and informal, and the role of the United States in Colombia.

DECEMBER 5, 1996

Why Are Death Squads Allowed to Roam Free in Colombia?

Capital Times
Madison, Wisconsin
[Editor's note: a few word order changes and identifying phrases have been added to this guest column.]

On October 16, at noon sharp, my friend Albeiro Bustamante was shot to death as he was going home for lunch.

He was a city alderman from Madison's sister community of Apartadó in Colombia. Albeiro was one of the sweetest persons I have ever known and the personification of a nobility of heart so rare these days. He never meant to harm anybody. He was a member of the Colombian alternative party Unión Patriótica and he wanted peace, democracy and a better life for those Colombians who are poor and disenfranchised.

Albeiro graciously received Madison delegations when he was president of the City Council in Apartadó—people like Wisconsin State Representative Tammy Baldwin and former Dane County Board Member Mark Pocan, who have visited our sister community.[1]

But Albeiro was killed. And the killings continue. They go on and on to the indifference of the whole world because it has already been decided: The killings in Colombia are *only* drug-related. Simple and easy. No analysis and no need to do one. On September 16, the executive board members of the Balsamar Cooperative, a humble peasant cooperative started by members of what is now called the Peace Community of San José de Apartadó, that sells cocoa beans to chocolate factories and which was painfully organized with the help of Dutch solidarity, were called outside their homes and killed by a group of 50 men who did not even bother to wear masks. The following week, an adorable peasant leader, 67-year-old Don Bartolome Cataño, founder of San José de Apartadó, another elected alderman from the Unión Patriótica, was killed.

In the last week of September, celebrating a week calling for peace, when Mayor Gloria Cuartas was in a patio of the school surrounded by school children doing a project called "Let's Do the Homework for Peace," two men dressed as civilians came, took a child and beheaded the child in front of Gloria and the other children.

Colombia is hailed by the State Department as the oldest Latin American democracy. And it certainly fulfills the formalities. It holds elections every four years. It has three branches of government. It is a member of the United Nations and the Organization of American States and has signed all kinds of international treaties on human rights, women's rights, children's rights, the environment, etc.

But this façade of a constitutional regime covers a militarized society.

If you read the *Wall Street Journal*, you will start to find explanations for Colombia's brand of democracy. Reporter Thomas Vogel wrote on August 20 that despite political turmoil, Colombia boasts 65 years of continuous economic growth, "by far the best in Latin America and perhaps in the world."

Blessed with rivers, with different climates and soil where crops can be grown all year around and with many minerals and rain forests, Colombia certainly has all the resources to provide for its citizens' basic needs. Violence in Colombia is the result of deep inequalities because there is an absolute lack of political will to implement a significant transformation in the social and

1. Tammy Baldwin subsequently was elected to the Wisconsin Legislature and to the U.S. House of Representatives. In 2012, she won a seat in the U.S. Senate, where she continues to this day. After serving on the Dane County Board, Mark Pocan won election to the Wisconsin State Assembly, and in 2012, was elected to the House of Representatives, where he currently serves.

economic structures of the country. Public investment in education, health, housing, food distribution and other social programs is very low, and the steady economic growth and stability have not been employed to resolve the most basic problems of poverty and social exclusion. Drug trafficking and a guerrilla movement are the results of this disgraceful situation.

Most modern democracies permit freedom of association. Colombia's democracy features two political parties, the Conservative Party and the Liberal Party, that might as well be considered one party with two heads because there is absolutely no ideological difference between them. A challenge to these parties came in 1985 with the Unión Patriótica Party, which appealed to a broad range of Colombian citizens who felt the traditional parties did nothing to represent their interests. Because the Unión Patriótica enjoyed extensive success in elections, the killings started. More than 3,000 elected members of the party have been killed. Political killings have also taken the lives of labor leaders, lawyers, political activists, teachers, peasants, actors, journalists, priests, nuns—anybody who thinks. Who kills them? Paramilitary groups, trained and organized and left free by members of the Colombian Army allied with drug lords and some landowners who in Urabá (where Apartadó is located) are banana plantation owners.

So while you eat Colombian bananas bought in Madison grocery stores, Colombians enjoy the bullets of the American arms given to the Colombian Army in the name of the so-called "War on Drugs."

What kind of "War on Drugs" is this where generals who plan massacres and collaborate with drug traffickers enjoy total freedom?

• • •

Let's take the case of Gen. Rito Alejo del Río, the military commander in the region of Urabá. His forces who control movement in Urabá have never apprehended Carlos Castaño, the drug lord who is the organizer of death squads there.

How come death squads move freely in a region that is totally militarized?

Will somebody please finally listen to me?

OCTOBER 2016

Are We Going Back to Square One?

"We will see each other after the next 10,000 deaths."
—Alfonso Cano, head of FARC[1] delegation for peace talks in 1992, to members of the Colombian government's delegation when peace conversations were broken off in Tlaxcala, Mexico.

Last Sunday, October 2, 2016, there was a plebiscite in Colombia in order to obtain the people's approval of the Agreements for ending the war between the FARC guerrillas and the Colombian government, with the hope of closing the last war in existence in the Western Hemisphere and starting a new form of making politics in Colombia without recourse to guns. The plebiscite was not necessary, as the Colombian Constitutional Court indicated. Advisers told the President not to do it, given the fact that the Constitution considers peace as a right of the citizens and seeking it a duty for whoever becomes President.

After 52 years of war, the results are 1,906 villages destroyed by massacres, seven million campesinos displaced, 280,000 civilian deaths by the three armed actors (paramilitaries, guerrillas and the Colombian Army), 45,000 disappeared, thousands of victims of kidnappings, thousands of false

1. Editor's note: FARC, Fuerzas Armadas Revolucionarias de Colombia (Colombian Revolutionary Armed Forces)

positives, that is, civilians assassinated by the Colombian Army with the goal of increasing their body count, and thousands of women raped and humiliated. Then, we ask ourselves, why did the voters in a country destroyed by war and pain, with millions of victims, reject this peace offer?[2]

The Agreement was signed after four long years of intense negotiations in Havana. Cuba and Norway played very important roles as guarantors of this process. The Agreement had the support of the international community and shows a complex system of multinational verification. Besides, it has been considered as an example for conflict resolution. It was born from the valiant and risky challenge by President Juan Manuel Santos, who certainly played all his political capital with this initiative to achieve a durable peace in Colombia.

The Agreement has six points:

1. Policies of agricultural development
2. Participation in politics by the guerrillas
3. Guarantees for security
4. Solution to the problem of drug-trafficking and the production of illegal drugs
5. Implementation and Verification of the Agreement
6. A system of Transitional Justice with truth, justice, reparations and guarantees of no repetition.

Two other aspects make this Agreement a model: the focus and inclusion of the victims of all the armed actors (guerrillas, paramilitaries and the Armed Forces) and the inclusion of gender in all of the six points. In other words, it means that all the components of the Agreement were considered from the point of view of the rights of women and of persons from different sexual orientations.

It is worth remembering that in Colombia to be a leader of the left implies to give your own life. In 1946, Jorge Eliécer Gaitán, leader of the Liberal Party, generated a big socialist movement, popular and democratic, that possibly would have taken him to the presidency, if it were not for the fact that he was assassinated on April 9, 1948. His assassination was the cause of a popular revolt that was the origin of the so-called *Violencia* period that resulted in the

2. Editor's note: The exact numbers of the plebiscite vote, as discussed on pages 277ff of this article, were, "NO: 6,431,376;" "YES: 6,377,482." "NO" won with 50.21 percent of the votes. The question voted upon was whether to approve the Peace Agreement which had been negotiated between the government of President Juan Manuel Santos and the leadership of the FARC guerrillas. For context see the article by Annette Idler in the *Washington Post* of October 3, 2016.

killing of 250,000 Colombians. As a consequence of this situation, peasant guerrillas were born which then in 1964 became the FARC. In other words, the FARC were not a life accident; they were born from the abuses and injustices in the rural areas as a consequence of policies of arrogance and exploitation, which made it impossible to make opposition by another way which was not violence. In the 1980s, the Conservative government of Belisario Betancur negotiated a peace agreement with the FARC so they would become a political party. The FARC accepted and created a party called Unión Patriótica (U.P.). After the following elections, many of their elected mayors, city council members, deputies and senators, were systematically assassinated, as were two Presidential candidates of the U.P. This was a unique case of political genocide that cost the lives of more than 3,000 people.

In Colombia, 53 percent of the land lies in the hands of 2,300 persons. Given this situation it is understandable that these landowners deeply dislike to hear that, according to the Peace Agreement, 10 million hectares are going to be provided with title to poor, landless peasants. During the conflict, seven million hectares were taken from their owners and have never been returned. The Agreement also presumes the elimination of the daily expense released for war needs of about seven to eight million dollars, to be redirected to social investment, infrastructure, health and education. An argument against the Agreement is the supposed impunity it may bring. On the contrary, it is the first time that an integrated system of justice and truth is agreed to in a Peace Process where all those who took part in the conflict—members of political organizations, combatants and noncombatants, people from economic groups, agents of foreign governments and others—should give account of their responsibilities. Those, who from their comfortable offices in Bogotá and Medellín used the war for their political and economic benefit, are the ones who now rail against "guerrilla impunity." Those are the same persons who financed and instigated the creation of paramilitary groups who, in their massacres, dismembered their victims alive with chainsaws. Those paramilitaries are responsible for 50 percent of the victims of the conflict.

In spite of the insistence of the polls that the YES would win, the result could not have been more discouraging. The NO won with 6,431,376 votes, that is, with 50.21 percent of the votes. The YES had a total of 6,377,482 votes. The difference was only some 53,894 votes.[3] The country is essentially divided in half. In the rural areas where the war was more intense, such as Cauca, Nariño

3. BBC News for October 3, 2006, "Colombia referendum: Voters reject FARC peace deal."

and Putumayo provinces, the YES vote won, and in the urban areas, where most of the population is concentrated, the NO vote won, with the exceptions of Bogotá, Cali and Barranquilla. The urban world, for whom the war is something as remote as the one in Syria, decided to continue the war that exists in the rural world. So the question is: Are we going back to square one? Are we postponing the problem for another 10 years? Is all of this to maintain the economic and political interests of a minority?

Going back to the elections, one feels moved first of all by the incredible number of abstentions. For 62 percent of the nearly 34 million citizens with the right to vote, out of a population of 48 million people, their immediate and more worrisome problems are the ones related to their daily lives, their poverty and their defenselessness. They do not feel represented by or integrated into public institutions. Justice does not arrive, the Police repress them instead of protecting them, they have poorly paid jobs and barely survive. Or they voted NO out of fear, clientelism or resentment. These are people without hope, and without hope resistance does not exist. Without rights how can you demand participation? What kind of democracy is this one? For them it is the same whether the war continues or peace is achieved, particularly in the big urban centers. The weather also contributed to the abstentions, especially on the Caribbean coast where hurricane Matthew prevented even the setting up of voting places in some towns. Without infrastructure or adequate transportation, many people in the rural areas could not vote.

There is an imminent danger that the war will continue. Just since this year began, 51 defenders of the peace process and of human rights have been assassinated. According to the United Nations Office for Human Rights, at least 17 of them were defenders of the peace dialogs between the government and the FARC.[4] They were killed because they were considered "guerrillas dressed as civilians." Both Minister of Interior Juan Fernando Cristo and the Ombudsman's office condemned these killings, and for the FARC commanders these killings were not isolated but part of a strategy against social leaders. What this shows is the urgency of implementing in the territories the agreed measures on the special point of security in the final Agreement.

The more the days pass, the more details we are learning of the NO campaign led by former President Álvaro Uribe-Vélez. On October 5, 2016, the director of this campaign gave an interview to the newspaper La República in which he declared that their central message was to cause the indignation

4. "Report of the United Nations Office for Human Rights," 2016

of the voters, especially using the social networks, and that following on the advice of some strategists from Brazil and Panamá, they decided not to explain the Agreement, but adapted their messages according to social classes.[5] On radio stations listened to by the high and middle class strata they spoke of the impunity, the eligibility of guerrillas to run for Congress and of the tax reform that will make them pay more taxes. On the radio stations listened to by the lower classes the message was that their subsidies were going to be taken away in order to give them to the guerrillas. These leaders of the NO campaign deliberately lied in order to cause the sensation of fear among the electorate through fictitious scenarios. The campaign director declared that these distortions of the truth were also done by the proponents of the YES vote. On the contrary, the proponents of the YES vote carried out workshops, seminars, congresses, conferences, etc., explaining the Agreement.[6]

Some of the messages would be humorous if it were not for the tragedy behind all of this. For example, there were suggestions that "Castro-Chavismo" will come, that we will become like Venezuela, that Timochenko, the FARC leader, would be our next President, that people would lose their property. Political illiteracy is fed by manipulation on the part of the mass media in the hands of the private sector. Programs full of vacuity, superficial and lacking in depth, such as soap operas and contest programs like *Survivors*, are the daily bread of TV. Besides, for 52 years on a daily basis, the FARC were demonized to the point that this attitude had a perverse influence on the implementation of reconciliation. It's not that the FARC are saints. There are no saints in war. But many of the horrible massacres and crimes committed by the paramilitaries were kept silent, and almost all you heard of on the news were the crimes committed by the FARC.

The Christian extreme right, along with the Catholic Church, played a diabolical card, attributing gender ideology to the Peace Agreement in order to associate it with the establishment of a society governed by gendered interests. In other words, they suggested that the Peace Agreement would generate homosexual relations and would facilitate the creation of a sort of "feminist social dictatorship." I feel a lot of respect for representatives of the Catholic Church who in remote regions are almost the only consolation for the victims. Many priests and nuns have given their lives defending the weak

5. *La República*, Bogotá, Colombia, October 5, 2016.

6. Editor's note: For a detailed analysis of the vote and the campaign against a "Yes" vote, see El Triunfo del No por Andrei Gomez-Suarez, Icono, 2016.

in this war. But the hierarchy of the Catholic Church, with some exceptions, decided not to support the YES because they were "neutral"... this in Colombia, where since the time of the *Violencia* period we still remember the words of bishops preaching that it was not a sin to kill Liberals!

After the *Violencia* that started in 1948, leaders from the two parties, Liberal and Conservative, made a political pact in 1957 called *Frente Nacional* (National Front) in order to stop the violence. According to this agreement, government bureaucracy was divided into two equal parts, with equal numbers of representatives from the two parties and the Presidency alternating between the four-year electoral periods. Nobody mentioned badly needed structural reforms that would change inequality and the use of land. Don't get me wrong: Santos, a son of the country's classical elite, does not represent change. Santos represents a civilized and modern right, while Uribe represents a barbarian right with no scruples. Uribe tried his best to weaken FARC in order to take them to the border of extinction because he was seeking their destruction. An element that is almost never mentioned is the modern war technology provided both by the United States and Israel. After the assassination of several guerrilla leaders, it became obvious to the FARC that not even the deepest jungle would protect them. Santos decided on peace negotiations because he knew that this was the only reasonable way to achieve peace when neither of the two sides was able to exterminate the other, and even more, when a civil war makes the work of reconciliation more complicated.

After the plebiscite with its minimal majority of 53,894 "no" votes, President Santos agreed to meet with Uribe's party, called Centro Democrático, in order to reconcile what was agreed to in Havana with the requests of Uribe. This is an almost impossible mission, given the antagonism of the two positions. This dialogue with the opposition should be made as soon as possible, given the fact that for reasons of the agreed verification, it cannot wait. The United Nations observers were already located in the different regions, and the guerrillas were preparing to give them their arms. The ceasefire was supposed to be maintained, but how will it be done if the Agreement is not approved and put into effect? To the credit of both parties, the President declared that he would maintain the ceasefire, and the FARC declared that their struggle was now with words and not with arms.

For Uribe, the Havana Agreement opened the door for the terrorists to participate in politics. That was precisely the reason for the negotiations, that politics be made without the need to have recourse to arms! That is, to exchange bullets for votes. Another point made by Uribe concerns the subject of justice in the Agreement. It includes a chapter for state agents and their parties that have links with the conflict. Uribe sees this as equating the armed forces and civil society with terrorism. For Uribe, drug trafficking used to finance terrorism is not a political crime and should not be pardoned. But the Supreme Court indicated that drug trafficking by the guerrillas was connected to rebellion since it was used to finance insurgent organizations. For Uribe it is not enough for the guerrillas to "lay down" (dejar) their arms, the term to be used should be "deliver over" (entregar), because in his view the words "lay down" means to leave the terrorists with their arms. It was agreed in Havana that the UN will monitor the laying down of arms. The Transitional Justice Agreement, according to Uribe, accepts that delinquents responsible for atrocities do not go to jail, and this is unacceptable to him. He suggests that this system equates the treatment of the military and business people with that of the "bandits". For the FARC, it would be difficult to accept these changes because they did not negotiate with the idea of going to jail or being extradited to the United States. There are many other options, as shown in the peace agreements in Northern Ireland and South Africa.

Another closed and elitist pact that excludes the common people cannot be accepted because it will be a certain road to another cycle of violence. What is needed is a generous national dialogue for peace that brings closer all the forces to build a durable peace. The Nobel Peace Prize awarded to Santos is a recognition of his efforts during all these years. The President said he shared it with the victims and to them he will donate the money he is going to receive. Colombia does not lose hope. The courage, dignity and greatness of the victims who all said YES to the Agreement, both in the countryside and in the cities, demonstrated their willingness for pardon and reconciliation, showing that armed confrontation is not the way out of the conflict but civilized and respectful dialogue is. Basic measures to reincorporate guerrillas into civil society, according to the international rules of Transitional Justice, are the minimal requirement to end the war and should be implemented as soon as possible.

A broad front where all peace organizations converge must call for the participation of all segments of Colombian society in order to end this war of pain and suffering. The victims movement, youth, academics, women, sectors of the NO who thought they were defending the family without measuring the consequences that this decision will bring for Colombia, all ought to participate. And this is happening; the huge demonstrations from civil society in Bogotá and other cities asking for reconciliation and the reconstruction of Colombian society, in a kind of Colombian spring, are showing it. Fully 40,000 persons filled Bolívar Square in Bogotá in absolute silence, which was only broken when they tearfully sang the national anthem.

A pact among elites linked to defend their interests should not be accepted. Peace is a right. Now more than ever Colombia needs the vigilance and accompaniment of the international community to monitor this process and to continue its support. Going back to war is not possible.

JANUARY 28, 2002

Taliban in Colombia

I have followed with great interest most of the news about the Peace Process in Colombia. I read the editorials, look at the photos, analyze the articles and think deeply about how my beautiful land, so full of sorrow, will be rebuilt. I am glad to see even a glimmer of light coming from the exhausted warriors.

I think a lot about the children and the women, and for their sake I pray for a just peace. For all of them and the relatives of the displaced, the kidnapped, the disappeared, the ones who have lost their homes and have witnessed atrocities, I hope there will be peace. Nevertheless, something is missing when I think about the Peace Process. Suddenly, I realize what it is when I look at the photos. There are no women participating in the conversations. Looking at the photos one can conclude that the Taliban are alive and well in Colombia.

Colombian men have demonstrated extensively and with full evidence before the whole world that they have an extraordinary capacity, energy, creativity and incredible talent for killing one another. They hold the patent for some of the most horrible methods that have ever existed to kill a human being, such as cutting people in pieces with chainsaws. Should we trust these men when they get together to talk about peace?

In like manner, Colombian women have demonstrated an extraordinary capacity to build hope and life from the depths of misery, despair, loneliness and cruelty. They have shown to the world, with the same energy, creativity and talent that the Colombian men have, that they are capable of forgiveness, kindness, generosity and strength when the world collapses around them. They have shown great talent for organizing and administering when everything is destroyed ... But they are nowhere to be seen in the Peace Process.

It seems as though the warriors from all sides believe that women should only appear "for activities related to their sex." In all these years, who has picked up the bodies? Who has cried over them? Who has buried them? Who has gone to search for food, for shelter and shreds of clothing? Who has taken care of the children? It is said that the FARC is 40 percent women. Why are they absent from the negotiations? The Colombian government prides itself on the fact that women are a priority. Where are the women when it comes to discussing the future of the country?

Who is going to ask questions such as: How many schools are going to be built with the money to buy a Blackhawk helicopter? How many teachers will be well paid with the money spent on cars for the generals? How many of the soldiers are going to be trained in agriculture or public health? When are the FARC going to rebuild the towns they destroyed? When are they going to ask for forgiveness from the relatives of the kidnapped? Who will pay the therapists and counselors required for the children who saw their parents beheaded? Forgive me! But women are needed.

MAY 1-2, 2009

The Return of the Crematoriums

Cecilia Zarate-Laun, Colombia Support Network:
Panel at Conference for 100th Anniversary
Celebration of Progressive Magazine
Monona Terrace Conference Center
Madison, Wisconsin

Throughout time, wealth has been accumulated and territories controlled with the help of pirates, bandits and Mafiosi. Their influence has been crucial in the formation of states. They have helped to protect acquired wealth, to force individuals to submit to the domination of their leaders, and to expel unwanted populations from territories. Kings and emperors recognized the services of such persons, and eventually, some were assimilated into the formal power structure and became members of the elite. Similar methods of acquiring and maintaining wealth are still being used in our times—now to further globalization. In no place are the practices more brutal than those being used in Colombia.

For the last 60 years, Colombia has been ravaged by a non-declared civil war. This conflict is in part due to a structural problem within Colombian society that has prevented the majority of the population from enjoying social, political, economic and human rights. This is the origin of the two guerrilla movements that have, along with the paramilitary forces created to combat them, committed many atrocities in the name of a war of liberation.

This war is being fought in a very wealthy country and within the framework of a democratic façade. Elections are held regularly, the three branches of government function, and all kinds of international treaties are signed to show the government's dedication to protecting women's rights, the environment, labor rights, etc.

Unfortunately, none of this has a connection to reality.

The following data clearly illustrate the true state of affairs in Colombia. There are more than four million internally displaced people in the country, which represents 10 percent of the total population. This is the highest number in the world after Darfur. Since 2002, the Army has extra-judicially executed more than 1,500 people. Soldiers kidnap and kill lower-class Colombians, generally unemployed youth or campesinos, and then dress them in uniforms and present them as "guerrillas killed in combat" to make themselves eligible for bonuses and leaves of absence. In 2002 alone, 184 trade unionists were killed. In the last 20 years, 50,000 people have been disappeared. This includes political activists, human rights defenders, journalists, teachers, opposition party members and "undesirables" such as beggars, prostitutes, homosexuals and drug addicts, killed during "social cleansing" campaigns. Does this sound like fascism? In testimony given to the Colombian Supreme Court by former paramilitary leader Salvatore Mancuso this week, he explained that during meetings with politicians, "high level personalities," and members of the military, it was decided that crematoriums would be built in order to burn bodies and thus erase all traces of the "cleansing campaigns" since "it would not look right."

Methods of execution that have been used include beheading, cutting people up with chainsaws while still alive, and other forms of torture I do not wish to describe. Women have been gang raped. Children have been made to watch the atrocities. Food crops have been fumigated with Monsanto products in the name of the so-called War on Drugs. People have had to flee their beloved land, too afraid to ever return. And thus areas have been "cleansed" and made ready to welcome multinational corporations, agribusiness, mining companies and builders of hydroelectric dams.

It is worrisome to me to hear the statements coming from the U.S. government concerning the situations in Iraq and Afghanistan. Are they preparing the armies of those countries to become proxy armies once the U.S. troops leave, just like the Colombian Army has become? Are they aiding in the development of democratic façades in these countries, like the one that exists in Colombia? It seems that this method of implementing globalization, by means of proxy armies protecting and furthering the interests of corporations, is seen as desirable because it is cheap and politically "safe." When the eyes do not see the heart does not feel.

I want to end this presentation with a message of hope. This hope comes from the same rural communities that have suffered so much. In order to avoid being displaced from their beloved land, many courageous people have decided to organize themselves into communities practicing non-violent resistance. In a country so used to violent resistance, this is a very admirable step. These are the communities that Colombia Support Network is working with to develop sister-community relationships with communities in the United States.

MADISON, FEBRUARY 21, 2005

The Forgotten Power of Public Education

Generally speaking, public education is one of the most significant achievements of the modern world. Before the French Revolution, education was reserved as a privilege for elites and members of the clergy. Women in general were not raised to be educated, and the few who were represented the exception to the rule.

Public education is an instrument to be feared. Even modern democracies fear the education of the masses. I still remember some years ago when a prominent Colombian politician called for less investment of the budget for public education. From his point of view it made perfect sense. Educated people raise questions that are not supposed to be raised. Educated people use the knowledge they have accumulated to propose changes in the structure of societies that should not be proposed.

People might demand revolutionary things such as more investment in health, the young or the environment. Educated people might rationalize that wars are not the answer to the problems of this planet. Educated people might influence public opinion on issues that might better be left to the decisions of the policy makers. Issues such as priorities in the budgets of a country, the right to organize, the solutions to pollution, the use of public lands and how public resources must be handled. Ownership of the public airwaves is better left to be decided by publicly elected servants who, once elected, forget their obligations to the people who elected them and serve only the interests of the ones who pay for their services.

Educated people cannot be scared easily with fake threats that come with manipulations to use the resources of a country unwisely. Education is a resource that does not produce profits except that in the long run, it enhances the capacity to produce, and therefore the capacity of a country to benefit economically from investing in education.

Public education deserves attention, care and investment if we look at it from the point of view of our faith in humanity. It enhances our dignity as human beings and makes us appreciate how far we have evolved since the beginning of time. Think about something as common today as a computer. To a modern young person it is a very common thing. But a computer is the result of thousands of years of human knowledge that has evolved since the time the Phoenicians counted marbles and the Chinese used the abacus, passing through the Renaissance bankers to the adding machines of last century. Every computer is the display of this little knowledge here and that little knowledge there from the passing of centuries of collective knowledge.

The same can be said of radio or television. Nowadays it is very common to hear criticisms of radio and television. Rightly we rage against the vulgarity of television. But radio, television and computers are not bad per se: they are bad because we do not use them well. Just imagine how it would be if TV were dedicated to spreading the masters of art, music, literature, theater and intelligent debates. Imagine if we, instead of the barbarity of football, had the beauty of an Ibsen play.[1] Or Arthur Miller's incisive and sharp works of art. It is up to us to make proper use of technology.

Let us talk about categories in public education. Of course there is public education that is formal and public education that is informal. I want to focus on informal public education. There is a special reason for this selectivity, and it has a lot to do with all of us.

By all of us I refer to all of us who have had access to public formal college education. It is our duty to become educators. We, all of us. Since we are the beneficiaries and users of the public's strong belief in the need to have public universities, therefore our duty is to return this benefit to the community.

---

1. Editor's note: Cecilia was appalled at the violence of football in the United States, but she approved of fútbol (soccer) in Latin America and Europe.

We all are fed up with policies that do not address the needs and expectations of the general population. We do not own large newspapers or radio and television networks. But we do own our imaginations, our minds and our hearts. We are the owners of our passion, and we should channel it in the right direction. Are we tired of the way the environment is handled? Let us resort to street theater, mime, plays, protest music, painting, photography, short-term classes, forums, everything open to the participation of the public. Let us include the elderly and the children. It is important to learn their perspectives since they have a lot to contribute.

I close this part with an example that I hope illuminates my point. A year ago, President Álvaro Uribe of Colombia wanted to pass a referendum that contained many clauses which were highly detrimental to Colombian society, particularly to the weaker and more needy members, who would end up paying for the privatization of the public sector. Adjustment plans that were imposed by the IMF, and the offer of models that extract natural and energy resources which diminish sovereignty, such as Plan Colombia, and so on, were the pattern. The economic model presented to be voted upon in this referendum increased exclusion, discrimination and poverty.

The referendum was defeated soundly, to the fury of President Uribe. Public popular education led by university students, women, grassroots organizations, unions and community and indigenous movements developed many creative ways to educate the general public about the harm the approval of the referendum would do to all of them as society. Street theater played a very important role in awakening the conscience of the people to vote a resounding NO to the proposed referendum.

Artists drew their best murals, musicians wrote their best songs, and round-tables, debates and teach-ins flourished all over the country in spite of efforts by armed thugs threatening to disrupt them. Some were killed. But the education continued through community radios, marches, demonstrations and town meetings. Is there a message here?

2002

A Military Peace

On January 25, 2002 at 2:50 p.m., across from the gas station Gato Negro in the town of Tame, Department of Arauca, 12 heavily armed men killed Ángel Riveros Chaparro and two other men. Ángel was president of the local Peasant Association of Tame. I met Ángel, a quiet and dignified man, when he came to Chicago to testify at the International Tribunal of Opinion held at Northwestern University in September 2000 on the bombing of the village of Santo Domingo. Ángel's death illustrates in a microcosm the ultimate trend of the Colombian war, which has never ceased to be the elimination of popular civilian leaders whose activities challenge the status quo.

Meanwhile, newspapers around the world debate, discuss and analyze the breakup of the peace talks in Colombia on February 21. A negotiated peace has many enemies both inside and outside Colombia. We have to look at the evolution of this war to understand the recent events. First, the war originated as a classical class war when peasants demanded their right to land. In 1965, the peasants, allied with the Colombian Communist Party, formed the FARC (Fuerzas Armadas Revolucionarias de Colombia, Revolutionary Armed Forces of Colombia). Answering to overtures from the Colombian government to become a political party, FARC created the Unión Patriótica in 1985. The killing of more than 3,000 activists from the new party reflected the most basic characteristic of Colombian society, which is fundamentally exclusionary and ostracizes the majority of its population from their social, political, economic and human rights.

FARC's strategy has always been ultimately to win power by the use of arms. Its messianic attitude, combined with dubious methods such as the kidnapping of many people, the indiscriminate use of bombings, extortions and selective killings, has created immense pain in Colombian society and the rejection and isolation of the movement by Colombians from all ways of life. From being excluded for so long, FARC leaders themselves became exclusionary.

Fed up with the extortions and kidnappings, cattlemen, hacienda owners, industrialists and the recently nouveau-riche drug barons decided to create a counter-guerrilla which would attack FARC with its own methods, the dreaded AUC (Autodefensas Unidas de Colombia, United Self-Defense Forces of Colombia). The Colombian Army has been proven a close ally of these thugs who on many occasions do the dirty work for them, such as in the case of Ángel. When Colombia Support Network called to inquire why paramilitaries killed Ángel in broad daylight in a region totally militarized, Colonel Gustavo Matamoros said to us, "I do not have to answer to you," and hung up the phone.

Colombians saw with incredulity peace negotiations that continued in the middle of a never-ending war, where both sides refused to concede anything. The establishment would not give up its privileges. FARC would keep trying to conquer power by war. President Andrés Pastrana made people believe that peace was an easy task and could be accomplished quickly. Colombians desire peace more than anything. But peace can be achieved only when all sectors of Colombian society are incorporated in negotiations that address fundamental changes, such as social investment and land distribution. A quick, shallow and militarized peace will only take more deaths. The recent decision by the U.S. government to give 98 million dollars to strengthen the XVIII Brigade in Arauca in order to protect the pipeline of Caño Limón, which carries oil pumped by Occidental Petroleum, brings the war to a new level: the protection of multinational corporations such as Occidental Petroleum in the name of protecting us from terrorists and classifying Ángel as a terrorist. In the meantime, the paramilitaries keep killing peasants while your tax dollars protect Occidental. A military peace is no peace at all.

2005

Would the United States Support Al Qaeda?

We all have carved in our minds the images of horror. When the airplanes sliced through the air like swords obsessed by hate, and penetrated the buildings of the Twin Towers on September 11, 2001, we all cried together seeing the images of the innocent who were assassinated without pity as they went about their daily lives. We think about the poisonous gasses that killed the firemen while they were rescuing victims. We remember the infernal heat, the voices of the thirsty clamoring for water without a compassionate hand giving them something to drink. The cries of terror, the expressions of pain and desperation on the faces of the rescued.

Would the United States consider supporting Al Qaeda, a terrorist organization that targets the civilian and unarmed population of the United States? A population which has no power to decide the policies designed by its elected leaders? Policies that seem insane and irrational to the rest of the planet and that do not reflect the sovereignty and genuine kindness of the American people?

At a recent meeting for donor countries in the historic city of Cartagena de Indias in Colombia, apparently there were observers from the Bush administration promising help for the demobilization of the paramilitaries of the AUC (Autodefensas Unidas de Colombia), which like Al Qaeda has been declared a terrorist organization by the United States.

AUC members are the most brutal expression of a traditional sector of Colombian society that wants to maintain at all cost their economic and political interests, excluding the majority of the population of Colombia. For many years an unholy alliance of members of the Colombian Army, cocaine dealers, landowners, industrialists, representatives of multinational corporations and cattlemen have financed the AUC, with the result that 20 persons are killed daily for political reasons and three million internally displaced people have been forced out of their base and off their lands.

The AUC steals the land in areas coveted by multinational corporations or in areas which are the site of infrastructural projects that favor the FTAA (Free Trade Agreement of the Americas) because of Colombia's privileged geographic location and its huge natural and biological resources. President Uribe's government is negotiating a demobilization of the AUC, responsible for horrendous massacres where they butchered peasant leaders alive using chainsaws. AUC members are the main producers and dealers of cocaine in Colombia.

I will briefly mention some randomly chosen examples of the AUC's brutality. On November 22, 2000, a humble fishermen's town called Venecia, near Colombia's Atlantic coast, was left with 300 of its previous 4,000 inhabitants after a visit paid to them by the AUC. Thirty-eight victims were left beheaded and cut into pieces with machetes while others were used as living targets. Their crime? They were suspected of being friends of the guerrillas.

On April 10 and 11, 2001, during Holy Week, 20 persons were tortured, beheaded and cut into pieces by AUC forces in the Alto Naya region. Their crime? To live in that region. Gladys Ipia's hands were cut off with machetes and then her head was cut off. Cayetano Cruz, a town alderman, begged to save his friends' lives. He was shot and his body cut into pieces with chainsaws.

On January 7, 2004, at 10 a.m. in the town of El Tarra, elements of the AUC committed their first massacre of the year in the region of Catatumbo near the border with Venezuela, where there is a rain forest famous for its biodiversity, coal mines and oil. Six people were killed in front of their relatives. All of this happened while the AUC was holding peace conversations with the Uribe government to demobilize. Moreover, four units of the Colombian Army control the region. The Colombian Army receives millions in military aid from the United States to fight terrorism.

On January 14 of this year, 2005, at 9:35 p.m. in the town of Funza, just 35 kilometers from Bogotá, in front of his wife and two little girls aged six and eight years, Aldemar Campos was killed by armed men belonging to the AUC group headed by a man called "El Águila" ("The Eagle"). Astonishingly, this group has demobilized and holds a safe-pass from the government. Campos had been president of the city council, led demonstrations against privatization of public services and campaigned for people to abstain on the referendum proposed by President Uribe a year ago. He was running to be Mayor of the town on the ticket of the opposition party, the Polo Democrático.

The despicable war tactic of sowing terror, torture, beheading and execution of grassroots leaders in front of their families, friends and neighbors is used to force people to leave their lands or to cooperate in silence in order that the paramilitaries and their allies may control Colombia for the benefit of the same people who have always controlled Colombia, and for their foreign allies. These tactics seek to promote establishment of the Free Trade Agreement of the Americas.

These demobilized paramilitaries will receive only divine justice, because when it comes to human justice, they will go free to enjoy their ill-gotten lands. Peace without justice and reparations has no meaning. United States' support for the AUC paramilitary demobilization, including providing funds for this process, effectively helps a U.S.-designated terrorist organization. It is almost as if the United States were financing Al Qaeda.

2000

Speech on U.S. Policy for Colombia

I want to thank the organizers of this event today for inviting me to talk about Colombia. Although it has barely been present as a relevant subject in the debates and I am sure will not be discussed at the Town Hall meeting today, it is present in many people's minds due to the fact that the United States is giving more than one billion dollars in aid to Colombia. Aid for whom? Let's look carefully at who is receiving aid. A War on Drugs? Let us analyze that in depth.

First, before I attempt to answer these questions, I must say that the war in Colombia goes back to the 1940s, when peasant and indigenous communities decided to arm themselves when their lands were taken with the expansion of coffee haciendas. That same struggle for land with new actors and new elements is still persisting today.

The war in Colombia is the result of an exclusionary society that excludes the majority of its population from their social, political, economic and human rights. It is a war caused by the structure of a deeply unjust society in a very wealthy country where the majority of its population live in absolute poverty.

President Clinton and the U.S. government insist that they support Colombia in order to defend the oldest democracy in Latin America. It is the oldest but only on paper, since in a country with so much inequality it is impossible to build democracy. Colombia is a democracy where the two political parties, Liberals and Conservatives, act as if they were one party with two heads. These two parties hold absolutely the same agenda in social, political and economic issues, so for us Colombians, it does not matter which one is in power. It is a democracy where a vibrant third political party, the Unión Patriótica (UP), born from an agreement with the guerrillas to enter the political process in the mid-1980s, went to elections. Thousands were elected to city councils, Congress, etc., only to be hunted down thereafter and killed one by one all over Colombia. More than 4,000 UP elected officials were killed, making it a case of political genocide unparalleled in the Western Hemisphere. What democracy is the U.S. supporting in Colombia?

Let's talk about drugs. The U.S. government says that it needs to give money to Colombia in order to stop the drugs coming to this country. Let's look at that carefully.

Drugs became an element in the Colombian war only in the 1970s when, due to its privileged geographic location, the only country in mainland South America with coasts on both the Atlantic and Pacific Oceans, Americans bringing cocaine from Peru and Bolivia used Colombia as a stopover and a refining place for their business. Soon elements of the Colombian mafia allied with their new partners, took over the business and made millions in drug profits. It is impossible to have this business without some collaboration from several elements of the Colombian Army. In order to legitimize their money, the drug people, seeking respectability, started to evict peasants and take their land, creating a displaced population which today numbers two million persons, one of the largest displaced populations in the world. To protect their lands, drug people, landowners, cattlemen and multinational corporations use private armies called paramilitaries to defend their newly acquired lands. These paramilitaries are very closely allied with the Colombian Army, which passes information to them, patrols with them and looks the other way when they are committing atrocities such as taking people at random in rural communities and cutting them alive with chainsaws in order to terrorize the population and get them to leave their land to the new owners.

This same Colombian Army which has declared a war against the Colombian poor is the defender of the poor? Is this the same Colombian Army which has declared a war against the Colombian poor and those who defend the poor? Every year in Colombia, during the last 10 years, an average of more than 3,000 people have been killed for political reasons, which is more than those killed in the 17 years of Pinochet in Chile. Is the Colombian Army, which will receive the bulk of the American aid, to be the one to stop drug trafficking? How will this happen if they are closely allied with the paramilitaries, who are deeply involved in the drug business? The guerrillas in the southern part of the country charge taxes to cocaine laboratories or to coca growers and also kidnap people to make a lot of money, which they use to buy arms. If all sides of the Colombian war make money with drugs, why is Plan Colombia being applied in the south and not in the north where the paramilitaries are? Why this selection? Where is the logic? There must be another reason to give aid to have peace by creating more war. An aid which proposes to provide funds for the refugees who are created by that very increased warfare. Does that make sense?

Where do the displaced people go? The displaced peasants in Colombia go to the Colombian rainforest, which is part of the Amazonian rainforest, where they cut the rainforest to plant the only economic alternative allowed to them: coca. The production of coca in Colombia is the result of the desperation of the poor in the very same way that the people who sell cocaine in the streets of the U.S. are also the same poor people who have been abandoned by their own society, which is a democracy like Colombia. The two oldest democracies have abandoned their poor. So, in this peculiar way both the supply side and the demand side of the drug business reflect tremendous inequalities and injustices. Where is the logic? If there is something that will result from Plan Colombia it is an increase of drugs on the streets of the U.S. because Plan Colombia is not being applied in the north where the paramilitaries are located. Plan Colombia is being applied selectively in the rainforest where the bulk of the guerrillas are. Why? Who will benefit from Plan Colombia? Here is the answer: the multinational corporations.

In other words, the war in Colombia is a war for implementing NAFTA and globalization in this hemisphere. The long and bloody Colombian civil war is an obstacle to globalization. President Clinton himself said so in a speech to a group of Latin American ambassadors, members of the State Department and Council of the Americas and business leaders on May 3 of this year. I quote him: "The globalization of our societies is presenting us a lot of new challenges...We need to win in Colombia...We have to win the fight for a Free Trade Area of the Americas...We have to prove that freedom and free markets go hand in hand."[1]

1. Remarks by President Bill Clinton at the 2000 Washington Conference on the Americas, May 3, 2000.

If you look at the Colombian map and look carefully at areas where people are being displaced by paramilitaries, you can clearly see that these areas happen to be areas or territories where multinational corporations are present or will be present. Drummond Coal Co. and Exxon seek to protect their access to coal in the Guajira; gold companies seek access to gold deposits in the Serranía de San Lucas; Boise Cascade seeks protection for its lumbering interests in the Chocó; Occidental Petroleum seeks to force the U'Wa indigenous people off their historic homelands to drill oil wells there. Likewise for Bechtel, Mobil, British Petroleum, communications companies, fashion industry moguls and many, many more who are present in Colombia. Plan Colombia has not forgotten companies based in the U.S. such as Sikorsky from Connecticut and Bell in Texas which make helicopters, and your own Monsanto, which makes millions of dollars every year by selling Roundup to be spread in the Colombian rainforest to which the peasants are fleeing.

Last but not least, I want to mention the chemical and biological war of the U.S. against Colombia. The rainforest, rivers and animals are contaminated; birds and fish die; people suffer with upset stomachs and eye infections; babies are born deformed. Saddam Hussein is not the only one with biological arms. Plan Colombia has a component to finance the use of biological funguses to be used to kill coca plants. There are more than 200 wild relatives of coca in the rainforest and if you destroy even one link of the biological chain, you break the chain and may destroy the ecology of the whole planet. You can recall armies, but you cannot recall biological weapons. Once released they cannot be detained. We are witnessing the destruction of one of the richest biological environments on Earth in the name of making a false peace for a false democracy. Let us open our eyes and help to stop this madness.

2003

My Turn

I love public libraries. I think they are one of the best institutions in the United States. They invite a person to think and meditate in the middle of a busy day. I learned that several libraries I use in my neighborhood are going to be closed for lack of money. I ran into a neighbor who talked to me about all the money she has to spend each month for prescribed medicines that her insurance does not cover. There is not enough money to provide healthcare for the people.

But there is a lot of money for wars. Wars, wars, wars. I wonder if the American people know what war means? There are no survivors of the Civil War to tell them what war in this country could be like. War is death, blood, tears, anguish, suffering, pain, cruelty and brutality. Since the Gulf War people have made a game of war as if it were a pinball machine.

No war has been more unproductive and destructive than the so-called War on Drugs. For how long are the American people going to put up with this façade of a war? I read the Colombian press daily. In November 2002 it was reported that Colombian Police confiscated three tons of cocaine and then, for a large bribe, returned them to the drug dealers. The drug dealers in turn paid another bribe for the names of the DEA (Drug Enforcement Agency) informants whom they subsequently murdered. This is not the first time that this has happened.

But there is a lot of U.S. money for the Colombian Police and Army which have a very cozy relationship with the paramilitaries who moonlight as drug dealers. This is money that is desperately needed here for the people who seek treatment for their addiction to drugs. Attempting to end the long and bloody Colombian conflict, the Colombian government drafted a bill encouraging the armed groups to lay down their weapons, counting upon political and economic support from the United States.

The leftist guerrilla group Fuerzas Armadas Revolucionarias de Colombia (FARC) and the right-wing paramilitaries, the Autodefensas Unidas de Colombia (AUC), are both terribly guilty of crimes against humanity and of dealing with drugs. So far the government has been negotiating with the AUC who, according to highly respected human rights organizations such as Amnesty International, commit most of the killings. The AUC's favorite method of killing is cutting people live in pieces with chainsaws. Rape, torture, theft and displacement have been the AUC's trademark. Three million peasants, mainly women and children, roam the country because the AUC took their land and killed their husbands and fathers. In most cases the land taken is used to plant coca, to build cocaine laboratories or for cattle raising.

What are the displaced peasants going to do? They become beggars, prostitutes, street children, or they go to the Amazon rainforest to plant coca in order to survive. By planting coca, not only do they become the target of both the FARC and the AUC again, but they are the victims of crop spraying paid for with U.S. taxpayers' money.

The Colombian government's proposed bill is intriguing. It offers what is called "alternative punishment," which basically means that the criminals do not serve one single day of jail time as long as they offer to confess their crimes and promise not to get near their victims, which should be easy to promise given the fact that their victims were killed a long time ago.

High-ranking officials of the American Embassy have met with representatives of the AUC. The American people and the American Congress must know what these conversations are about. Since the AUC are not only heavily involved in drug trafficking but have been declared terrorists by the State Department, are they receiving different treatment than other terrorist groups?

When it comes to the War on Drugs, the United States suddenly becomes a socialist country looking only at the supply side of the issue. In capitalism one produces what sells. The production of drugs in Colombia is directly related to the desperation of the poor who become victims of the drug trade. It is not a military problem. Therefore, the solution should not be a military solution. It is about time that this country asks itself the most difficult questions, which are: Why is this society the largest consumer of drugs in the world? Is there too much loneliness? Is it competing with each other that makes our young people consume drugs? Is it to escape reality? Is it lack of spiritual values?

A new political season is coming, and with it, politicians crisscross the country. It is the perfect opportunity to ask them to put the money here for the many needs of this society and not in unnecessary and futile wars that only result in a hatred of the United States. The American people deserve better.

SPRING 2002

Statement for Peace in Colombia

Action on Colombia

We would like to express our solidarity with the Colombian people at this crucial moment in the history of their country.

We call upon the government of Colombia, the FARC guerrilla movement and Colombian society in general, to maintain the conversations for peace in Colombia, for their future and their children's future.

To listen is an essential part of reconciliation for both sides. The Colombian government and the FARC should try to understand the requests of each other. Perhaps if the Colombian establishment looks at the pain and injustice that the poor of Colombia suffer and recognizes the need to make structural changes that will benefit everyone, we can talk about a future with peace in Colombia. If the insurgent movements understand the immense suffering all their violent actions cause and hear the voices of those who have suffered from them, then we can talk about a future with peace in Colombia. Colombian women and children, particularly, have suffered the consequences of the violence in Colombia. It is time to take their interest into account and to achieve peace for their sake.

We appreciate the courage and persistence of President Pastrana in pursuing peace negotiations with both the FARC and the ELN.

We strongly believe in the spiritual power of nonviolence, and thus we encourage the efforts made by communities such as the Peace Community of San José de Apartadó, the communities returning to the Cacarica River Basin, the displaced community of La Balsita and the Development and Peace Program of the Middle Magdalena.

Colombian people are all part of the human family. The rest of humankind has a lot to learn from their enormous creativity, their boundless energy, their generosity, their hospitality, their love for life and their kindness. The children of Colombia cannot keep growing up in the middle of war. Colombia is not alone. The whole world is watching very carefully and asking the major players not to abandon all they have accomplished in the peace process until now.

We ask you to continue serious negotiations for peace and to do all in your power to achieve peace with justice, so the future generations of Colombia may realize their full potential.[1]

1. Editor's note added to the Spring 2002, Action on Colombia newsletter: The Peace Process, which had been in process in Colombia since 1998, broke down the night of February 10, 2002, when the FARC hijacked a plane carrying 30 passengers and kidnapped a Colombian senator. At 10:00 p.m., President Pastrana announced that the Peace Process with the FARC was over and that the Colombian Military would take back the "zona de despeje" at midnight. We invite you individually or as an organization to sign on to the "Statement for Peace in Colombia."

WINTER 2002

Sister Community "Disappears"

Action on Colombia newsletter

Last year, after Colombia Support Network (CSN) representatives visited the displaced community of Ciénaga del Opón, CSN along with PDPMM (Programa de Desarrollo y Paz del Magdalena Medio; Development and Peace Program of the Middle Magdalena) recommended this community as a sister community to the budding CSN chapter in Duluth, Minnesota. This community had all the requirements of a sisterhood project.[1]

1. Editor's note: In the late 1990s, the Colombia Support Network entered into a relationship with the Programa de Desarrollo y Paz del Magdalena Medio (PDPMM), an organization founded by Father Francisco de Roux, a Catholic priest whom CSN had become acquainted with when he was the Director of CINEP, a Jesuit think tank based in Bogotá. The PDPMM was established to foster and support development programs in communities in the Middle Magdalena region, several of which were on the Magdalena River. CSN was invited to undertake a sister-community project, matching CSN member communities in the United States with communities in the Middle Magdalena region with which the PDPMM was working. Several of these sister community relationships were developed, and visits by members of CSN chapters to their Colombian sister communities took place. This cooperative program was terminated by the PDPMM leadership after the incursion of paramilitary forces into the Middle Magdalena region. The development and end of CSN's collaboration with the PDPMM in the Middle Magdalena region is documented in CSN's *Action on Colombia* newsletters in the late 1990s and the early 2000s, available on the CSN webpage.

However, war realities took over, and the hopes of the group that took refuge in the empty Normal School building are lost. Almost two years after having fled their homes, the 40 families are convinced they cannot return to their place of origin.

Ciénaga del Opón was a nice little village where the community lovingly built, with their own resources, a small building for a school and another for a community health center, where they dreamed of constructing their lives with a future together. All of that is gone. When the armed actors, both FARC (Fuerzas Armadas Revolucionarias de Colombia) and the AUC (Autodefensas Unidas de Colombia),[2] started to enter their village to threaten them, burn their homes and kill some of their members, they fled to the security of Barrancabermeja. All the time the community dreamed of going back. The cramped, old and inadequate building in which they were staying was not at all suited for the children to live comfortably. Peasants such as Benjamín Jiménez dreamed of going back—back to his little farm where he cultivated plantain, corn, and cassava and fished all the fish he wanted in the nearby Opón River. In that place there was always something to eat, and there he felt that "there is no life other than the Opón." But the families who were in Barranca felt there was not enough food for them there, and they suffered greatly in the school—especially the children.

At the beginning of this year, they were asked to pay the ultimate sacrifice. Their leader, Manuel Francisco Sampayo, was taken by the AUC and has not been seen since. It was his leadership and commitment which had kept their hopes to return to their village alive. Since his "disappearance," their dreams are also gone. Maybe that is exactly why he was taken away.

Without him the community has lost their compass, and the desperate community believes that their fear of returning is stronger than their hunger. At any moment "the armed actors who want our land will come back to evict us, and we cannot live like that with so much uncertainty and fear." Besides lack of food, another worrisome item is the schooling for their children since in Ciénaga the teachers were the first to be threatened. They have made a decision. There will be no return, and the community is disbanding.

CSN has never had this situation before. We learn from this experience and can ponder together about the cruelty and insanity of war—the anguish and

2. Editor's note: FARC is a revolutionary group in Colombia and AUC is a paramilitary group. They are enemies of one another, the AUC generally working alongside government forces or for landed and corporate interests.

desperation of the people who, once their means of livelihood and organizing are taken from them, have no more illusions in life and see a bleak future for themselves and their children. We should see from this example the tragedy and pain that thousands of humble people in Colombia experience constantly. Their lives are destroyed forever for the lack of justice.

Their land will be taken by people who support another way of looking at life. A way where only the individual is important and life as a community has no value.

This example will reinforce our commitment for peace with justice in Colombia and for a negotiated solution to the conflict in the hopes that children will have a school, a roof, food and laughter. The cruelty experienced by Ciénaga del Opón shows the real strategy for the peasant communities in Colombia, which is: either accept the new rules of the new society led by the paramilitaries or leave and become displaced.

SUMMER 1999

Another War for Globalization

Action on Colombia newsletter

The United States government pursued a policy of bombing Yugoslavia, supposedly to curb human rights abuses by the state security and military apparatus of President Slobodan Milosevic. Yet in Colombia the same U.S. government supports an Army that has long been engaged in very serious human rights abuses in collaboration with paramilitary death squads. In fact, Colombia is the third largest recipient of U.S. military aid, after Israel and Egypt. These death squads target teachers, members of legal political movements, priests, nuns, human rights leaders, labor leaders, journalists, academics and thousands of peasants. While the U.S. government supported the KLA rebels to stop ethnic cleansing in Kosovo, it indirectly and knowingly provides support to paramilitaries in Colombia engaged in similar "cleansing" activities.

Why don't we hear more about the situation in Colombia? First, because the Colombian government, unlike Milosevic's government, is considered "friendly" to the U.S. Secondly, the U.S. government is intentionally misleading in its public pronouncements on the reasons for the war in Colombia. Rather than a "War on Drugs!" featuring the Colombian Army and Police against drug traffickers and guerrillas, the conflict in Colombia is a class war which has been underway for about 60 years as the product of a very exclusionary society that does not willingly accept social, political and economic reforms.

The facts behind U.S. policy in both Yugoslavia and Colombia have much more to do with globalization policies than human rights or drugs. In the Balkans the U.S., through NATO, appears to seek to protect access to oil supplies in the Caspian Sea and continues to play a decisive role in defending a status quo which has greatly benefited this country. In Colombia, the U.S. seeks to protect access to natural resources, especially oil and gold, and to make the area safe for U.S. investments by supporting the narrow economic and political elite which controls power and limits access to the political process. The U.S. continues to use a proxy army—the Colombian Army and Police—to advance a neoliberal agenda which includes access to mineral wealth (gold, oil, coal, platinum, etc.) in the Middle Magdalena region, the Chocó and other strategic regions of the country. Completion of the Pan-American Highway in the northern coastal area together with vast development programs in environmentally sensitive areas are also means to control Colombia's unique geographic advantage of being the only country in mainland South America with coasts on both the Atlantic and Pacific Oceans.

It is significant that U.S. military aid is clearly given to defined geographical areas. These areas are guerrilla territories whereas other areas, such as the one controlled by drug lord and paramilitary leader Carlos Castaño, are left unattended.

Why is Milosevic condemned and not Carlos Castaño? Is the U.S. funding a war on drugs or a counterinsurgency war?

In the meantime, the war rages on with nearly two million internal refugees, 201 massacres (incidents in which four or more people are killed) in 1998 alone, "disappearances" and torture. In the last 10 years, there have been a total of 37,165 political killings in Colombia as a result of the war to control and exploit the Colombian people and Colombian resources. Long live globalization!

2004

The Department of Colonies

The year 1959 was a very important one for Latin America. This was the year that the Cuban Revolution began and the revolutionary winds of change swept the continent. The U.S., reacting angrily to the Cuban challenge, used the Organization of American States (OAS) as their controlling political arm, causing the beloved leader Ernesto "Che" Guevara to rename the OAS the "U.S. Colonies Department."

The historical issue comes to mind when I read the current Colombian news. On January 24 the leading Colombian newspaper in Bogotá, *El Tiempo*, reported that the Secretary General of the OAS, former Colombian President César Gaviria, decided to sign an agreement with the government of Álvaro Uribe Vélez. According to the agreement, the OAS commits itself to support the "peace process" of President Uribe. The OAS will supervise the cease-fire, the cessation of hostilities, the disarmament and the return to society of Colombian paramilitary groups. The agreement, signed at night and behind closed doors, lacks the approval of the OAS member countries. In particular, the approval of those who specifically support the Colombian peace process in the hemisphere is absent: Argentina, Mexico, Brazil and Canada were not informed of its creation.

This agreement is a very serious one because it legitimizes a process that no respected international organization, including the European Union and the United Nations, has wanted to support. Uribe's "peace process" gives total freedom to individuals who have committed horrendous crimes with no regard for the consequences of their actions. The truth of what happened might therefore never be acknowledged, justice is not served and victims remain uncompensated.

What is worse, the umbrella paramilitary group called Autodefensas Unidas de Colombia (AUC) was declared "terrorist" by the U.S. Department of State, which requested that the leaders be extradited on drug-trafficking charges. The process in place is one that is dictated by the paramilitary leaders themselves, who set the conditions and constantly make a threat to step out of the negotiations if these conditions are not met.

César Gaviria, the OAS Secretary-General handpicked by the Clinton Administration in a notorious selection that generated a lot of controversy from the member states, has shown no respect for the fragile inter-American organization and has further weakened it. The U.S., meanwhile, has kept a suspicious silence during all of this. Could it be possible that Mr. Gaviria is following orders from Washington?

Currently, the AUC keeps busy spreading death and destruction throughout the Colombian countryside. Human Rights NGOs in Colombia report assassinations, disappearances, massacres and criminal abuses from the members of the AUC on a regular basis. All of this in the middle of a "peace process" with the Uribe administration, aided by the blessing of the OAS. There is not the slightest sign of shame on the part of the Colombian government toward the international community.

The newspaper *El Independiente* from Mexico reports that the Mexican government was not informed about the agreement. But what does Gaviria have at stake involving Mexico? The precise function of the Department of Colonies is to keep its population happy. It would not be surprising if the U.S. was sending this intriguing message to the rest of its colonies in the hemisphere: When it comes to defending its interests, such as the expansion of the Free Trade Area of the Americas (FTAA), a hemisphere at peace is needed. Small things such as truth, justice and reparations are not important. What is important is to have obedient and cynical secretaries such as César Gaviria. The rest is inconsequential.

PART F

Cecilia's Remembrance of lost friends.

WINTER 1996

My Friend Silvio

A Remembrance for Silvio Salazar
Killed January 13, 1996

On January 13 at 3:40 p.m., in front of the offices of Convivir, Silvio Salazar was assassinated for unknown reasons. Once again, one of Colombia's most dedicated and beloved grassroots leaders was eliminated by the insane violence that plagues the country.

I initially met Silvio when he came to Madison in the Spring of 1992. He immediately struck me by the generosity of his spirit and a kindness that reflected the beauty of his soul. He spoke to me at length about his peasant roots, his inner desire for peace and the absolute need to fight for it continuously. Silvio told me how he started to care about his community when as a child he was prepared for his First Communion by a liberation theology priest. Then as an adult he drove a taxi in Medellín and was shocked one day, when starting his daily rounds around 4 a.m., he found 30 bodies of young teenagers who had just been killed. The bodies were still warm. One of them apparently was carried to his execution place with his fingers smashed by the car's door. Silvio's horror found no limits and he started to cry. His crying reflected desperation, sadness, horror, anguish and pain. Starting at that moment Silvio dedicated all of the beautiful qualities that he possessed to the struggle for peace, love and reconciliation.

Along with other communal leaders of the popular neighborhoods of Medellín, he founded Convivir[1], trying to generate processes of integration and development in the community, always looking for practical and civil solutions to the problems. His killing was received with indignation and profound sadness.

Silvio was a friend of Colombia Support Network, and he welcomed several of us at the Medellín airport when we went to Apartadó. He was interviewed by George Vukelich for his Isthmus column 'Listening In' in June 1992. George entitled the story "Bang Bang Bang," expressing the violence that a few years later would kill Silvio also. Personally, I feel very sad and enraged at the killing of such a beautiful human being. The Colombia Support Network invites everyone to a memorial service for Silvio on April 19 at Edgewood College.[2] He leaves a wife and two little girls.

1. Editor's note: Silvio Salazar's neighborhood organization, named *Convivir*, should be distinguished from Álvaro Uribe's "convivir" structures, which were paramilitary organizations, initially legal but later classified as illegal. Silvio's neighborhood organization, *Convivir*, was initiated prior to Uribe's paramilitary organizations of the same name, and was a neighborhood support organization, the opposite of a paramilitary organization.
2. Edgewood College is in Madison, Wisconsin.

FALL 2008

Mourning Orlando Fals Borda

Colombia Support Network deeply mourns the passing last August 14 of the celebrated sociologist Orlando Fals Borda at age 83. Two years ago, we mourned the death of his wife, sociologist Maria Cristina Salazar. They were two dear friends of this organization.

I first met Orlando many years ago at the wedding of my cousin, Sara Ortiz, with Orlando's younger brother, Juan Fals Borda, in Bucaramanga. His unaffected manner and his kindness were evident to me from that moment on. My dinners with Orlando and Maria Cristina when I visited Bogotá were always a great pleasure, as we reminisced and analyzed the situation of the moment in Colombia. Once, Orlando told me that he had escaped from a long imprisonment thanks to an amulet which indigenous friends from the Amazon had given to him. Orlando and Maria Cristina responded with great dignity to the torment of their persecution, torture and the false accusation against them by the military that they were M-19 guerrillas.

On another occasion, Maria Cristina proudly showed me the framed oil painting of the Marquise de Valdchoyos that one of her descendants had given to Orlando. The donor had first wanted to throw the painting away in the trash, but then thought, correctly, that Orlando would appreciate it more, given his studies of the history of the Coast.

But enough of anecdotes. Orlando Fals Borda was above all a Colombian who felt an immense responsibility for his country, without ever bragging or claiming credit for his contributions. With the force of his spirit and his knowledge, he and Father Camilo Torres founded the first Sociology department in Latin America. A leading university professor and investigator, he was the author of many books and articles, including his 1955 doctoral thesis at the University of Florida, "Peasant Society in the Colombian Andes: A Sociological Study of Saucio" and the pathbreaking two-volume study of Colombia's civil conflict, *La Violencia en Colombia*, which he co-authored with Germán Guzmán Campos and Eduardo Umaña Luna.

His scientific focus and analysis, always objective, rational and ethical, characterized his work. Rigorously and with sensitivity, Orlando concluded that social scientists also had political responsibilities. It was not sufficient to conduct an exhaustive investigation of a community and then give it a warm goodbye. His methodology of Investigación Acción Participativa (Investigation and Active Participation) is in essence the ethical duty which in Orlando's eyes required giving back to the community being studied, repaying them for their generosity toward the researcher and empowering the community to take into its own hands its development. It was in that spirit that Maria Cristina received several CSN delegations when she was working with women flower workers. Orlando was a member of the National Constituent Assembly which produced the 1991 Constitution and was until his death the Honorary President of the Polo Democrático Party.

In his scholarship and his role as an educator he will be greatly missed. But we particularly valued his unceasing commitment to the search for justice and to achieving a more equitable Colombia. May he rest in peace.

APRIL 17, 2023

Conclusion

Jack Laun
Middleton, Wisconsin

Dear Reader,

I am honored that you have given your time and attention to this book. My wife, Cecilia Lucia Zarate-Laun, considered her life work to be trying to do what she could to end the daily conflict in her beloved Colombia. She conceived the idea of starting a human rights organization to address the unrelenting violence in her home country. She and I had come to live in my home state, Wisconsin, where I had practiced law for several years before going to Bogota to do research for a thesis on urban housing policies. Cecilia had received a scholarship to study nutritional science at the University of Wisconsin in Madison and we became acquainted there in 1973.

In 1976 we married in an old colonial church in the city of Girón in Cecilia's home province of Santander. The next year we returned to the United States and Cecilia began her human rights activity. She and a close friend, Angela Kellner, started an empanada production and sale business in Madison known as Coquitos Corporation. Meanwhile Cecilia responded to her felt necessity of doing what she could to help bring peace to Colombia, which had suffered from conflict between rival political factions since 1948. She joined the Women's

International League for Peace and Freedom (WILPF) and she and I founded the Colombia Support Network in 1987.

The organization established a sister community for Dane County, in which the city of Madison is located, its sister being the community of Apartadó, Colombia. Two members of the Dane County Board at that time, Tammy Baldwin and Mark Pocan, now respectively a United States Senator and a member of the House of Representatives, were instrumental in establishing an official sister community relationship, which continues to this day.

Cecilia conceived of her role in life as having a focus upon doing what she could to end the conflict in Colombia. She responded to a strategy implemented by Ana Teresa Bernal who developed an organization, Redepaz, of community chapters working for peace in their communities. Several of the chapters in this book describe the activities of the CSN chapters and their sister communities.

Cecilia felt keenly that it was important to form CSN chapters in the United States and match them with Colombian communities in areas of conflict. The chapters would work with their sister communities in Colombia for an end to the conflict. Several of the articles in this book focus on this work. It was important for Cecilia to undertake efforts at peace in these communities.

To support her work in Colombia she approached Noam Chomsky, who responded with wonderful support and on two occasions went to Colombia with Cecilia. The inspiration he provided to Cecilia was a great gift. Her activities, and the focus behind them, owe a great deal to Professor Chomsky.

Fundamentally important from the very beginning of Cecilia's human rights activity has been Father Javier Giraldo, a Jesuit priest who has devoted a lifetime to working for peace and establishing relationships to promote peace, while reporting on threats to peace and honoring the many Colombians who lost their lives as a result of their activism in pursuit of peace.

Important support for Cecilia's work was also provided by Father Roy Bourgeois, founder of the School of Americas Watch, some of whose annual gatherings at Fort Benning, Georgia, Cecilia attended. As well, Father John Dear provided important moral support for Cecilia's work. For Cecilia it was important that the work to which she devoted her life continue after she passed away. In answer to this concern, members of the Board of Directors of the Colombia Support Network have responded by giving of their time and energy to continue CSN's activities. Eunice Gibson, a former Madison City Attorney and a great friend, has for many years as Secretary provided support for Cecilia's work and for the continued activity of CSN. This is also true for other members of the CSN Board of Directors, without whose commitment of time and energy Cecilia could not have done the work she did and written what became the chapters of this book.

Printed in the United States
by Baker & Taylor Publisher Services